Feminist Human Rights

Feminist Strategies: Flexible Theories and Resilient Practices

Feminist Strategies encourages original work in contemporary philosophical feminism that recognizes that while women have achieved a significant measure of equality, discrimination nonetheless persists through the intersection of gender with other systems and practices of oppression. Such work includes the formulation of theories that are sufficiently flexible, and the promotion of practices sufficiently resilient, to address these changing contexts and forms of oppression. The volumes that comprise this series thus examine current practices, actual cases, and historical episodes of discrimination in which gender has intersected with systems of oppression including those involving feminism and disability; women, animals, and emotion; extended cognition and feminism; women and depression; motherhood, and the new materialist feminism.

Titles in the series

Feminist Human Rights: A Political Approach, by Kristen Hessler
Shame, Gender Violence, and Ethics: Terrors of Injustice, edited by Lenart Škof and Shé M. Hawke
Ethics, Emotion, Education, and Empowerment, by Lisa Kretz
Transcultural Feminist Philosophy: Rethinking Difference and Solidarity through Chinese-American Encounters, by Yuanfang Dai
Antagonizing White Feminism: Intersectionality's Critique of Women's Studies and the Academy, edited by Beth Hinderliter and Noelle Chaddock

Feminist Human Rights

A Political Approach

Kristen Hessler

LEXINGTON BOOKS
Lanham • Boulder • New York • London

Published by Lexington Books
An imprint of The Rowman & Littlefield Publishing Group, Inc.
4501 Forbes Boulevard, Suite 200, Lanham, Maryland 20706
www.rowman.com

86-90 Paul Street, London EC2A 4NE

British Library Cataloguing in Publication Information Available

Library of Congress Cataloging-in-Publication Data

Names: Hessler, Kristen, author.
Title: Feminist human rights : a political approach / Kristen Hessler.
Description: Lanham : Lexington Books, [2023] | Series: Feminist strategies | Includes bibliographical references and index.
Identifiers: LCCN 2023011243 (print) | LCCN 2023011244 (ebook) | ISBN 9781498592307 (cloth) | ISBN 9781498592314 (ebook)
Subjects: LCSH: Feminist theory. | Human rights--Philosophy.
Classification: LCC HQ1190 .H485 2023 (print) | LCC HQ1190 (ebook) | DDC 305.4201--dc23/eng/20230323
LC record available at https://lccn.loc.gov/2023011243
LC ebook record available at https://lccn.loc.gov/2023011244

Contents

For Allen Buchanan

Acknowledgments

My debts to Allen Buchanan for his mentorship and intellectual influence are manifest on every page of this book. Allen's pathbreaking work on the philosophy of international law and human rights shaped my development as a philosopher, and the deep commitment to equality that is the hallmark of his political philosophy continues to inspire me as a human being.

Jon Mandle has my immense gratitude for helping me think in novel ways about political philosophy over the years we have been colleagues. Jon closely read more than one draft of nearly everything in this book. His incisive criticisms helped me make the arguments a million times better than they were, and his generous commitment to seeing the best in my arguments gave me the confidence to keep working.

I'm particularly grateful to Andreas Føllesdal for organizing a workshop on a late draft of the entire manuscript. The critiques and encouragement I received from the participants—including Andreas, Cindy Holder, Avery Kolers, Jon Mandle, Fleur Johns, Alejandro Chehtman, Harlan Cohen, and Neus Torbisco-Casals—helped me improve the manuscript immensely.

All of the following people generously read and discussed drafts of various chapters over Zoom during the global pandemic: Matthias Brinkmann; Allen Buchanan; Andreas Føllesdal; Fleur Johns; David Lefkowitz; Nahuel Maisley; Jon Mandle; Carmen Pavel; Steven Ratner; Antionette Scherz; Jiewuh Song; Oisin Suttle; Pauline Westerman, Johan Vorland Wibye; and Alain Zysset. I'm immensely grateful for their constructive criticisms.

Many thanks to audiences and commentators at the IVR World Congress in 2019 in Lucerne, the 2020 Central APA meeting in Chicago, where Steven Ratner provided excellent commentary, and in Geneva in 2021, where I am particularly indebted to Alejandro Chehtman, Neus Torbisco-Casals, and Stéphanie Hennette Vauchez.

I'm deeply grateful to Professor Lisa Pruitt for her communications and for sharing documents from the *Akayesu* file that I had trouble locating otherwise, including her own memos that played an influential role in securing the testimony needed to indict and ultimately convict Jean-Paul Akayesu on sexual violence charges.

Thanks to my editor at Lexington Books, Jana Hodges-Kluck, for her patience and encouragement, and to an anonymous reviewer for very helpful comments.

Farha Khalidi provided extremely helpful research assistance, and helped format the notes and bibliography, as did Mel Galvin, Derek Delaney, and Jo Wunderlich.

I am grateful to the University at Albany (SUNY) for providing a sabbatical leave to complete the manuscript, and to my department chair, Brad Armour-Garb, for his enthusiastic support.

Kimberly Van Orman was my coach and confidante as I was first getting started in the writing process. Her encouragement was invaluable.

Derek Delaney inspired me with his passion for work and life, supported me when writing (and life) was difficult, and believed in me every step of the way.

Infinite gratitude to my daughter, Jo, who always shows me new ways to see the world, reminds me of what is important in life, and inspires me to live accordingly. And I have never enjoyed editing as much as I did when she was helping me on this book.

My cats, Dasher and Turtle, generously, if insistently, offered their companionship during the writing process. They didn't even mind when I deleted the revisions they suggested by walking on my keyboard, though some may well have been improvements.

And finally, I'm deeply grateful to everyone who provided encouragement, support, help, and cheer throughout the long illness I experienced while completing this manuscript, especially Derek and Jo, my mom and my dad, and my friends Karen, Jon, and Susan.

Chapter 1

The Orthodox/Political Debate and Its Methodological Assumptions

One of the most pressing and divisive questions in the philosophy of human rights concerns philosophy's relationship with human rights practice—that is, the many ways that the idea of human rights is deployed in various social, political, and legal contexts. International human rights law is the most obvious real-world manifestation of this idea, and the one that has received the most attention from philosophers. Encompassing multiple international treaties and conventions enumerating the legal rights of all persons, beginning with the 1948 Universal Declaration of Human Rights, international human rights law (or IHRL for short) also includes institutions that interpret and monitor the implementation of human rights within states. However, the concept of human rights also plays important roles in many other domains beyond IHRL, including international politics, foreign policy decisions by individual states, human rights activism, and other branches of international law, including humanitarian and criminal law.

So-called "orthodox" philosophers of human rights argue that human rights practice, especially international human rights law, is animated by the inherently philosophical idea of universal moral rights—moral rights possessed by all persons, regardless of nationality, citizenship, class, sex, race, ethnicity, or any other distinguishing features. On the orthodox view, the point of philosophical theorizing about human rights is to develop a systematic account of this idea, using the traditional tools of moral philosophy to determine which universal moral human rights really exist and how they are to be justified. It is relatively uncontroversial to defend the existence of a moral human right against torture, for example, but there is more disagreement about whether there is a moral human right to an adequate standard of health. Orthodox theories aim to develop sophisticated philosophical theories that explain how moral human rights can be justified, thereby providing reasoned resolutions to such debates, including debates about which legal human rights international law should embrace.

Against this orthodox methodology, so-called "political" theorists argue that philosophical theorizing about human rights should defer in important respects to the idea of human rights as it appears in the practice. Political theorists are motivated by the concern that even sophisticated philosophical accounts of the idea of universal moral rights may not speak to the real moral problems and questions arising in human rights practice, thus risking irrelevance to the ways in which human rights actually function in law, politics, and society. Their aim, therefore, is to develop a philosophical theory of human rights that is based on an accurate reconstruction of the role that the idea of human rights plays in these domains.

My objective in this chapter is to situate my own approach—ultimately, a kind of political approach—in terms of this debate. In the first two sections, I explain in more detail the debate between orthodox and political theories of human rights, focusing in particular on their different understandings of the relationship between philosophy and human rights practice. My account is limited to a few canonical examples of each approach, and is not intended to be representative of the rich literature that has developed these approaches in more detail.[1] Rather, my objective is to sketch the main contours of the debate as a way of motivating the approach I develop later in the book.

In the section "Facts, Values, and Philosophy," I argue that the roots of the orthodox/political debate are intertwined with persistent questions in academic philosophy regarding the nature of the distinction between facts and values, and about philosophy's distinctive contribution to understanding and theorizing moral practices. I will try to show that this debate has been structured by an overly stark distinction between facts and values, which in turn implies a disciplinary division of labor according to which philosophy's distinctive work is to provide abstract moral analysis that is needed to guide human rights practice and scholarship in other disciplines. My objective is to challenge this presumed division of labor, relying on two strategies for doing so. First, it is helpful to theorize human rights as a thick concept, containing both normative and descriptive elements. On this view, the moral idea of human rights cannot accurately be understood (at least insofar as it is relevant to human rights practice) without due attention to the descriptive features of that idea within the practice. Second, I argue that the orthodox/political debate can be transformed by making room for philosophical arguments in which both descriptive and normative claims from within human rights practice may stand in evidentiary relationship to moral claims in human rights theory. My approach therefore regards the practice as a source of both descriptive evidence and normative claims that philosophers of human rights have good reason to take up into their theorizing about human rights morality.

I then show how a commitment to an overly stark version of the fact/value distinction manifests in the orthodox/political debate in two ways: first, in a commitment by orthodox theorists to theorizing human rights at a high level of abstraction, rather than by addressing more contextualized moral issues embedded in the practice; and second, a narrow focus (by both orthodox and political theorists) on answering ontological questions about which moral human rights exist and how they are to be justified. Regarding the first, I argue that the orthodox method of conducting moral inquiry as if it were neatly extractable from the practice runs the risk of developing irrelevant or even misleading theories of human rights morality. Regarding the second, I argue that a narrow focus on ontological questions about moral human rights contributes to the neglect of other ways of theorizing human rights morality, especially including its institutional and egalitarian elements.

In this chapter's final section, I argue that rethinking the nature of the fact/value distinction can point philosophers toward novel research questions and methods, and toward an alternative methodology that provides a way out of the current impasse. Emphasizing the pragmatist elements of existing political approaches, and building on arguments from Allen Buchanan about the nature and scope of the practice, I propose a methodology that provides a compelling account of its own normativity (which practical approaches are accused of lacking), while squarely addressing the question of relevance that constitutes the distinctive challenge facing orthodox views. On my approach, the work of the philosopher is neither to provide an account of the normativity of moral human rights from outside the practice, nor is it confined to providing a systematic reconstruction of the practice's aims as they currently exist. Instead, philosophy can contribute to understanding human rights morality by theorizing the multiple and contested moral visions of human rights that animate the practice itself.

ORTHODOX THEORIES

Orthodox (or traditional) theories begin with the idea of human rights as moral rights possessed by all human beings, along with the conviction that this is the moral idea that animates and motivates human rights law and practice. As John Tasioulas has argued regarding IHRL, "human rights laws . . . typically presuppose an extra-legal conception of human rights, one that is a benchmark against which the laws themselves are to be assessed."[2] The goal of orthodox theorizing is both to illuminate this extra-legal conception of human rights as a philosophical project in its own right, and to provide moral clarity and guidance to the practice, via careful philosophical argument about the values that ground moral human rights.

James Griffin's theory is generally considered an exemplar of the orthodox approach, and is therefore worth considering in some detail.[3] Griffin begins with the idea of moral human rights as it emerged from the Enlightenment tradition of natural law, according to which a human right is "a right that we have simply in virtue of being human."[4] This idea emerged in the Middle Ages, and was a precursor to the idea of natural rights possessed by all human beings found in, for example, the American Declaration of Independence and the French Declaration of the Rights of Man and the Citizen. The Universal Declaration of Human Rights, and the subsequent treaties comprising international human rights law as it developed during the twentieth century, are the descendants of this same tradition, animated by the core ethical concept of universal moral rights.

For Griffin, the intellectual history of this moral idea establishes the connection between twentieth-century human rights practice and philosophical theorizing about moral human rights: namely, that the moral core of IHRL just is the philosophical idea of moral human rights. For this reason, Griffin differentiates his approach from philosophical projects (such as Kant's or Mill's) that attempt to "derive [universal rights] from one, or a few, highest-level moral principles."[5] Rather than explicating the idea of human rights as we know it via the intellectual pedigree that Griffin traces, Kant and Mill (he argues) are simply "commandeering the term 'human rights' (or 'natural rights' or, in Mill's case, just plain 'rights') to do service in the exposition of their own general moral theory."[6] In contrast to such "top-down" philosophical approaches, Griffin describes his own view as "bottom up"—in other words, one that starts instead from the idea of human rights inherent in international human rights practice. On his methodology, "one starts with human rights as used in our actual social life by politicians, lawyers, social campaigners, as well as theorists of various sorts, and then sees what higher principles one must resort to in order to explain their moral weight, when one thinks they have it, and to resolve conflicts between them."[7]

In Griffin's view, the most important contribution to be made by philosophers of human rights is to give more specific normative content to the still-indeterminate idea of human rights that international human rights law has inherited from Enlightenment philosophy. Because this is the moral idea that animates the practice, its indeterminacy generates intractable practical conflicts, for example, about basic questions like which moral human rights really exist, and even about what should count as relevant considerations in answering such questions. The appropriate philosophical contribution to remedying this state of affairs is therefore to "complete" the historical idea of human rights: "We need an account of human rights with at least enough content to tell us, for any such proposed right, difficult borderline cases aside, whether it really is one and to what it is a right."[8]

The specification of the Enlightenment idea that Griffin's own theory proposes is to see them as protections for human beings' "normative agency," that is, "our capacity to choose and to pursue our conception of a worthwhile life."[9] In his view, the moral importance of this capacity covers "the spectrum from deliberation to choice to action to outcome."[10] Human rights, therefore, "have their ground in the three values of personhood: autonomy, liberty, and minimal provision":[11]

> To be an agent, in the fullest sense of which we are capable, one must (first) choose one's own path through life—that is, not be dominated or controlled by someone or something else (call it "autonomy"). And (second) one's choice must be real; one must have at least a certain minimum education and information. And having chosen, one must then be able to act; that is, one must have at least the minimum provision of resources and capabilities that it takes (call all of this "minimum provision"). And none of this is any good if someone then blocks one; so (third) others must also not forcibly stop one from pursuing what one sees as a worthwhile life (call this "liberty").[12]

While these "personhood values" provide the foundational values for moral human rights, Griffin does not think that this account is sufficient for specifying a moral human right in a determinate enough way that it can serve as "an effective, socially manageable claim on others."[13] Therefore, he provides a role for what he calls "practicalities" in determining the content of moral human rights. These are "features of human nature and of the nature of human societies" that are relevant to determining what a particular human right is a right to.[14]

Taken together, the personhood values Griffin specifies, together with the relevant practicalities, justify a list of moral rights that is shorter than the lists of legal human rights embodied in international human rights declarations and treaties. While his list of *bona fide* moral human rights endorses the broad categories of human rights represented in international law, including both welfare rights and political rights, Griffin criticizes the lists of human rights in international law as too "lavish," for including rights that cannot be justified on the basis of his personhood account.[15] For example, while the Universal Declaration of Human Rights proclaims a right to work, Griffin writes that:

> on my account, there is no right to work. There is certainly a right to the resources needed to live as an agent, but those resources do not have to come from work. If in an advanced technological society there were not enough work for everyone, and those without it were adequately provided for, then, on the face of it, no one's human rights would be violated.[16]

It might seem odd for Griffin to critique the idea of human rights operative in the practice, given that his goal is to theorize that very idea. However, a basic commitment of Griffin's methodology is that a philosophically defensible theory of moral human rights (like the one he offers) is needed to provide normative guidance for the practice. In other words, a normatively disciplined human rights practice would declare as human rights only those that can be justified according to a philosophically defensible account of the core normative concept of moral human rights.[17] Griffin of course recognizes that a philosophical theory of moral human rights cannot in fact bring about the reform of international human rights law in the ways that his theory recommends. Acknowledging that "[a] solitary author, especially a solitary philosopher, is most unlikely to be able to bring about a rethinking of the whole of the international law of human rights," Griffin nonetheless argues that philosophical theories of moral human rights can contribute to the "gradual critical process" inherent in law itself. This process, presumably driven primarily by international lawyers and judges, "can turn a cold shoulder to laws or sections of treaties that it thinks deeply flawed; it can sometimes eventually make dead letters of them. Or it can wait for courts to remedy ambiguity and confusion in the law."[18] Based on his personhood theory of moral human rights, Griffin recommends the legal "cold shoulder" for many rights claims in international law that his theory classifies as "unacceptable" or "debatable," but also argues that "[m]any rights are so badly drawn that they need interpretation tantamount to redrafting."[19]

Other orthodox theories of human rights generally agree with Griffin's on methodological issues, but disagree with him about the existence conditions and grounds of moral human rights. Their views therefore generate different lists of genuine moral human rights, which they argue should serve as the standard of moral justification for international human rights law. For example, John Tasioulas's theory has a similar overall structure as Griffin's, but Tasioulas argues that multiple human interests (not just an interest in personhood) can ground moral human rights. Regarding Griffin's rejection of a moral human right to work, for example, Tasioulas questions whether Griffin's personhood account really considers all the relevant values that might ground such a right:

> Certainly, considerations of liberty and autonomy are among them . . . , but why not also, for example, other values such as accomplishment, understanding, deep personal relations and enjoyment? Why can't the right to work or to options to live one's life in a productive, interesting, enjoyable way derive from the combined effect of a number of values, of which the values of personhood are only two?[20]

Tasioulas's view therefore differs from Griffin's regarding the inter-related questions of *fidelity to the practice* and *rights inflation*. Orthodox theorists critique human rights practice for including legal human rights that cannot be justified on the basis of a theory of moral human rights. Insofar as Griffin's theory justifies a relatively narrow range of legal human rights, it is subject to the criticism that it is revisionist (in a minimalist direction) with respect to the practice. Tasioulas's view, by contrast, justifies a longer list of moral human rights, and in that respect exhibits greater fidelity to the practice, but for this reason his theory (like the practice itself) is susceptible to the reverse critique that it enables or engages in a problematic tendency to rights inflation—that is, to proclaim human rights without adequate normative justification, thereby "cheapening" the moral value of "genuine" human rights.[21]

Importantly, for orthodox theorists, questions about whether the practice is justified in proclaiming the existence of particular legal human rights are not ones that the practice has resources on its own to resolve. Instead, any adequate resolution of these issues requires a philosophical account of moral human rights that engages in moral theorizing at a more detailed level. For example, regarding the charge of rights inflation, Tasioulas argues that Griffin erroneously assumes that "the only way to avoid profligacy is to restrict the category of values that can figure in the justification of human rights."[22] Against this assumption, Tasioulas argues that moral human rights may be grounded in a wide range of interests, but only when those interests "are weighty enough to justify the imposing on others of duties to respect and further those interests in various ways."[23] His view therefore avoids "profligacy" of the kind that might contribute to rights inflation on the basis of "judgments of importance" regarding the interests that ground human rights, rather than by limiting which interests can ground human rights.[24] However, the point here is not so much about the details of these particular philosophical arguments. Rather, what matters for our purposes is to draw out the orthodox methodological assumption that a philosophical theory of moral human rights is needed for determining which human rights the practice should embrace. Again, this is because the point of a philosophical theory of human rights, according to orthodox methodology, is to offer a theory of moral human rights that specifies their existence conditions and that generates normatively justified and coherent lists of moral human rights, all as a way of constructively theorizing the inchoate idea of human rights found in international law and practice.

This methodology, however, raises rather urgently the important question of how a philosophical theory of moral human rights is supposed to provide normative guidance for international human rights law or other aspects of human rights practice. As Charles Beitz argues, orthodox conceptions of human rights "are question-begging in presuming to understand and criticize an existing normative practice on the basis of one or another governing conception that does not, itself, take account of the functions that the idea of a human right is meant to play, and actually does play, in the practice."[25] Joseph Raz puts the same point rather baldly: "The problem [for orthodox theories] is the absence of a convincing argument as to why human rights practice should conform to their theories. There is no point in criticizing current human rights practice on the ground that it does not fit the traditional human rights ethical doctrine. Why should it?"[26]

By way of an answer to this question, Tasioulas has recently argued for what he calls the "formative aim thesis" as the "guiding aspiration that characterizes the distinctive nature of IHRL": "IHRL's integrity as a department of international law consists in the fact that it is primarily concerned with giving effect to universal moral rights, insofar as it is appropriate for international law to do so through the technique of assigning a uniform set of individual rights to all human beings."[27]

Given philosophy's expertise in moral theory, its distinctive contribution to understanding human rights practice is (on this view) to offer a philosophical theory of moral human rights, thereby helping to render the central, animating idea of the practice more determinate and consistent. Orthodox theorists therefore regard theories of moral human rights not only as worthy philosophical projects in their own right, but also as the appropriate contribution from philosophy to interdisciplinary scholarship about human rights practice—again, because a theory of moral human rights is essential to understanding the moral point of international human rights law and practice in the first place.[28]

In addition to the formative aim thesis, orthodox theorists have separately articulated at least three additional reasons why a philosophical theory of moral human rights—the central contribution of orthodox theories—is relevant to and normatively authoritative for the practice, especially including international human rights law. The first is that a plausible theory of moral human rights has practical significance for the broad success of human rights culture, given widespread skepticism about the moral legitimacy of human rights claims. According to this argument, observers and stakeholders are justifiably critical of a practice that seems normatively undisciplined but nonetheless challenges traditional norms of state independence and autonomy, and aims to substantively influence the internal political culture and laws of states.[29] Orthodox theorists argue that developing a theory of moral human rights that explicates the aims and goals of the practice in a normatively coherent way is a powerful step in alleviating skepticism about it, especially if that theory can be put to use in actually disciplining the practice's development. For example, Griffin argues that

> [m]any persons have still to be convinced of the case for human rights. There is cynicism about the whole discourse, which, being so fatally malleable, is exploited as a weapon in power politics. . . . And there are doubts, not always groundless, about how firmly based some of the claims to human rights are. One way to join in advancing the cause of human rights is to make the case for them as intellectually compelling as one can.[30]

Tasioulas argues, similarly, that "human rights culture might achieve enhanced 'efficacy'—higher levels of acceptance and compliance throughout the globe—precisely through being furnished with a rational justification that [is] able to win over individuals, states and cultures currently resistant to the idea of human rights or beset by confusion and perplexity about it."[31]

The second argument concerns the interpretation of international human rights law. As Griffin notes, the sources of international law include not only treaties and customary law, but also basic commitments of justice (called *jus cogens* norms in international law). Insofar as international human rights law incorporates moral norms, then, its interpretation by international courts will necessarily involve making moral judgments. And those judgments, if they are to be themselves normatively coherent, need to be guided by a respectably coherent theory of the relevant moral values, which is exactly what orthodox theorists are offering. As Griffin argues: "an international court willing to heed expert opinion or considerations of humanity or *ius cogens* is driven to take seriously basic considerations of justice, the meaning of the 'the dignity of the human person,' and how justice and rights are related. The decisions of international courts are not an alternative to answering my questions; they require it."[32]

Third, orthodox theorists worry that an account of moral human rights is necessary to avoid legal positivism about international human rights law. As Griffin argues, for example: "No matter who we are we cannot establish a human right just by declaring it to be one. Not even the Universal Declaration of Human Rights by the United Nations in solemn assembly is enough. We—whoever we are—can get it wrong, and we owe attention, therefore, to the criteria for right and wrong here."[33]

Without a theory of moral human rights, Griffin implies, we will lack such criteria, leaving ourselves no standard for what count as "genuine" human rights other than the positive lists of human rights proclaimed in international human rights law. Tasioulas echoes this view, arguing that the broader point of orthodox theorizing is "to oppose the tendency among many, especially human rights lawyers, to bypass the question of whether something really is a human right, in the moral sense, by treating the law as dispositive on the matter."[34]

For orthodox theorists, then, developing a defensible theory of moral human rights is the appropriate philosophical contribution to understanding and guiding the practice, because the central point of the practice is precisely to "give effect" to this inherently philosophical idea. On this view, orthodox theorizing taps into philosophy's distinctive expertise, and is not only deeply relevant to the practice, but essential to appreciating its moral point in the first place and to specifying its moral requirements in particular contexts.

POLITICAL THEORIES OF HUMAN RIGHTS

Political (or practical) theories of human rights reject the orthodox assertion that human rights can be adequately theorized independently of their role in the practice. Despite their shared commitment to theorizing human rights in terms of their role or function in the practice, however, political theories are a much more heterogeneous group than orthodox theories. They do not necessarily agree about the appropriate relationship between philosophy and the practice, or on the range of philosophical questions about human rights to which the practice is relevant. As I'll explain below, John Rawls (on one reading) and Joseph Raz conceive of human rights in a remarkably orthodox way as a subset of universal moral rights, where political considerations are relevant primarily to defining the subset of moral rights that count as human rights. By contrast, Charles Beitz, and possibly John Rawls (on a different reading), reject the orthodox idea that human rights should be considered a species of universal moral rights at all, opting instead for an account of human rights that derives more directly and fully from the practice. I describe these views in this section in order to bring out the essential contrast between them and orthodox views. I move quickly over the subset views (or at least, the subset interpretations of Raz and Rawls) in order to concentrate on the political approach's more radical methodological innovations.

Rawls's account of human rights is widely regarded as the inspiration for political approaches. In *Law of Peoples*, Rawls develops his account of human rights as part of his ideal theory of a foreign policy for liberal societies, or, as he puts it, "an ideal conception of a Law of Peoples for the Society of well-ordered Peoples."[35] His account of human rights is deliberately minimalist in order to cater to the specific role they play in this larger, ideal theory, where they provide standards that specify which peoples are entitled to toleration on the world stage and which are not. As Rawls defines them, human rights are "necessary conditions of any system of social cooperation,"[36] with the implication that *if* a non-liberal, but "decent," people is a conceptual possibility, then such a people would be entitled to toleration in international politics precisely because they respect human rights.[37] (So-called outlaw states, that is, states that violate human rights [in Rawls's minimalist sense], are not entitled to toleration.)[38]

Rawls connects human rights so understood to the practice of human rights by noting that the primary function of human rights in international relations in the late twentieth century was to justify emerging limitations on the internationally recognized prerogatives of state sovereignty, which had traditionally been understood to include both the right to pursue state aims via warfare and the right to complete autonomy regarding how a state treats its own citizens. Since Rawls's larger aim in the *Law of Peoples* is to develop an ideal theory of international relations (from the perspective of a liberal society), he decides to "leave aside the many difficulties of interpreting these rights and limits, and take their general meaning and tendency as clear enough. What is essential is that our elaboration of the Law of Peoples should fit these two basic changes, and give them a suitable rationale."[39] Ultimately, then, this rationale is provided in Rawls's ideal theory by his minimalist conception of human rights, which he relies on to mark the difference between decent and outlaw peoples, or, ultimately, between societies that enjoy traditional sovereignty rights against external interference and those that don't.[40]

In this way, Rawls essentially operationalizes the term "human rights" to play a particular role in his theory of fair terms of cooperation among societies or peoples. It may therefore be appropriate to understand his project as "top-down," in Griffin's sense. Griffin himself endorses this reading, arguing that Rawls, just as much as Kant or Mill, simply appropriates the language of human rights in service of his own ideal theory (in Rawls's case, his own ideal theory of international relations for liberal states). And, as many critiques of Rawls's account of human rights have noted, it is beset with perplexities if it is interpreted as a "bottom-up" theory of human rights practice. One of these is the fact that his list of human rights is notoriously extremely short, including only rights to life, liberty (understood negatively as freedom from slavery, serfdom, and forced labor), personal property, and formal equality before the law.[41] In this respect, Rawls's view fares very poorly indeed on the standard of fidelity to the practice. However, given the functional role of human rights in his broader theory, there is ample reason to keep the list of human rights short. As Rawls notes, "[a]n outlaw state that violates these rights is to be condemned, and in grave cases may be subjected to forceful sanctions and even to intervention."[42] Therefore, only a very limited list of human rights can be justified on this account, given the limited circumstances in which interventions should be justifiable in a moral theory of international politics.

While criticisms of Rawls's view as revisionist of human rights practice may be misplaced if his theory is not actually attempting to theorize the practice in the first place, it is nonetheless worth spending some time on his view as if it were such a theory, if only because many political theorists take Rawls's account of human rights in *Law of Peoples* as pioneering the political approach. Understood as a "bottom up" theory of human rights, then, Rawls's view has two notable features. First, as we just noted, Rawls's view has been widely criticized from nearly all quarters for being deeply revisionist with respect to the practice. Like many of Rawls's critics, Griffin notes that Rawls's view leaves out very many different roles that human rights play in international politics: "For example, they quite obviously have [a] point intra-nationally: to justify rebellion, to establish a case for peaceful reform, to curb an autocratic ruler, to criticize a majority's treatment of racial or ethnic minorities."[43] Griffin and other critics have also argued that Rawls's concern that human rights should avoid parochialism need not result in his particularly short list of human rights, since (as Griffin argues), "the continued spread of the largely Western-inspired discourse of human rights that we have witnessed over the last sixty years" holds out the promise of producing a "measure of convergence" from members of different societies and cultures on both the lists of human rights endorsed within the practice and their justifications.[44] "Why, then," Griffin asks, "does Rawls commandeer the label 'human rights' for his shorter list? For no sufficient reason."[45]

While orthodox views have been widely criticized by political theorists as having only questionable relevance to the practice, Rawls's account therefore arguably exhibits even *less* engagement with human rights practice than many orthodox theorists do. For a purportedly "political" view, then, Rawls's theory is surprisingly disengaged from any details about human rights practice. As Tasioulas notes, "it is hard to shake off the suspicion that Rawls means by 'human rights' something very different from what, on any half-way charitable construal, most people, including the Declaration's framers, mean by that phrase."[46] However we interpret Rawls's theory, Tasioulas's point is apt: Rawls's understanding of human rights is not at all one that is closely informed by or that even resembles how human rights are understood in practice.

Second, Rawls unambiguously views human rights as moral standards. As he notes: "they are intrinsic to the Law of Peoples and have a political (moral) effect whether or not they are supported locally. That is, their political (moral) force extends to all societies, and they are binding on all peoples and societies, including outlaw states."[47] Indeed, Rawls refers to human rights as "a special class of urgent rights."[48] Tasioulas, responding to this feature of Rawls's view, categorizes his theory as a "subset" view: one that characterizes human rights as those universal moral rights that also meet the further condition of playing "the political role that such rights perform" in international politics.[49]

Joseph Raz, while critical of Rawls's view in some respects, emulates (this reading of) Rawls by also defining moral human rights as a politically defined subset of universal moral rights. As Raz argues, "[t]he task of a theory of human rights is (a) to establish the essential features which contemporary human rights practice attributes to the rights it acknowledges to be human rights; and (b) to identify the moral standards which qualify anything to be so acknowledged."[50] Like Rawls, Raz also emphasizes the role of human rights in justifying international intervention. He argues that "while human rights are invoked in various contexts, and for a variety of purposes, the dominant trend in human rights practice is to take the fact that a right is a human right as a defeasibly sufficient ground for taking action against violators in the international arena."[51] In this respect, then, Raz follows what he takes to be Rawls's lead by identifying aspects of human rights practice (specifically, the role that human rights play in international politics) that (in his view) specify which universal moral human rights qualify as human rights.

By contrast, Charles Beitz rejects the interpretation of Rawls as a subset theorist. As Beitz puts it, "[t]here is no appeal to any independent philosophical conception of a human right in Rawls's account of the content or authority of the doctrine."[52] Instead, Beitz sees the "basic insight" of Rawls's view as rejecting reliance on a theory of universal moral rights, and embracing instead the transformative idea that

> we might frame our understanding of the idea of a human right by identifying the roles that this idea plays within a discursive practice. We attend to the practical inferences that would be drawn by competent participants in the practice from what they regard as valid claims of human rights. An inventory of these inferences generates a view of the discursive functions of human rights and this informs an account of the meaning of the concept.[53]

By aiming to develop a theory of human rights that follows this interpretation of Rawls's approach, Beitz's innovative methodology is to look to the practice of human rights in international law and politics in order to construct a conception of human rights that is true to the practice itself, rather than to an independent, pre-existing normative ideal in philosophical theory. His approach therefore reconstructs the meaning and significance of human rights within the practice as the standard for determining what human rights are and which human rights exist. As Beitz describes it, the point of a practical method is to take

> the doctrine and practice of human rights as we find them in international political life as source materials for constructing a conception of human rights. It understands questions about the nature and content of human rights to refer to objects of the sort called "human rights" in international practice. There is no assumption of a prior or independent layer of fundamental rights whose nature and content can be discovered independently of a consideration of the place of

> human rights in the international realm and its normative discourse and then used to interpret and criticize international doctrine.[54]

This view therefore amounts to a decisive rejection of the orthodox notion that human rights practice aims to "give effect to" pre-existing moral human rights.[55] In this sense, political theorists aim to start from scratch, using a close interpretation of the concept of human rights as it is used in the practice as the subject of their theorizing. Cristina LaFont aptly describes this central commitment of practical views as follows: "By grasping the aims of the practice and understanding its significance we obtain the central interpretative clue that allows us to answer the question of what human rights actually are through the indirect path of figuring out what distinctive functions they play in practice."[56]

FACTS, VALUES, AND PHILOSOPHY

Beitz's rejection of the idea that the practice's central, guiding aim is to realize a pre-existing concept of moral human rights contests the two key claims that orthodox theorists make in justifying and defending their approach. The first is the claim to an impeccable normative pedigree, on the grounds that orthodox theories of moral human rights are soundly rooted in philosophical accounts of value and traditional philosophical reasoning. The second is the claim to unimpeachable relevance to the practice, on grounds that the idea of moral human rights constitutes the moral core of the practice itself, so theorizing that idea just is theorizing the central moral point of the practice.

However, political approaches that follow Beitz's example take on a significant argumentative burden of articulating in convincing detail how their methodology is supposed to account for the normativity of human rights. On their own accounting at least, orthodox theorists get this normativity for free, since the concept of moral human rights they theorize is both the normative core of the practice (on their view) and an uncontestably normative concept. But even if political theorists are correct in arguing that human rights should be defined by their role within the practice, they then need some further account of how their theories can accommodate the radical, transformative potential and moral authority of the idea of human rights to criticize the world as it is, rather than simply accounting for the contingent uses to which that idea has been put in the practice as we know it.

As orthodox theorists argue, this transformative potential is a key element of the moral point of the practice in the first place, but the practice can go wrong in attempting to implement it. If political theories amount to simply describing the idea of human rights in the practice, it is hard to see how they provide any convincing account of this transformative moral idea. For example, Pablo Gilabert argues that "the political approach runs the risk of taking too much for granted from the status quo and of failing to make sense of the universalist moral aspirations that are crucial to render the practice of human rights a progressive development in modern politics."[57] Similarly, David Luban has argued that

> ILHRs [international legal human rights] cannot be decoupled from moral human rights, although they almost certainly can be decoupled from any specific philosophical theory of moral human rights. If legal human rights are just another bit of positive law, then why should anyone invest time and money, let alone risk their lives, to mobilize around ILHRs?[58]

In fact, Beitz himself concedes that this creates a burden of proof for practical approaches; as he describes it: "A practical view holds that human rights should be understood in relation to their discursive role within the practice. The question is how the fact that human rights play this role bears on the reasons we have to act, assuming that we have any, when a human right is violated."[59]

On a standard view of this debate, then, political theories purchase their relevance to the practice at the cost of taking on an argumentative burden to establish the normativity of their accounts. Orthodox views, by contrast, lay claim to both normativity and relevance, seeing (by their own lights at least) no tradeoff between the two.[60]

However, I want to question this received view by arguing that it, along with the orthodox/political debate itself, has been framed by an overly sharp version of the distinction between facts and values, which in turn presumes a particular disciplinary division of labor in conceptualizing philosophy's signature contribution to theorizing human rights. This is manifested in two interrelated ways. First, the claim that philosophy needs "critical distance" from the practice is often overstated, or at least unanalyzed, in this debate. This claim implies, quite plausibly, that philosophers should theorize normative questions arising from the practice by abstracting away from the detailed empirical realities of the practice itself in order to better focus on the moral questions at stake. But too many participants in this debate understand the need for critical distance to imply a more extreme view: namely, that philosophical theorizing about human rights may (or even must) fully extract any distinctively normative questions and then analyze them separately from the contingencies of the practice. This view conceptualizes the moral and the practical aspects of human rights practice as distinct, separable elements that can be understood independently from each other. Putting this point in terms of the fact/value distinction, this reflects the tendency of philosophers to think that reliable moral inquiry may (or even must) be (more or less) "fact-free," emphasizing the need for moral theorizing to proceed independently and at an appropriately wide critical distance from existing social or political practices, rather than in connection with them.

The second, related phenomenon is the tendency to underestimate the extent to which the practice itself contains normativity of any kind that deserves philosophical attention. In terms of the fact/value distinction, this is the tendency to see the practice as (more or less) value-free, at least to the extent that it is regarded as incapable of generating normatively authoritative accounts of its own core values. In other words, while philosophers recognize that participants in the practice are making moral claims, they view those claims as suspect unless and until they are validated by a philosophical perspective that is appropriately external to the practice.[61] The view that the normative perspective internal to the practice may in some respects be at least presumptively authoritative regarding human rights morality simply has no room in standard philosophical methodologies. Instead, the standard approach regards factual claims made by participants within the practice as largely irrelevant to the philosophical project regarding human rights, which is distinctively normative. As I will argue, this hampers the ability of philosophical analysis to learn from the forms of moral reasoning inherent in human rights practice, which include participants making, responding to, and analyzing moral claims, often via institutionalized channels that intentionally encourage the participation of voices whose moral claims may be unheard in other forums (including in mainstream or traditional academic philosophy).

The orthodox critique of practical views as lacking any obvious normative authority of its own is therefore based on twin assumptions: that authoritative moral principles can (or even should) be developed without close engagement with the specific practices in which they are intended to be authoritative; and that human rights practice is essentially a consumer but not a producer of credible value claims, and is therefore in need of normative guidance from moral philosophy.[62] Insofar as they understand moral theorizing as illuminating what *ought to be*, while other disciplines are concerned to investigate and explain what *is*, orthodox theorists resist suggestions that detailed knowledge about human rights practice is relevant to the distinctly philosophical work of generating theories of human rights morality. They therefore presume philosophy's *asymmetrical disciplinary independence* from scholarship in other relevant disciplines (such as political science and law), and from the practice itself. In other words, they presume a disciplinary division of labor that assigns to philosophy the role of providing authoritative moral guidance to these other disciplines and to human rights practice, even while holding that this guidance need not (and perhaps should not) be informed in any substantive way by those disciplines or by the practice in order to play this role appropriately.

The prominence and persistence of the assumption of philosophy's asymmetrical disciplinary independence can be explained by pointing to entrenched views within philosophy about the nature of moral reasoning. As Elizabeth Anderson has argued, philosophers historically have tended to adopt a conception of moral inquiry that draws a sharp boundary between facts and values:

> If Anglo-American philosophy can claim moral inquiry as a proper part of its mission, this is largely because it conceives of the academic division of labor as assigning responsibility for discovering the empirical facts to the natural and social sciences, while it works on a priori truths and value judgments. Philosophy no less than the other disciplines operates under the shadow of the fact-value dichotomy, even when it accepts the legitimacy of moral inquiry.[63]

As Anderson argues, while the idea of "applied ethics" in philosophy was intended to provide a way for philosophical inquiry to engage directly with the real world, it nonetheless preserved the role of moral inquiry as primarily a matter of abstract moral reasoning, rather than close engagement with actual practices in the world:

> This conception of moral inquiry preserves the fact-value dichotomy because it takes empirical inquiry into the facts and experiences of living up to the ethical norms embodied in actual social practices as irrelevant to the justification of the moral principles that "apply" to these practices, and because it assumes that the actual state of these practices has nothing to do with whether the norms they embody are reasonable or apt.[64]

Using Anderson's framework, we can understand orthodox approaches to theorizing moral human rights as operating on a traditional model of moral philosophy, where human rights represent a moral concept to be explicated using the methods of abstract reasoning typical of philosophical inquiry. To the extent that such theories engage with human rights practice, this engagement tends to assume the model of applied ethics, according to which abstract philosophical reasoning is deployed to guide or correct the functioning of the practice, which itself is not taken to be morally instructive.

Kimberly Hutchings has argued that this division of labor manifests itself in a particular way within political philosophy, which assigns to itself the role of identifying and defending authoritative principles of justice, while seeing the work of political science as measuring the gap between the world as it is and the world as it should be according to philosophical principles of justice. This division of labor leaves the work of figuring out how to close that gap, and actually closing it, to activists, policy makers, and others immersed in politics.[65] (Of course, philosophers may partake in these tasks, for example, as activists, but in that capacity they are not representing the distinctive disciplinary contribution of philosophy.[66]) According to Hutchings, this division of labor embraces the assumption that political philosophy functions as "the source of moral commands, which it is the task of political scientists and political actors to help actualize."[67] In other words, normative theory is taken to provide guidance and moral coherence to the work of political scientists and activists, even while neither empirical evidence discovered by political scientists nor activists' struggles are regarded as essential to philosophical theorizing about how the world ought to be. On this view, then, the work of political scientists, lawyers, and activists should respond to the work of political philosophers and theorists, but the reverse is not true. Hutchings's description of this disciplinary division of labor echoes Anderson's critique of traditional ways of doing "applied ethics" within philosophy, where "[e]mpirical evidence may be accepted as relevant to the question of how to apply an ethical principle but almost never to the question of whether the ethical principle is justified in the first place."[68]

There are at least two ways to contest the overly sharp fact-value distinction as it has been deployed in the philosophy of human rights. The first is to consider the moral concept of human rights as a *thick concept*, one that includes both descriptive and normative elements. For example, the idea of "cruelty" implies not only a thin normative analysis as wrongful or vicious, but also only accurately applies to behavior exhibiting (as a descriptive element) the "intention to make some creature suffer."[69] Similarly, for any theory that aims to provide informed normative critique and guidance for contemporary human rights practice, accurately theorizing human rights requires both normative and descriptive elements, including essential descriptive reference to the role of human rights in the practice. While very many evaluative terms are thick in this way (so the concept of human rights is not particularly special in this regard), the salient point is that any theory that aims to be normatively authoritative for the practice should theorize the descriptive elements of human rights claims in terms that are recognizable to competent participants in human rights practice.

Second, while the fact/value distinction has an appropriate role to play in preventing illicit logical inferences from facts to values (or vice versa), it is important to recognize that factual premises may legitimately stand in evidentiary relationship to moral conclusions. As Anderson argues:

> There is a conceptual distinction between "*x* exists" and the report "I see *x*," where *x* is an object that exists independent of the mind. Hence, one is always logically entitled to reject the usual inference from the report "I see *x*" to "*x*

> exists." However, if one insists on rejecting this inference without offering reasons to doubt the evidence of one's senses, one simply is not engaged in empirical inquiry. Similarly, if one insists on rejecting the usual normative inferences licensed by thick evaluative judgments without offering reasons to doubt, for instance, that cruelty is bad, one simply is not engaged in ethical inquiry. In both cases the entitlement to infer one claim from another is not logical but inferential.[70]

On Anderson's (broadly pragmatist) model of moral reasoning, facts may provide *evidence for* the truth of certain claims about value, even though it would be illegitimate to infer any value claims as a direct logical implication of any factual claims. For example, the fact that living according to a particular value makes one's life go well can function as defeasible evidence for the claim that this value is in fact worthy of one's endorsement. Similarly, collective experience of social life under a particular regime of laws can provide evidence regarding the moral justifiability of such laws. In terms of human rights theory, the lesson here is that we may legitimately look to evidence from human rights practice for insights about substantive dimensions of human rights morality. Philosophers have tended to focus on questions about (to paraphrase Griffin) whether some putative human right really is one, and what it is a right to. But, as I will argue, we can legitimately and productively look to human rights practice to illuminate a broader range of questions that have been less-thoroughly explored in the philosophical literature, saliently including how to interpret the foundational values of human rights morality.

The central point of this section is that, where descriptive and normative claims overlap, as in much of our everyday discourse about morality generally and about human rights in particular, insisting on a sharp distinction between them may hamper moral inquiry in the practical settings where normative guidance is most needed. Moral theories constructed at too great a distance from practical moral questions may offer normative guidance that is questionable in itself or of dubious relevance to the circumstances in which we find ourselves. This possibility suggests that moral investigation of human rights that is relevant to the practice and to other disciplines should, as Anderson puts it, "enlist[. . .] moral and political philosophy in a common project with social and humanistic studies."[71] My aim in this book is to sketch a methodology for theorizing human rights morality as just such a common project (albeit from my own perspective as a philosopher). I pay particular attention to how this methodology expands the range of normative questions that are seen as legitimate objects for philosophical inquiry, while at the same time inviting more genuine collaboration from outside of philosophy in addressing these questions.

ASSUMPTIONS ABOUT THE FACT/VALUE DISTINCTION IN THE ORTHODOX/POLITICAL DEBATE

The aim of this section is to provide a clearer picture of how to broaden and enrich philosophical inquiry regarding human rights morality by uncovering in greater detail two ways that the commitment to an overly sharp understanding of the fact/value distinction has constricted this debate. The first is the orthodox methodological thesis that an account of human rights morality that is instructive for the real world can be supplied using philosophy's traditional methods, in particular, via sophisticated reasoning about questions of moral theory that abstract a considerable distance away from concrete problems and issues concerning human rights in the real world.

Recall Tasioulas's formative aim thesis: "IHRL's integrity as a department of international law consists in the fact that it is primarily concerned with giving effect to universal moral rights, insofar as it is appropriate for international law to do so through the technique of assigning a uniform set of individual rights to all human beings."[72] This view, which animates the orthodox approach in general, positions philosophical questions about moral human rights—their existence, foundations, content, etc.—as *separable from* and *normatively prior* to other questions that arise about or within the practice. Orthodox theorists intend their accounts of moral human rights to illuminate the foundational aims of the practice, conditions for its normative legitimacy, morally desirable paths for its future development, and moral ideals for political activism. The normative guidance provided by a philosophical theory of moral human rights can also, on this view, extend beyond human rights law; for example, some orthodox theorists, moved by the idealism of activists and dissidents whose missions are articulated in terms of human rights, argue that philosophical theories that connect human rights to more foundational values can help to validate and legitimate these movements and the moral significance of human rights practice in a broad sense.[73] As Gilabert puts this point:

> I claim that moral human rights provide a characteristic and powerful resource to orient and justify human rights practice. This justification is characteristic, as most central human rights are commonly seen by practitioners (activists, lawyers, legislators, and the public more broadly) either as expressing moral rights or as specifications of consequences of them in various contexts.[74]

At the same time, however, while fully intending to provide normative guidance to the practice, orthodox theorists rely primarily on the abstract moral reasoning characteristic of traditional philosophical methods in constructing theories of moral human rights. To this extent, the orthodox approach does not regard expertise about human rights practice to be necessary to philosophical theorizing about moral human rights. Consider, for example, James Griffin's gesture of intellectual modesty regarding international law in his book's introduction: "My argument is that ethics must make a contribution too, not that it alone will do the job. We will not reach sufficient determinateness of sense without contribution from ethics. That I do not say much about international law is simply because I do not know much about it."[75] Similarly, in addressing the relationship between "legal, political, and moral discourses" about human dignity and human rights, Gilabert argues that his own philosophical contribution to understanding these relationships should be seen as only part of an ongoing interdisciplinary dialogue: "I do not deny the great importance of legal discourse. If, in this book, I devote more space to moral philosophy and political theory, it is because I am more competent in these areas. My arguments should be seen as humble and fallible hypothetical moves within a larger, interdisciplinary debate which also includes legal scholars."[76]

Remarks like these, fully intended to be modestly realistic about the appropriate limits of philosophical expertise, at the same time reveal an important methodological assumption: that the need for interdisciplinary inquiry regarding human rights practice does not require philosophers to attend closely to international human rights law, activism, or other aspects of the practice in developing their own theories of human rights morality. A further assumption is that the work of actually connecting philosophical theories of moral human rights with law, activism, or other scholarly disciplines can be assigned primarily, if not solely, to non-philosophers.[77] To the extent that philosophical theories of moral human rights are intended to function as a contribution to interdisciplinary scholarship or as normative guidance for the practice itself, relying on traditional philosophical methods in constructing theories of moral human rights leaves the work left to be done in "applying" these theories entirely to other scholars, presumably those with the relevant expertise in these other areas. These approaches therefore reveal a commitment to the view that philosophical theories of moral human rights that are intended to be instructive for the practice may nonetheless be developed nearly or entirely independently from the "real world of human rights."[78]

But is this diagnosis really fair? Recall that orthodox theorists explicitly refute the charge that their theories of moral human rights are insensitive to the idea of human rights in the practice. As we saw, for example, Griffin styles his own view as "bottom up," in the sense of being rooted in the historical idea of human rights used by "political theorists, politicians, international lawyers, and civil servants," as opposed to "top down" philosophical accounts untethered to this idea.[79] Moreover, both Tasioulas and Gilabert take pains to argue that the moral theories they develop are philosophically sophisticated accounts of the values articulated within the practice itself.[80] I should clarify therefore that I do not mean to imply that orthodox theorists simply appropriate the language of human rights while ignoring its public culture and practice, as in the methodology that Griffin imputes to Kant or Mill (or Rawls). Rather, my claim here is that even when orthodox theorists begin their theoretical work by focusing on moral ideas present in the practice, their method from that starting point onward straightforwardly utilizes the abstract moral reasoning typical of philosophy and largely in isolation from the procedures and norms of human rights practice or from expertise in other disciplines that study the practice.

We can see this point a bit more clearly by considering Griffin's description of orthodox methodology. According to Griffin, even when a philosopher aims to theorize the idea of human rights found in international human rights treaties and conventions, "in determining the content of human rights, especially in seeing how to resolve conflict between them, the bottom-up approach will have to rise considerably in theoretical abstraction."[81] Insofar as theorizing of any kind requires abstraction, this is of course not itself an objection to this method. Notice, however, that a "considerable" increase in theoretical abstraction creates room for untethering the philosophical moral analysis from the moral concepts that began the inquiry in the first place. The question is whether orthodox philosophers deploying traditional philosophical methods have any methodological controls in place to ensure that the results of their theorizing remain relevant to the practice, especially when these results are supposed to guide the reform or further development of the practice. Given that orthodox theorists conceptualize moral human rights as an essentially philosophical concept, rather than a thick concept with both normative content and descriptive ties to the practice, the answer to this question appears to be "no." Importantly, then, while the starting points for this methodology are rooted in human rights practice, the account of normativity it provides may end up being developed entirely independently from the practice.

Orthodox theorists might challenge this charge for a different reason. That is because they do in fact provide a role for the practice in specifying the content of human rights in particular contexts. As we saw, in Griffin's account, "practicalities" play an essential role in specifying human rights claims in a determinate enough way that they can serve as "effective, socially manageable" claims.[82] Similarly, Tasioulas has argued that "pure moral reasoning" is not capable of yielding "a fully adequate specification" of human rights claims, maintaining that "a workable standard must, to a large extent, be the product of social decision-making, whether conventional or legal."[83] However, it is not at all clear that this move in fact reduces the distance between orthodox theorizing and the practice in any substantive way. The question hinges on whether this move—recognizing practical contexts as sites of norm specification—constitutes a concession in the direction of recognizing any normative authority within human rights practice, or whether it preserves the division of labor in which abstract philosophical theory is seen as morally authoritative for the practice in a unidirectional fashion. There is good reason to suspect the latter. For example, Tasioulas's further claim that "any such specification through social fiat must operate within tolerably determinate parameters set by moral reasoning" suggests that the specification provided by "practicalities" or "social decision-making" in these theories is merely a mechanism for selecting one particular specification from a range of equally morally acceptable ones, as determined by the philosophical theory of moral human rights at work in the background.[84] So does his argument that "we should acknowledge that at the level of pure moral reasoning, there may be an ineliminable indeterminacy in the deontic content of any given right, . . . so that the formulation of a practically workable standard will require us to supplement such reasoning with positive legal norms or social conventions."[85] Ultimately, there is no obvious mechanism within orthodox methodology that would explain why the outcomes specified by the relevant forms of social decision-making should be regarded as normatively justified *for that reason*. The absence of any such account appears to be further evidence that the process of norm specification within the practice does not make any substantive moral contribution of its own, but is rather simply a morally arbitrary process of selection among equally acceptable alternatives.

The second methodological assumption of orthodox views that is predicated on an overly sharp version of the fact/value distinction is that any adequate philosophical account of human rights morality must be a theory of moral human rights. This assumption simply ignores other aspects of human rights morality, most saliently including its institutional and egalitarian dimensions, which, as I will argue, are not easily accounted for within a theory of moral human rights. Moreover, this assumption also provides one further reason to doubt that orthodox theories regard some sort of practice-based specification of human rights norms as a form of normativity within the practice. This is because orthodox theorizing confines philosophical interest in the practice to what may be called ontological questions about moral human rights—that is, questions about which moral human rights exist and how they are to be justified, and perhaps (to some not-fully-specified degree) what substantive claims they enable rights holders to make. Again, according to the orthodox methodology, these questions are the distinctive expertise of philosophers, so not ones that the practice is likely to have anything morally instructive to contribute to answering.

Perhaps surprisingly, however, the focus on ontological questions about moral human rights is characteristic of both political and orthodox views. In fact, it represents a point of agreement between the two camps on the assumption that the signature contribution from philosophy to interdisciplinary theorizing about human rights is a normatively authoritative list of justifiable human rights. Orthodox theorists focus on ontological questions as a result of their methodological thesis that the idea of moral human rights is the central, motivating concern of the practice. They are naturally preoccupied with questions about which moral human rights exist and why, simply because (in their view) these questions are both the distinctive focus of international human rights law and the distinctive expertise of philosophy. As Tasioulas notes, for example, "philosophers focus on these questions not because they take them to be the most important in some unqualified sense, but rather because they are those with which, as philosophers, they are best equipped to make headway."[86] Subset views (Raz's and perhaps Rawls's) focus on ontological questions for the same reasons that orthodox theories do, given that the sense in which these views are "political" is simply that they harness political considerations as a way of determining which universal moral rights should be considered human rights. While Beitz's view is more thoroughly practice-oriented, the central methodological thesis of his view is nonetheless focused on defining and specifying particular human rights, essentially revealing the same ontological preoccupation shared by the other approaches.[87]

My point here is not at all to discredit the goal of addressing ontological questions about moral human rights. Addressing such questions is of course a legitimate philosophical enterprise unto itself, and may also constitute (part of) a meaningful contribution to understanding and evaluating aspects of human rights practice. However, a narrow focus on ontological questions about moral human rights has sharply limited the contributions that philosophers have made to theorizing normative elements of human rights practice, and (as I will argue in Chapter 3) even distorts philosophers' reasoning about the foundational values of human rights morality. Moreover, this narrow focus seems to stem from, and risks further contributing to, a misleadingly narrow view of human rights practice as consisting primarily of the lists of human rights in international treaties and conventions. As Allen Buchanan has pointed out, IHRL also includes the institutional processes that generate human rights treaties and conventions in the first place, and that specify how human rights norms are interpreted and specified for application to particular circumstances. Moreover, human rights *practice* more broadly includes agents as diverse as states' governments, international organizations created by international human rights law (like the Treaty Bodies that oversee implementation of human rights conventions within states), international courts, judges, and officials, individual human beings in their roles as citizens, government officials, and activists, civil society organizations including human rights advocacy groups, and more.[88]

Buchanan's broader view of human rights practice highlights the fact that ontological questions about moral human rights constitute only a very narrow sliver of the broad range of normative questions about the practice that philosophers might address. This narrow focus therefore leaves many other moral questions about human rights practice off the philosophical agenda. Notably among these, as Buchanan notes, are questions about the moral justifiability of the system of international human rights law, understood as a set of institutions that create, interpret, and (to some extent) enforce universal legal rights. Importantly, once philosophers turn their attention to these broader questions, there is no reason to think that the methodological resources of either orthodox or existing political approaches will be adequate to answering them. This is at least partly because the terms of evaluation for political and institutional contexts—including political legitimacy and equality in the sense that is important to human rights morality—are not necessarily reducible to a theory of moral human rights, as I shall argue in subsequent chapters.[89]

A PRAGMATIST, FEMINIST METHODOLOGY

Buchanan's larger point—that it is important to appreciate that human rights practice includes international legal institutions and their functioning over time—has a methodological significance beyond simply directing philosophers' attention to aspects of the practice that have been marginalized in the philosophical literature. As he argues, international human rights law, "like law generally, is an institutionalized form of practical reasoning that serves moral values while at the same time managing moral disagreement by constraining the types of reasons and evidence it admits as relevant and that has the resources for improving itself over time."[90] Importantly, the practice so understood is laden with normativity, deriving not only from an abstract philosophical idea of moral human rights, but also from the moral aims and goals of actors, and the processes of moral discovery and contestation, within the practice itself. In addition, the variety of actors in the practice enables the expression of a wide range of voices to be heard, not only from human rights lawyers and judges, but also including activists and ordinary individuals whose rights are violated or unfulfilled. Taken together, these points support an understanding of human rights practice as an ongoing social and political endeavor on the part of many and varied actors, that is both value-laden and at least partly institutionalized.

For this reason, I will argue that an appropriately broad conception of human rights practice reveals that it contains an internal moral perspective, which includes processes by which human rights claims are contested and adjudicated, not only by lawyers but also by activists and ordinary people (and their advocates) calling for greater recognition and realization of their own human rights. My larger methodological argument is that neither orthodox theories, nor political theories in their most familiar versions, can adequately embrace these processes as sources of moral knowledge which are essential to a full understanding of moral human rights, beyond their thinnest and most abstract formulations. By contrast, the methodology I am recommending suggests that philosophers have good reason to take up the normative claims that emerge from these processes into our theorizing.

In fact, a full appreciation of the complexity of the practice may suggest that it is misleading to refer to a singular human rights practice, which encompasses a complex and intertwined set of phenomena ranging from formal and institutionalized procedures and norms, to more informal, emergent, and contested claims inherent in human rights activism and protest. Indeed, the idea of human rights today features prominently in a wide variety of official and non-official domains, including the institutions and core documents of international human rights law, activism ranging from grassroots to global movements, summit-level international politics between states, and complex interactions between international and state-level law, politics, and civil society in all countries of the world. Within these various domains, actors such as judges, activists, lawyers, politicians, victims of human rights violations, and citizens of democracies and authoritarian states alike all face practical questions relevant to human rights (some of them urgent) on a regular basis. It is important to keep an open mind about whether all of these can be meaningfully characterized as part of a single practice with a unified set of aims and goals.[91]

This point has two further implications that are important to my understanding of human rights practice in this book. First, as Buchanan has argued, human rights practices are not static, even in their most formal, institutionalized manifestations. For example, the codified lists of rights in international human rights law continue to grow and develop, influenced by (among other things) human rights activism and formal jurisprudence regarding the interpretation and implementation of existing treaties (each of which may also influence the other). Philosophical theories of human rights practice should therefore somehow accommodate the fact of the practice's change over time, rather than treating it as a fixed, static entity.[92] Second, the complexity of human rights practice may also mean that it is not necessarily clearly demarcated by determinate institutional boundaries, and, as I have already indicated, that it is not synonymous with international human rights law. On one hand, social movements, operating outside of formal institutions, play a significant role in an appropriately broad sense of human rights practice. Even if we were interested only in international legal manifestations of human rights, however, the informal activities of social groups and movements may significantly influence the development of international law over time (for example, in the creation of new human rights treaties and conventions), and deserve attention for that reason at least. In addition, I will argue in later chapters that the idea of human rights plays an important role in other branches of international law, including humanitarian and criminal law.[93] Building on this expansive and dynamic conception of the practice, I will argue that philosophical theorizing about human rights morality should engage with the various, contested constructions of human rights in various aspects of human rights practice, including but not limited to their expression in (various branches of) international law.

In this respect, the methodology I'm defending aims to satisfy Brooke Ackerly's standard for a feminist methodology in political theory, as one that "develops normative arguments for improving our political lives together that are grounded in the lived experiences of human beings together."[94] As Hutchings argues, feminist methodology is committed to "the *democratization* not only of global political relations but also the *process of theorizing global justice*."[95] In turn, this implies "a radical displacement of the theorist's authority," requiring that theorists

> must take on board the implications of their own status as political actors in a complex, hierarchical and contested global order. . . . This means a re-thinking of the traditional division of labour between persons theorizing global justice, those studying global relations of economic and political power, and the global political actors, whether in formal or informal sectors.[96]

A feminist re-thinking of theorizing human rights morality, then, will require not only "specific and contextual knowledge about what is unjust to whom and how," but "also actively involve those experiencing injustice—the 'objects,' as it were, of theories of global justice—in the formulation of theory."[97] The methodology I'm arguing for is feminist in this sense, given that it attempts to ensure that theorizing about human rights morality has some mechanism for taking up the struggles toward equality and human rights within various aspects of the practice.

Importantly, the conceptual resources that I have marshalled in this chapter demonstrate that this sort of feminist methodology can satisfactorily address the normativity problem that plagues political theories of human rights as we know them. The voices of "those experiencing injustice" are not providing mere (value-free) "descriptions" of human rights morality as they happen to see it, but which have no legitimate role to play in philosophical theorizing. Instead, on my methodology, they provide essential evidence, in the form of testimony about lived experiences under various social, political, and legal contexts, that is directly relevant to normative theoretical conclusions about the substantive content of human rights morality. In other words, the pragmatist-influenced methodology I am recommending suggests that philosophers of human rights have good reason to take up into our theorizing the perspectives articulated by those empowered within the practice to testify to their experiences of human rights violations. The evidence provided by such testimony can itself be instructive for better understanding the full dimensions of human rights morality.

If this is correct, then theorizing moral human rights as if their moral dimensions are separable from the practice is actually not theorizing the idea of human rights as it appears in the practice, as orthodox theorists take themselves to do. Political views therefore need not purchase their relevance to the practice at the cost of abandoning their ability to provide normative guidance to the practice. Rather, in addition to indexing the meaning of human rights norms to the practice, political approaches to theorizing human rights may in fact tap into a different, and largely unrecognized, strand of normativity inherent in the practice itself. In this way, we (as philosophers) can learn about the morality of human rights from the uses to which human rights practice is put, especially when leveraged by members of marginalized groups advocating for their own human rights. At least, that is the hypothesis that guides the inquiry in the remainder of this book.

NOTES

1. The literature on this debate has ballooned in recent years. Recent collections addressing this debate include Rowan Cruft, S. Matthew Liao, and Massimo Renzo, eds., *Philosophical Foundations of Human Rights* (Oxford: Oxford University Press, 2015); Tom Campbell and Kylie Bourne, eds., *Political and Legal Approaches to Human Rights* (New York: Routledge, 2017); Johan Karlsson Schaffer and Reidar Maliks, eds., *Moral and Political Conceptions to Human Rights: Implications for Theory and Practice* (Cambridge: Cambridge University Press, 2017); and Adam Etinson, ed., *Human Rights: Moral or Political?* (New York: Oxford University Press, 2018).

2. John Tasioulas, "Towards a Philosophy of Human Rights," *Current Legal Problems* 65, no. 1 (2012): 2.

3. Though John Tasioulas has argued that Griffin's theory can also be seen as a "reductive" view, according to which "to say that there is a human right to X ultimately amounts to asserting that in the case of all human beings enjoying or having access to X serves some value that can be more perspicuously specified independently of the notion of a right." John Tasioulas, "On the Nature of Human Rights," in *The Philosophy of Human Rights,* eds. Gerhard Ernst and Jan-Christoph Heilinger (Göttingen: De Gruyter, 2012), 21.

4. James Griffin, *On Human Rights* (New York: Oxford University Press, 2008), 2.
5. Griffin, *On Human Rights*, 2.
6. Griffin, *On Human Rights*, 3. This is not necessarily a criticism of Kant and Mill, so much as pointing out that they are engaged in a different project than Griffin is. As Griffin notes (see later this chapter), Rawls's *Law of Peoples* (on one reading of it) does exactly this.
7. Griffin, *On Human Rights*, 29.
8. Griffin, *On Human Rights*, 20.
9. Griffin, *On Human Rights*, 45.
10. Griffin, *On Human Rights*, 48.
11. Griffin, *On Human Rights*, 51.
12. Griffin, *On Human Rights*, 33.
13. Griffin, *On Human Rights*, 38.
14. Griffin, *On Human Rights*, 38.
15. Griffin, *On Human Rights*, 206–9.
16. Griffin, *On Human Rights*, 207.
17. This is not meant to imply that Griffin is committed to the claim that legal human rights should "mirror" moral human rights, in a kind of one-to-one correspondence. Rather, the point is that the justification for any (set of) legal human rights should, on an orthodox view, be justified via a systematic theory of moral human rights. For deeper analysis of this point, see Allen Buchanan and Gopal Sreenivasan, "Taking International Legality Seriously: A Methodology for Human Rights," in *Human Rights: Moral or Political?* ed. Adam Etinson (New York: Oxford University Press, 2018).
18. Griffin, *On Human Rights*, 209.
19. Griffin, *On Human Rights*, 209.
20. John Tasioulas, "Human Rights, Universality and the Values of Personhood: Retracing Griffin's Steps," *European Journal of Philosophy* 10, no. 1 (2002): 93.
21. For example, see Maurice Cranston's claim that "[i]f rights are to be reduced to the status of ideals, the whole enterprise of protecting human rights will be sabotaged." (Maurice Cranston, "Are There Any Human Rights?," *Daedalus* 112, no. 4 (Fall 1983): 12.)
22. Tasioulas, "Human Rights, Universality," 96.
23. Tasioulas, "Human Rights, Universality," 96.
24. Tasioulas, "Human Rights, Universality," 96.
25. Charles Beitz, *The Idea of Human Rights* (Oxford: Oxford University Press, 2009), 8.
26. Joseph Raz, "Human Rights Without Foundations," in *The Philosophy of International Law,* eds. Samantha Besson and John Tasioulas (Oxford: Oxford University Press, 2010), 328.
27. John Tasioulas, "Exiting the Hall of Mirrors: Morality and Law in Human Rights," in *Political and Legal Approaches to Human Rights*, eds. Tom Campbell and Kylie Bourne (New York: Routledge, 2017), 81. This view expands on and specifies the basic idea behind Griffin's earlier claim that "[p]art of the ambition of international law is to incorporate rights that exist independently of positive law. So

international lawyers need a grasp of the existence conditions of those rights" (Griffin, *On Human Rights*, 204).

28. I return to Tasioulas's arguments for the Formative Aim Thesis in Chapter 2, where I argue both that he assumes rather than argues for it, and that it neglects institutional ways of conceptualizing the moral values that are foundational to international human rights law.

29. See, for example, Eric A. Posner, *The Twilight of Human Rights Law* (Oxford: Oxford University Press, 2014). See also Tasioulas's response to Posner and other critics to the effect that such criticisms "could be parried if IHRL were properly responsive to the important but limited objective described by the [Formative Aim Thesis]." (John Tasioulas, "Saving Human Rights from Human Rights Law," *Vanderbilt Journal of Transnational Law* 52 [2019]: 1194.)

30. Griffin, *On Human Rights*, 203–4.

31. Tasioulas, "Human Rights, Universality," 82. See also John Tasioulas, "Philosophizing the Real World of Human Rights: A Reply to Samuel Moyn," in *Human Rights: Moral or Political?,* ed. Adam Etinson (Oxford: Oxford University Press, 2018), 88–102.

32. Griffin, *On Human Rights*, 205.

33. James Griffin, "Human Rights and the Autonomy of International Law," in *The Philosophy of International Law,* ed. Samantha Besson and John Tasioulas (Oxford: Oxford University Press, 2010), 340.

34. Tasioulas, "Exiting the Hall of Mirrors," 80. See also Tasioulas, "Towards a Philosophy of Human Rights," 1, discussing "lawyers who unapologetically declare that a human right is nothing more than any norm denominated as such in a formally valid legal source, such as an international treaty."

35. John Rawls, *The Law of Peoples* (Cambridge, MA: Harvard University Press, 1999), 89.

36. Rawls, *Law of Peoples*, 68.

37. Rawls, *Law of Peoples*, 75 f.16.

38. Rawls, *Law of Peoples*, 80–81.

39. Rawls, *Law of Peoples*, 27.

40. Rawls, *Law of Peoples*, 80.

41. Rawls, *Law of Peoples*, 65.

42. Rawls, *Law of Peoples*, 81.

43. Griffin, *On Human Rights*, 24.

44. Griffin, *On Human Rights*, 24. See also Allen Buchanan, "Taking the Human Out of Human Rights," in *Rawls's Law of Peoples: A Realistic Utopia?,* ed. Rex Martin and David Reidy (Malden, MA: Blackwell Publishing, 2006).

45. Griffin, "Human Rights and the Autonomy of International Law," 342.

46. Tasioulas, "Towards a Philosophy of Human Rights," 3.

47. Rawls, *Law of Peoples*, 80.

48. Rawls, *Law of Peoples*, 79.

49. Tasioulas, "On the Nature of Human Rights," 45. See p. 49 for Tasioulas's categorization of Rawls as a subset theorist.

50. Raz, "Human Rights Without Foundations," 327.

51. Raz, "Human Rights Without Foundations," 328.
52. Beitz, *The Idea of Human Rights*, 99.
53. Beitz, *The Idea of Human Rights*, 102.
54. Beitz, *The Idea of Human Rights*, 102.
55. Again using Tasioulas's taxonomy, Beitz's view is therefore not a subset view (like Raz's), but rather a *sui generis* view. These "either reject, or are non-committal towards, the thesis that human rights are to be understood in terms of an underlying layer of universal moral rights." Tasioulas, "On the Nature of Human Rights," 45.
56. Cristina LaFont, *Global Governance and Human Rights* (Assen, Netherlands: Koninklijke Van Gorcum, 2012), 15.
57. Pablo Gilabert, *Human Dignity and Human Rights* (Oxford: Oxford University Press, 2018), 47.
58. David Luban, "Human Rights Pragmatism and Human Dignity," in *Philosophical Foundations of Human Rights*, ed. Rowan Cruft, S. Matthew Liao, and Massimo Renzo (Oxford: Oxford University Press, 2015), 268.
59. Charles Beitz, "The Practice and Its Authority: An Elaboration," *Critical Review of International Social and Political Philosophy* (2020); DOI: 10.1080/13698230.2020.1859220: p. 12.
60. I leave for Chapter 2 a consideration of Buchanan and Sreenivasan's instrumentalist approach, which solves the problem of normativity for political approaches by arguing that a system of international legal human rights can contribute to achieving morally desirable ends. Allen Buchanan and Gopal Sreenivasan, "Taking International Legality Seriously: A Methodology for Human Rights," in *Human Rights: Moral or Political?,* ed. Adam Etinson (New York: Oxford University Press, 2018).
61. I'm indebted to Jon Mandle for helpful discussion and suggestions on this point.
62. Tasioulas explicitly rejects this characterization of his methodology, arguing that "ordinary moral reasoning, in virtue of being 'natural,' need not be saddled with the futile ambition of wringing moral conclusions exclusively from value-free propositions about the natural world." (John Tasioulas, "Human Rights, Legitimacy, and International Law," *American Journal of Jurisprudence* 58, no. 1 [2013]: 3.) In response, my argument is not that he finds the practice literally value-free, but that he does not regard the practice as informative regarding moral principles at the conceptual level. (Tasioulas, "On the Nature of Human Rights," 48.) I consider Tasioulas's methodological arguments in more detail in Chapter 2.
63. Elizabeth Anderson, "Pragmatism, Science, and Moral Inquiry," *In Face of the Facts: Moral Inquiry in American Scholarship*, ed. Richard Wightman Fox and Robert Westbrook (Cambridge: Cambridge University Press, 1998), 10.
64. Anderson, "Pragmatism, Science, and Moral Inquiry," 11.
65. Kimberly Hutchings, "Global Justice," in *New Directions in Political Science: Responding to the Challenges of an Interdependent World*, ed. Colin Hay (Hampshire, UK: Palgrave Macmillan, 2010), 236.
66. I'm grateful to Jon Mandle for helping me clarify this point.
67. Hutchings, "Global Justice," 246.
68. Anderson, "Pragmatism, Science, and Moral Inquiry," 11.

69. Anderson, "Pragmatism, Science, and Moral Inquiry," 18.
70. Anderson, "Pragmatism, Science, and Moral Inquiry," 19.
71. Anderson, "Pragmatism, Science, and Moral Inquiry," 37.
72. Tasioulas, "Exiting the Hall of Mirrors," 81.
73. See Gilabert, *Human Dignity and Human Rights*, 23–25; Griffin, *On Human Rights*, 25.
74. Gilabert, *Human Dignity and Human Rights*, 15.
75. Griffin, *On Human Rights*, 6.
76. Gilabert, *Human Dignity and Human Rights*, 157.
77. See also Allen Buchanan's critique of "the assumption that a philosophical account of the system of international legal rights is by and large a matter of producing a theory of moral human rights and then leaving the supposedly much less interesting and less philosophical question of their proper implementation to lawyers." Allen Buchanan, "Why International Legal Human Rights?" in *Philosophical Foundations of Human Rights*, ed. Rowan Cruft, S. Matthew Liao, and Massimo Renzo (Oxford: Oxford University Press, 2015), 246.
78. This phrase is a reference to John Tasioulas's title: "Philosophizing the Real World of Human Rights."
79. Griffin, *On Human Rights*, 1.
80. See in particular Gilabert's Appendix: "Survey of Uses of 'Human Dignity' in Major Human Rights Documents." Gilabert, *Human Dignity and Human Rights*, 321–23.
81. Griffin, *On Human Rights*, 4.
82. Griffin, *On Human Rights*, 38.
83. John Tasioulas and Effy Vayena, "The Place of Human Rights and the Common Good in Global Health Policy," *Theoretical Medical Bioethics* 37 (2016): 374.
84. Tasioulas and Vayena, "The Place of Human Rights," 374.
85. John Tasioulas, "On the Foundations of Human Rights," in *Philosophical Foundations of Human Rights*, ed. Rowan Cruft, S. Matthew Liao, and Massimo Renzo (Oxford: Oxford University Press, 2015), 57.
86. Tasioulas, "Philosophizing the Real World of Human Rights," 88–89.
87. It is unclear why Beitz limits his approach in this way. Perhaps the reason is that this is how Rawls deployed his conception of human rights in *Law of Peoples*, combined with Beitz's goal of following Rawls's lead. I'm grateful to Jon Mandle for helpful discussions on this point.
88. Buchanan, *Heart of Human Rights*, 6.
89. I argue for an appropriately institutional conception of human rights morality in Chapter 2. In Chapter 3, I argue that human rights morality must include structural equality, an inherently institutional concept.
90. Allen Buchanan, *The Heart of Human Rights* (Oxford: Oxford University Press, 2013), 8.
91. For example, Andrea Sangiovanni argues that "we do better to treat the practice as embodying a multiplicity of contributing practices." Andrea Sangiovanni, "Human Rights Practices," *Critical Review of International Social and Political Philosophy* 25, no. 1 (2020): 50.

92. For example, Cristina LaFont has argued that the content of human rights should be understood as changeable over time in response to changing facts about standard threats to the basic interests that human rights protect, as well as to the institutional means available to protect them. LaFont, *Global Governance and Human Rights*. Similarly, Buchanan and Sreenivasan have argued that "the purposes the [international human rights legal] system serves may not be fixed, but subject to revision and perhaps even progressive development, as has sometimes been the case with domestic legal systems." Buchanan and Sreenivasan, "Taking International Legality Seriously," 228.

93. I substantiate this claim in more detail in Chapter 4.

94. Brooke Ackerly, *Just Responsibility: A Human Rights Theory of Global Justice* (Oxford: Oxford University Press, 2018), 158.

95. Hutchings, "Global Justice," 248 (emphasis original).

96. Hutchings, "Global Justice," 248.

97. Hutchings, "Global Justice," 246.

Chapter 2

Toward a Political Philosophy of Human Rights

The moral point of human rights takes shape within real-world social and political contexts, many of which are characterized by deeply entrenched social and political hierarchies. In turn, these hierarchies are often supported by widely accepted belief systems that naturalize and justify inequality. By itself, a philosophical account of moral human rights cannot adequately diagnose or address such systemic inequalities and their human rights implications. Instead, as I argue in this chapter, for this purpose we need to be able to understand human rights morality in explicitly political or institutional terms.

The first section of this chapter explicates the view that social and political institutions introduce novel, morally relevant considerations, especially inequalities of political and other forms of power, that are not apparent from a purely interpersonal perspective. Their distinctively political nature means that they cannot necessarily be adequately assessed using the same moral standards used to evaluate interpersonal morality or virtue ethics. This point, which was articulated by Rawls, and deployed more specifically in the context of human rights by Thomas Pogge, implies that a philosophical theory of human rights morality that aims to make sense of human rights practice must take seriously the social and institutional realities, including real-world power dynamics and deeply entrenched social and political hierarchies, that are relevant to understanding and realizing human rights in the real world. Explicitly institutional and political moral concepts are therefore necessary to an account of human rights morality, if it is to be able to critically assess many of the status quo realities that most concern human rights practice.

I then take a dialectical approach to supporting my thesis in this chapter—that political and institutional concepts are essential for theorizing human rights morality—by responding to several arguments by John Tasioulas, each of which purports to show that the philosophy of moral human rights should eschew political or institutional terms of analysis at the conceptual level. I argue in response that Tasioulas's (mostly) anti-institutional methodology prevents his theory from adequately accounting for the egalitarian dimensions of human rights morality.

In the final section of this chapter, I begin to sketch the outlines of a political approach to theorizing human rights morality. This approach follows a path blazed by Allen Buchanan in several key respects: first and foremost, by centering the value of status equality as a foundational value for human rights morality; second, by attempting to theorize human rights morality and practice beyond providing a theory of moral human rights; and third, by taking seriously the institutional system of international human rights law as an object of moral assessment. I then clarify three further features of my view: first, an emphasis on non-instrumental moral assessments of human rights practice; second, a broadly pragmatist account of the normativity in social and political practices; and third, a somewhat expanded conception of human rights practice that includes aspects of international criminal law.

POLITICAL PHILOSOPHY AND INSTITUTIONAL CONCEPTIONS OF HUMAN RIGHTS

Moral philosophy is the systematic approach to answering questions about value and normativity, including efforts to define right conduct and individual virtue. Political philosophy is a branch of moral philosophy that takes as its primary focus the moral evaluation of political institutions, and the background social and economic conditions that structure and enable interpersonal interactions. When considering how to respond morally to the plight of the poor, for example, moral philosophers focusing on individual virtue or interpersonal ethics might attempt to provide an account of our individual moral obligations to the poor, or of how virtuous individuals should respond to needy others. Political philosophers, by contrast, focus on the moral evaluation of background political, social, and economic conditions that not only structure the life chances of wealthy and poor individuals, but also create the conditions under which some become or remain rich or poor in the first place. These perspectives are, of course, not mutually exclusive. Regardless of the justice or injustice of background institutions, for example, individuals may still respond morally or immorally to needy others, so accounts of individuals' interpersonal obligations are complementary to (rather than competitive with) accounts of political justice or injustice.

Some philosophical approaches make no distinction between the evaluative parameters used to analyze questions of interpersonal and political morality. Aristotle's political theory, for example, is continuous with his moral theory in this sense. The aim of morality for Aristotle is to develop individual virtue, or excellence; in his view, the function of the state is an extension of what he took to be the organizing logic of all just human associations, namely, the moral goal of enabling and developing the virtues of all individuals according to their distinctive natures. Similarly, according to utilitarianism, the same basic mandate to maximize the good that governs interpersonal conduct also specifies the appropriate standard for political justice as well.

For the most part, contemporary political philosophers have tended to avoid unreconstructed versions of either classical utilitarianism or Aristotelian political theory, in part due to well-known difficulties with these views.[1] For example, Aristotle's political theory proceeds from the decidedly illiberal premise that "the better naturally rules over the worse," which in Aristotle's view justifies both slavery (for some human beings) and the subjection of women to men within the family.[2] For their part, utilitarian political philosophers must respond to John Rawls's criticism that the pursuit of best outcomes in the aggregate may permit or even require actions that sacrifice the liberties or essential interests of some for the sake of a greater good for others. As Rawls argued, according to utilitarianism, "there is no reason in principle why the greater gains of some should not compensate for the lesser losses of others; or more importantly, why the violation of the liberty of a few might not be made right by the greater good shared by many."[3] For this reason, Rawls argued, utilitarianism fails to take seriously what he called "the distinction between persons," and therefore cannot serve as an adequate political philosophy for determining just terms of cooperation among free and equal citizens.

Somewhat more seriously, both utilitarianism and Aristotelian approaches face a deeper challenge as grounds for political morality, given their commitment to substantive accounts of the good. Aristotelian approaches to politics, for example, face the task of defending an objective account of the human good that is authoritative in the political sphere. Perhaps the best-known such account is Martha Nussbaum's capabilities approach to justice and human rights. In her early work, Nussbaum accepted the challenge of defending a "frankly universalist and 'essentialist'" account of a good human life as the basis of a theory of justice.[4] This approach proved susceptible to a variety of critiques based on its commitment to an objective account of the human good; for example, that it is likely to be problematically parochial if it is intended as the basis of a universal account of human rights. The basic problem here is that moral justifications for social and political arrangements should be addressed to the people who are to be subject to their authority, but those justifications will not be successful if those people have good reason to reject their moral premises as, say, biased or parochial.

Similarly, classical utilitarians define the good as happiness, and then define right conduct as that which maximizes the good. As Rawls notes, while this might make for a sensible principle of rational choice from the perspective of an individual aiming to maximize her prospects over time, when applied in a political context it has the direct implication that it is not only permissible but under certain circumstances morally mandatory to sacrifice the interests of a few to maximize good consequences in the aggregate.[5] This of course is part of Rawls's argument that utilitarianism fails to respect the separateness of persons, which itself is an essential component of justice (as well as a foundational commitment of human rights morality).

This fundamental difficulty for both utilitarianism and Aristotelian political philosophy can be traced back to their shared commitment to utilizing the same standards of moral evaluation for political or institutional contexts as for interpersonal ethics or individual virtue. The idea is that the same evaluative standards that inform, say, Aristotle's conception of a good life, or the classical utilitarian conception of happiness, also provide appropriate standards of moral assessment for any object of evaluation: individual actions, character traits, public policy, or law. By contrast, Rawls has argued that there is no reason to expect that the moral principles that are appropriate for assessing individual conduct or virtue will be identical to those appropriate for the moral evaluation of institutions. As Rawls notes, "the correct regulative principle for anything depends on the nature of that thing."[6] Accordingly, Rawls's theory of justice insists that distinct terms of evaluation are required for social/political institutions than those appropriate for interpersonal conduct or individual virtue, because of the unique social relationships and interactions that political institutions introduce. In particular, the organization of human societies into political communities creates hierarchies among persons, and structures relationships between them, in ways that introduce novel moral concerns and considerations that cannot necessarily be appreciated or addressed from a purely interpersonal or individualist perspective. This fact raises an important distinction between distinctively political and non-political (or interpersonal) terms of moral analysis.

The question that this raises for our purposes is whether an account of human rights morality that is sensitive to human rights practice can be adequately theorized in the same terms that are appropriate for interpersonal conduct, or whether distinctly institutional concepts are necessary. Thomas Pogge has argued for the latter view, echoing the basic logic that distinct moral parameters are required for evaluating institutions. In his view, an "institutional" conception of human rights morality, rather than an interpersonal or "interactionist" one, is needed precisely to capture the distinct terms of moral analysis appropriate for institutions. In developing this account, Pogge draws on the distinctive focus of political philosophy on institutions, noting that

> [a]n institutional conception postulates certain fundamental principles of *social justice*. They apply to institutional schemes and are thus second-order principles: standards for assessing the ground rules and practices that regulate human interactions. An interactionist conception, by contract, postulates certain fundamental principles of *ethics*. These principles, like institutional ground rules, are first-order in that they apply directly to the conduct of persons and groups."[7]

In Pogge's terminology, an interactionist conception of human rights "presents human rights as placing the treatment of human beings under certain constraints that do not presuppose the existence of social institutions."[8] On an institutional conception, by contrast, moral human rights are understood "primarily as claims on coercive social institutions and secondarily as claims against those who uphold such institutions."[9] Asserting a human right to X, on this view, implies "that any society or other social system, insofar as this is reasonably possible, ought to be so (re)organized that all its members have secure access to X, with 'security' always understood as especially sensitive to persons' risk of being denied X or deprived of X officially: by the government or its agents or officials."[10]

Pogge's point here is not only that institutions are among the appropriate objects of assessment in terms of human rights. After all, interactionist conceptions of human rights may serve the purpose of institutional assessment, if, for example, the relevant institutions (or their officials) tend to commit, prohibit, or tolerate human rights violations in an interactionist sense. Rather, the importance of this distinction lies in the fact that even a full interactionist accounting of whose moral human rights have been violated, and by whom, will not suffice to inform us whether the relevant institutions respect the equality of all as human rights holders. To illustrate why not, consider the following contrasting cases:

> A person may fully enjoy X even while her access to X is insecure (as when persons relevantly like her, say blacks or vocal government opponents, are beaten or threatened). Conversely, a person may be temporarily deprived of X, through a crime by a rogue government official perhaps, in a society that is very effective in preventing crimes of the relevant type. Opposite to the interactional understanding, my institutional one regards only the first case as a human-rights problem.[11]

Pogge uses the term "human rights problem" in his analysis of these two cases because shifting to an institutional conception of human rights requires paying attention to whether human rights are securely fulfilled in the institutional order as a whole; information about the existence of discrete human rights violations (in an interactionist sense) will not suffice, on the institutional model, to establish (or disprove) the existence of a "human rights problem."

As Pogge interprets the institutional account of human rights, therefore, it links "human rights fulfillment with insecurity rather than violation": "On the interactional understanding of human rights, governments and individuals have a responsibility not to violate human rights. On my institutional understanding, by contrast, their responsibility is to work for an institutional order and public culture that ensures that all members of society have secure access to the objects of their human rights."[12]

The important moral point here is that an institutional perspective is necessary to assess the egalitarianism of human rights in practice. In other words, a specifically institutional focus is required precisely in order to assess how well the institutions in question are protecting human rights equally for all social groups.

Note that this view does not imply that human rights violations, in an interactionist sense, are of no moral significance. Nor does it entail that interpersonal conduct cannot violate human rights.[13] And importantly, an institutional conception of human rights assumes that there is independent sense to be made of whether "all members of society have secure access to the objects of their human rights." This presumes some account of what people may justifiably claim on the basis of their human rights. Rather than completely displacing all such questions, then, the point of an institutional conception of human rights is to illustrate the need for a distinctively institutional perspective in assessing the egalitarian dimensions of human rights in actual societies, structured as they are by social and political hierarchies of various kinds.

The tensions between an institutional perspective and orthodox theorizing may not be obvious at first glance. On one hand, there are ways in which orthodox theories do make room for institutions in various respects. For example, orthodox theories are perfectly capable of deploying the concept of moral human rights in assessing whether, for example, a state or economic regime is violating moral human rights, or to condemn officials or institutions themselves for failing to respond appropriately to (interactionist) human rights violations. In fact, orthodox theorists may even include reference to institutions in the justification of particular moral human rights. Tasioulas, for example, specifically leaves room for institutional facts to factor into the justification of particular moral human rights. This is because, on his view, "the question about which human rights exist can only be answered within some specified historical context."[14] Accordingly, Tasioulas recognizes that "very general facts about feasible institutional design in the modern world, for example, forms of legal regulation, political participation, and economic organization, . . . play a role in determining which human rights we recognize."[15] In this way, Tasioulas rejects the kind of thoroughly anti-institutional theory of human rights according to which "no account needs to be taken of individuals' special relationships to persons, groups, and institutions in determining which human rights exist."[16]

But the limits of the relevance of institutions to orthodox theorizing become apparent when we consider *how* they factor into a justification of moral human rights. As an example, Tasioulas's account of a moral human right against poverty begins by noting that severe poverty threatens a person's interests (including their interests in "health, physical security, autonomy, understanding, friendship, etc.").[17] Importantly for Tasioulas, a moral right exists only when the threat to a person's interests is "*pro tanto* of sufficient gravity to justify the imposition of duties on others, for example to refrain from impoverishing them, protect them from impoverishment, and assist those already suffering from severe material deprivation." These duties must also constitute "practicable claims on others given the constraints created by general and relatively entrenched facts of human nature and social life in the modern world." To the extent that these conditions are met, this account can then justify the existence of a moral right against severe poverty. Along the way, important "facts about social life in the modern world," some of them facts about relevant institutions, will have played a role in the justification. In this way, then, it is not quite true of Tasioulas's view that (as Pogge described interactionist views) it "presents human rights as placing the treatment of human beings under certain constraints that do not presuppose the existence of social institutions."[18] Instead, institutional facts may be relevant to Tasioulas's account of the existence of a human right if they make a difference to whether the duties assigned to others in service of the protection of the relevant interest are "practicable."

However, in this argument, institutional considerations are relevant to the justification of a particular moral human right only in a decidedly marginal way (insofar as they constitute various facts about the "modern world" that the assignment of concrete moral duties must accommodate). This aspect of Tasioulas's view does not, therefore, take up Rawls's point that the nature of the object of evaluation is important in determining the appropriate normative standards of evaluation. Instead, Tasioulas's orthodox methodology insists on the same terms of moral evaluation for evaluating individual conduct and institutions, specifically, in terms of an essentially interactionist theory of moral human rights.

This context helps to illuminate a remark by Tasioulas to the effect that "'to complete the Enlightenment project' of human rights—as James Griffin has put it—we need to go back, beyond the Enlightenment to an Aristotelian tradition of thought about the human good and the special protection it merits."[19] While Tasioulas intends for this comment to defend a conception of human rights based on a substantive account of the good (which will be relevant later in this chapter), at the same time it reflects the fact that Tasioulas's view is also thoroughly Aristotelian in its commitment to deploying the same terms of evaluation for political and non-political moral contexts. This commitment essentially commits Tasioulas to a conception of politics as a kind of ethics-writ-large, which (I will argue) in turn results in a blindness to structural inequalities and their implications for human rights morality.

Finally, Tasioulas explicitly objects to "linking human rights conceptually with particular institutional arrangements or roles."[20] This is because he is interested in theorizing human rights as a broader moral idea—"a human rights ethos that pervades our lives"—that, in his view, adequately accounts for the core meaning and moral point of human rights in both political and non-political contexts.[21] From this perspective, any specifically institutional terms of analysis for human rights will constitute a kind of conceptual straitjacket, preventing us from appreciating that human rights norms apply to a wide range of circumstances "across boundaries between public and private, society and state." I will consider this aspect of Tasioulas's view in more detail in the following section.

ORTHODOXY AND EQUALITY: RESPONSES TO TASIOULAS

In this section, I consider two of Tasioulas's arguments defending the (mostly) anti-institutional orientation of orthodox theories of moral human rights. First, Tasioulas has argued that only an orthodox theory of moral human rights, which interprets human rights as universal moral rights, can make sense of the value of status equality of persons as a grounding value for moral human rights. Second, he has also argued that the "feminist critique of human rights violations in the private sphere" supports an orthodox approach, since, on his view, such violations need not, "even pro tanto, be a matter for the law or for the state," thus vindicating the orthodox insistence that, at a conceptual level, moral human rights should not be defined by reference to states or other institutions.[22] I argue that these arguments are flawed but instructive. Exploring where they go wrong will lay the groundwork for constructing a positive argument defending a broadly political approach to human rights morality, one that better realizes both the value of equality relevant to human rights and feminist concerns regarding human rights in the private sphere.

Equality and Human Rights Morality

Allen Buchanan has argued that the two primary functions of international human rights law (IHRL) are to promote a form of universal moral equality for all human beings and to protect individuals' interests in living a decent life. More specifically, Buchanan argues that

> international legal human rights constrain sovereignty for the purposes of affirming and promoting the equal basic status of all people (the status egalitarian function) and helping to ensure that all have the opportunity to lead a minimally good or decent life by providing protections and resources that are generally needed for such a life (the well-being function).[23]

While agreeing with Buchanan that equality and well-being are core values of human rights morality, Tasioulas argues (in support of orthodox theorizing) that the "workability of the two functions identified by Buchanan appears to presuppose the idea of human rights as universal moral rights."[24] This is because these core values "can only contribute to the justification of IHRL by relying on the indispensable conceptual structure provided" by "the idea of a universal moral right."[25] For this reason, Buchanan's view presupposes the basic tenet of orthodox theorizing: that a theory of moral human rights is necessary for a moral assessment of human rights practice, including international human rights law.

The starting point for Tasioulas's argument is his claim that "[t]here are many ways in which status egalitarianism may be transgressed or not served, without this constituting a human rights violation, in the sense of the one that should sound in IHRL."[26] Tasioulas offers two separate examples of this. First, he considers the case of a "liberal racist" who "may behave impeccably towards blacks, yet harbor racist feelings toward them." This person, he argues, "is not obviously committing a human rights violation in virtue of his discreditable feelings, partly because it may not be possible for him to reform or self-police these spontaneous racist responses, partly because doing so is too costly to be demanded as of right."[27] His second example focuses on a person "confronted with the opportunity to promote the equal moral status of gay people in his community by risking his life, e.g., by 'coming out' as gay himself in circumstances that make it extremely dangerous to do so." Tasioulas argues that here again "it would not automatically follow that this sacrifice in the name of status equality is the kind of thing that may appropriately be demanded by IHRL." According to Tasioulas, each of these examples shows that the idea of promoting equality may "come apart" from both IHRL and moral human rights, since the conduct in question would promote status equality but is not plausibly a moral human right, and therefore could not be a requirement of IHRL (given Tasioulas's premise that "IHRL gives effect to universal moral rights"). The point of both examples is that "status equality is an important ground of both universal moral rights and IHRL, but the extent to which it is a matter of human rights (in both senses) is importantly constrained by the prior question: is there a universal moral right to basic moral equality being promoted or respected in this or that way?"[28]

Tasioulas's argument, then, starts with the claim that IHRL may create a legal obligation for someone to perform some conduct that supports status equality *only* in cases where there exists a prior moral right that someone perform this conduct. Any conduct that might promote status equality but cannot be demanded by others as a matter of a moral right is therefore illegitimate as a demand in IHRL. Therefore, a theory of moral human rights is necessary to account for when and in what ways the value of status equality may generate legal obligations in IHRL.

A first point to note in response is that Tasioulas's argument presupposes the truth of his "formative aim thesis," which holds that IHRL "is primarily concerned with giving effect to universal moral rights."[29] This is apparent in his premise that if a theory of moral human rights does not support the existence of a moral right to the conduct in question, then neither may IHRL demand it.[30] Of course, this is the reason that Tasioulas's own theory would give for determining which forms of conduct promoting status equality are appropriate for IHRL to demand and which not. However, in arguing that Buchanan's view presumes basic tenets of an orthodox view, Tasioulas seems to simply assume, rather than argue, that there is no way for IHRL to claim status egalitarianism as a grounding value without presuming the formative aim thesis. However, as I shall argue below, there exist relevant alternative theoretical structures that do exactly this.

A second point is that Tasioulas seems to presume as a premise of this argument that any behavior at all—private or public, interpersonal or institutional—that promotes a grounding value of a system of law could in principle be a requirement of that system of law, and for that reason, unless there exists some reason to block this presumptive inference. But it's not at all obvious why he would assume this. Suppose that a grounding moral value of U.S. criminal law is the principle that it is better to let a guilty person go free than to wrongfully convict an innocent person, and that certain key elements of criminal justice in the United States are structured in accordance with this value (for example, the strict presumption of the accused's innocence, until proven guilty as determined by a jury of her peers). Now imagine that a wealthy philanthropist whose primary passion is opera could choose to spend her fortune not on building new opera houses and music schools, but supporting state-of-the-art anti-bias training programs for judges and prosecutors that would help to reduce wrongful convictions and overly harsh sentencing of defendants on the basis of race.[31] Using Tasioulas's language, it would not automatically follow (to say the least) that this sacrifice on the part of the wealthy philanthropist in the name of this grounding value is the kind of thing that may appropriately be demanded by U.S. criminal law.

But what does this show? Tasioulas's argument would seem to commit him to arguing here that, just like in the case of IHRL, we need a theory of the (non-institutional) moral rights of defendants in order to explain what U.S. criminal law may and may not rightly demand from the philanthropist. If U.S. criminal law aims to give effect to the pre-existing moral rights of defendants (perhaps also of others, including accusers), then the inappropriateness of U.S. criminal law requiring wealthy philanthropists to contribute to its moral mission (in this example) can be explained by reference to the fact that no innocent defendants can rightfully make this claim, as a matter of a moral right, on any wealthy philanthropists. But this analysis misses an important point. In thinking about what U.S. criminal law may demand of wealthy philanthropists, it is perfectly natural to look not only to the grounding values of the relevant institutions, but also to the appropriate scope of the political function of those institutions, in order to determine the limits to the kinds of demands those institutions may make, and on whom. For example, a legitimate system of law may make demands only on those who are officially bound by that system of law, and may recognize as enforcers or judges in that system only those who are legitimate agents with official roles within it. It is therefore not at all mysterious why IHRL, or U.S. criminal law, may not legitimately demand anything of anyone, merely provided that the demand would advance one of the grounding values of that system of law. The point is that a system of law's demands on the private decisions of wealthy philanthropists (or "liberal racists," for that matter) are ruled out earlier in the reasoning process than Tasioulas's account allows: we only have to show that the demand is not appropriate given the legitimate boundaries of the institution or system of law, even though issuing the demand would advance the system's grounding values. Importantly, this explanation does not require spelling out in advance the contours of the specific moral rights that the system of law aims to give effect to, since the reason why these demands are inappropriate is not necessarily a function of the content of those rights.

We can express the same point in a different way. Tasioulas's formative aim thesis holds that international human rights law attempts to "give effect to universal moral rights" by "assigning a uniform set of individual rights to all human beings." A theory of universal moral rights is therefore, in his view, an essential component of understanding the defining basic aim of IHRL, namely, the assignment to all human beings of the same set of legal rights, which give legal effect to a doctrine of universal moral rights. On Tasioulas's view, then, the only way in which the foundational values of moral human rights are relevant to a uniform set of legal rights for all human beings is to figure out which moral human rights are justifiable on the basis of those values (which, for Tasioulas, means figuring out which aspects of those grounding values are weighty enough to justify imposing duties on others). In other words, the foundational values of human rights morality do not ground legal human rights directly, in Tasioulas's view, but rather only via the medium of an account of universal moral rights. This winnows down the respects in which IHRL is concerned with these grounding values.

But this approach ignores an alternative way to account for the relevance of status equality to IHRL—namely, to give this value a distinctively *political* role in justifying legal human rights. This route situates the grounding values of human rights morality within an account of the political morality of the relevant institutions. This move gives those values a direct role in assessing and guiding how those institutions (should) function, together with the appropriate political considerations inherent to the institutions (such as, for example, on whom they have the authority to impose legal duties of various kinds). This approach therefore allows the political function of institutions to limit the claims that may be made by those institutions in the name of their grounding values. Rather than conceptualizing IHRL as giving effect to moral human rights, then, a political account may instead conceptualize IHRL as giving *institutional* effect to the values of status equality and protection of individuals' interests via a system of uniform legal rights for all persons. A political account so described would therefore not depend on producing a philosophical theory of universal moral rights.

Even if the analysis thus far is correct, however, it only clears some conceptual room for the claim that the values that ground human rights (such as status equality) can be given a political interpretation, and need not be expressed via an account of moral human rights. I will defend this claim more substantively below, and in the rest of this book. For now I point out that if this possibility can be made good, then Tasioulas is mistaken to argue (as he did against Buchanan) that claiming status equality as a grounding value for human rights must rely on an orthodox theory of human rights.

Feminism and the "Private" Sphere

Tasioulas has described "the feminist critique of human rights violations in the private sphere" as holding that "[m]any sexist practices, such as those related to the distribution of domestic labour or decision-making processes within the family, may appropriately be assessed on human rights grounds without there being any implication that the enforcement of these rights should, even pro tanto, be a matter for the law or the state."[32] In his view, this feminist critique supports the orthodox rejection of political theorists' attempts to build references to states or other institutions into their conceptual accounts of moral human rights.

Tasioulas does not indicate which feminists' work he is drawing on in this argument.[33] And it is important to note that there is of course no single, unified feminist perspective. However, taken as a blanket statement about the range of feminist agendas regarding human rights and the private sphere, Tasioulas's premise in this argument is deeply misleading. While he is correct to argue that many feminists have lobbied for "private sphere" concerns, such as intimate partner violence or the gendered division of labor within the family, to be recognized as matters of human rights, by and large most feminist work in this area has aimed to establish precisely that such rights are indeed matters of state concern. The second-wave feminist slogan dating from the 1960s, "the personal is political," includes among other implications the idea that the private sphere, consisting of personal and intimate relationships, the structure of the family, and the like, should not be conceived as a sphere beyond the concern or reach of law or policy. Indeed, feminists have taken pains to argue that the private sphere is itself *constructed by* law and policy (including divorce and family law, public policies regarding child care, whether jobs are structured in ways that accommodate caregivers, and the like). For that reason, many feminists would argue that it is not only misleading but pernicious to conceptualize the private sphere as a realm beyond or outside of state control, since "[t]he myth that state power is not exercised in the 'private' realm . . . masks its control."[34]

Many feminists also argue that the concept of the "private" sphere is often deployed in deeply and problematically gendered ways that tend to both presume and entrench women's lesser social, political, and economic standing. As Lucy Ferguson argues, for example, "the delimitation of a public and private sphere [is] a gendered construction that has served to establish the borders of what is considered work, based on assumptions about whether work is considered *productive* (men's paid work in the market) or *unproductive* (women's unpaid work in the household)."[35] Along the same lines, in summarizing feminist critiques of traditional liberal political philosophy, Jean Hampton argues that "the effect of liberal reasoning and liberal reluctance to involve the state in personal relations has played an important role in allowing practices of subordinating women to men not only to continue, but even to flourish."[36] As Hampton notes, "the idea that the state should stay out of the private affairs of individuals (e.g., in families, clubs, or businesses)" gives "men a powerful tool to prevent the state from interfering" with accepted social practices that elevate men and subordinate women. She concludes that: "at the deepest level, feminists are challenging liberals to rethink what is 'political' and what is 'private,' where the jurisdiction of government ends and where the private and personal decisions of each autonomous individual begin, in order to secure a genuinely free and equal society."[37]

While Hampton's examples in support of this claim primarily concern U.S. court cases in which the state declined to interfere in cases of intimate partner violence or rape (which many would likely agree are properly matters of state concern), Susan Okin applies similar reasoning to forms of "private" subordination that are closer to Tasioulas's examples of "the distribution of domestic labour or decision-making processes within the family."[38] Like many feminists, Okin emphasizes that these patterns of expectations and behaviors (and the "private sphere" itself) are in many cases actually created and sustained by official law and policy (for example, regarding divorce) as well as by institutional expectations in the workplace and other "public" spheres (for example, that workplace expectations and reward structures do not tend to accommodate the needs of primary caregivers). Accordingly, Okin's proposed remedies for the injustices of the gendered division of labor in the private sphere are, overwhelmingly, policy proposals, and therefore matters of state concern: that "public policies and laws should generally assume no social differentiation of the sexes"; that public funding be available for "high-quality day care, subsidized so as to be equally available to all children"; that "[e]mployers must be required by law not only completely to eradicate sex discrimination, including sexual harassment" but "should also be required to make positive provision for the fact that most workers, for differing lengths of time in their working lives, are also parents, and are sometimes required to nurture other family members, such as their aging parents"; that public schools must ensure "that women's experience and women's writing are included in the curriculum" and "provide high-quality after-school programs"; and, fairly radically, that law should ensure that, for married couples, "both partners have equal legal entitlement to all earnings coming into the household."[39] As this broad range of proposals demonstrates, many feminists' concerns regarding sources of inequality in the so-called private sphere tend to focus squarely on law, policy, and the role of formal and informal institutions more broadly, as both the causes of, and possible solutions to, systemic gender inequality, including its manifestations in the so-called private sphere.

On the whole, then, feminist concerns about human rights and the public/private distinction tend to pull in exactly the opposite direction than the one Tasioulas thinks they do: toward the necessity of political and institutional theorizing for an adequate understanding of women's equality and feminist perspectives on human rights, both moral and legal. This point, while stated here as a critique of Tasioulas's argument, is also a central claim of my positive argument (which I develop below and in Chapter 3) that an institutional perspective is necessary for theorizing the value of status equality as a foundational value of human rights morality.

Human Rights in Ordinary Discourse

As I mentioned earlier in this chapter, Tasioulas might respond by arguing that a non-institutional moral conception of human rights is more basic or conceptually foundational than any explicitly political understanding of human rights. For example, he argues that an orthodox approach provides "a purer, moral concept of human rights, free of any such specific institutional entanglements."[40] The point of theorizing moral human rights at this more abstract, conceptually "pure" level is to be able to make sense of the plurality of ways in which this idea is employed in real life. This in turn, he argues, "maintains an important distinction between moral principles and the political structures that embody them, thereby respecting the great diversity of ways in which the language of human rights operates in ordinary discourse."[41]

Two points are important to make in response. First, Tasioulas's reference to the "distinction between moral principles and the political structures that embody them" implies that political structures are morally inert without reference to pre-existing moral values. This point simply ignores the possibility (discussed earlier in this chapter) that political situations and institutions may generate unique and specific moral requirements and possibilities for realizing them. Once we begin to ask institutional or political questions—for example: What terms of engagement or cooperation would treat all participants in a sociopolitical arrangement as moral equals?—we require terms of moral evaluation that are sensitive to this political context, and there is no reason to think that our theories of interpersonal morality or "ordinary moral reasoning" will be adequate to ground an account of political morality.

Second, Tasioulas's legitimate concern to accommodate the wide range of uses of the idea of human rights can be addressed by adopting a pluralism about conceptions of human rights, where appropriate. That is, we might admit that people often employ conceptions of human rights that are not institutional, while at the same time insisting that an institutional account is essential to capture the moral force of the central idea of human rights that animates international human rights practice, including not only IHRL but also much activism (including feminist and anti-racist activism) and critique of the practice itself. Tasioulas, however, in attempting to construct an overarching conception of human rights that can capture such a broad range of usage, clearly aims to theorize one substantive, non-institutional account of moral human rights as the correct, foundational one.[42] The arguments in this chapter suggest that this ambition may be misguided.

Ordinary Moral Reasoning

One important implication of the foregoing discussion is that Tasioulas's "liberal racist" argument neglects the possibility of giving a political interpretation to status egalitarianism as a grounding value for moral human rights. Structural inequalities like racism are established and maintained via public and habitual assumptions and expectations, as well as by networks of laws and policies (and the rationales behind them) that systematically subordinate some social groups to others.[43] Absent a social structure of inferiority and superiority, all there would be in the mind of a "liberal racist" would be a bizarre and idiosyncratic hatred, dislike, or distrust of a group of people based on socially insignificant physical features they happen to share. It would be the equivalent of someone's distrust or dislike or hatred of people whose second toes are longer than their first—vicious, but idiosyncratically so, and with no further social or political significance.[44] Tasioulas's construction of the liberal racist example therefore presumes, without noticing, that the society in which his example is situated is itself structured by formal and informal institutions that embody, create, and sustain substantive inequalities between people based on race. But his moral analysis of the human rights implications of this example (as well as the examples about homosexuality) proceeds entirely within the confines of interactionist moral claims.

Tasioulas's take on feminist accounts of human rights in the private sphere also neglects the distinction between the political and the interpersonal. As I argued earlier, the construction of the private sphere as a realm outside of state control or concern is revealed by much feminist work (with an explicitly political focus) to be a pernicious myth, in large part dependent on pre-theoretical assumptions that presume the social inferiority of women: for example, that is more important for the state to protect the domestic authority of the head of a household (frequently presumed male) than women's bodily security and safety within the home; or that the work done within the home, traditionally and still primarily performed by women, is not the kind of work that ought to be counted in economic assessments of productivity; or that the gendered division of labor and other structural features of the traditional family and "private" life are freely chosen by both women and men, rather than deeply constrained by political and social norms and institutions of all kinds. Feminist critiques of the private sphere therefore aim to reveal the role that such ideologies and practices of women's subordination play in constructing widely accepted perceptions of men and women's natures; in other words, feminists aim to reveal such gendered ways of thinking as already deeply political and institutional.

These arguments suggest that there are good reasons to explore an explicitly political account of human rights morality, which in turn would require explicitly institutional thinking. However, one further feature of Tasioulas's method pulls even further in the opposite direction. This is his commitment to what he labels Proposition O: "The existence and content of human rights is to be determined primarily by ordinary moral reasoning, assisted and supplemented as may be necessary by empirical, philosophical, or legal reasoning."[45] By way of clarification, Tasioulas specifies that Proposition O rules out reliance on "both divine revelation on one hand and the myriad forms of 'artificial' reasoning generated by social conventions and institutions on the other."[46]

While there are a number of ways to interpret Tasioulas's meaning here, two distinct interpretations are directly relevant to our discussion. Both interpretations accommodate the limited role that orthodox theories provide for institutional forms of reasoning in the specification of the full content of moral human rights. On the first interpretation, Proposition O might be intended as a justification for insisting upon utilizing the same moral standards for interpersonal and institutional objects of evaluation. On this interpretation, ordinary moral reasoning is "ordinary" by virtue of the fact that it eschews explicitly institutional or political concepts in theorizing human rights morality. It is an objection to the methodology I have been suggesting insofar as it repudiates the idea that the foundational values of human rights morality play a direct role in the assessment of international human rights law and other institutional elements of human rights practice. One possible justification for Proposition O, so understood, is the idea that ordinary, non-institutional moral reasoning seems more reliable from the perspective of moral epistemology, and perfectly capable on its own of developing appropriate moral standards for deployment in both interpersonal and institutional contexts. However, as many theorists of oppression have labored to demonstrate, ordinary moral reasoning, understood as moral reasoning that eschews any explicitly institutional or political focus, will often fail to reveal what are in fact structural and institutional patterns of bias, exclusion, and disrespect. For Tasioulas's methodology in particular, this matters insofar as he maintains that moral human rights are to be justified by moral reasoning about which particular interests justify imposing duties on others. If Proposition O insists that this moral reasoning should be carried out in non-institutional terms, the view risks providing an analysis of human rights that ignores the background social and political inequalities that are deeply relevant for an adequate understanding of the requirements of human rights morality in the world as we know it. As demonstrated by the earlier analysis of the public/private distinction, ordinary moral reasoning in this sense may simply fail to apprehend the broader systemic significance of seemingly innocuous attitudes, behaviors, or choices of individuals. Ordinary moral reasoning in this sense therefore risks failing to take seriously the real-world implications of status egalitarianism for human rights morality.

The second, somewhat narrower interpretation of Proposition O understands it as rejecting a different component of the methodology that I have been suggesting, according to which institutions as they function in the real world play a morally generative role in philosophical reasoning about which moral standards are appropriate for assessing international institutions or particular legal human rights. The point of Proposition O, understood as a rebuttal to an institutional account of human rights in this sense, is to insist on the power of reason (rather than politics) to determine moral truths. The implication is that resorting to either "divine revelation on one hand and the myriad forms of 'artificial' reasoning generated by social conventions and institutions on the other" are both simply different ways of abandoning philosophical standards of truth in moral reasoning.[47] Indeed, there is an important sense in which a profound commitment to these philosophical standards underlies the orthodox view of what the philosophy of human rights is for and how it should proceed, and that underwrites its claim to normative authority for the practice.

My first response is simply to deny that providing such a role for institutions in a theory of political morality constitutes an abandonment of the power of moral reasoning to arrive at moral truth. Tasioulas's Aristotelian methodology requires that political values rely for their ultimate justification on a substantive account of what has intrinsic moral value. However, this is not the only possible structure for a theory of political morality. For example, my approach relies on the claim that part of the point of human rights morality is to provide standards for assessing institutions (at least in part) on the basis of the foundational value of universal status equality understood as an aspect of political morality. The difference between this kind of political conception of human rights morality and Tasioulas's orthodox view is not that the latter is grounded in moral values and the former is not. Rather, the key differences are, first, whether those values constitute a substantive account of the good that is supposed to apply to both interpersonal and political contexts and, second, whether they need to be filtered first through a theory of moral human rights. Answering "no" to these questions need not put the theory outside the realm of truth-seeking philosophy.

Tasioulas would likely respond by arguing that his critique here is primarily that "institutional reasoning" in this sense illegitimately deputizes political institutions to do the work that ought properly to be done by philosophical reasoning. However, notice that Tasioulas's deep commitment to the view that institutional processes can provide little to no insight regarding questions of political morality is itself part and parcel of the persistent refrain in orthodox methodology that treats social practices (including human rights practice) as (more or less) value-free, at least in any way that is worth philosophical attention. On one hand, the argument in this book as a whole is my response. On the other hand, I suspect that, at a certain point, these arguments cannot be fully resolved by rational argument. What might be required instead is stepping back to examine our assumptions about the nature of philosophy, what it contributes to the world, and who it is for. One motivation for my approach is an appreciation of the fact that philosophical inquiry is only one form of engagement with the moral elements of human rights practice. My ambition is to (begin to) sketch a plausible and philosophically respectable methodology whereby philosophical inquiry can both contribute to and learn from moral discourses within human rights practice and scholarship. The orthodox route, by contrast, insistently forecloses on the possibility that there is anything of substantive moral interest that philosophers can learn from the practice. Looked at in this way, it may be that it is actually the formative aim thesis that turns out to be a conceptual and methodological straitjacket, inhibiting the development of more productive collaboration between philosophers, scholars from other fields, and participants in human rights practice.

A SKETCH FOR A POLITICAL PHILOSOPHY OF HUMAN RIGHTS

So far, I have argued that it is at least a conceptual possibility to give the values that ground human rights morality a direct and distinctively political role in the normative justification or critique of international human rights law and practice. Moreover, in my version of such an approach, the functioning of institutions in the real world may help to inform philosophical reasoning about which moral standards are appropriate for the moral assessment of those institutions.

This approach is intended to answer Allen Buchanan and Gopal Sreenivasan's exhortation "that moral and political philosophers interested in theorizing about human rights should take the international legality of human rights seriously."[48] By this they mean that at least one important objective of philosophical theorizing about human rights morality is to enable the moral justification (or critique) of particular international legal human rights and, more broadly, the existing system of international human rights law as a whole (or something relevantly similar to it). As Buchanan notes, philosophers have tended to overestimate the contribution that theories of moral human rights can make toward this goal. This is partly because, as Buchanan points out, IHRL includes not only the substantive human rights norms of international treaties and conventions, but also procedures and institutionalized practices for developing and applying legal human rights, such as human rights courts like the European Court of Human Rights or the Inter-American Court of Human Rights, or any of the Treaty Bodies established to guide States Parties to various conventions as they implement them in domestic law.[49] Taking the *system* of international human rights law as the primary object of moral theorizing therefore raises important normative questions that a narrowly ontological account of human rights by itself tends not to notice, and is not equipped to address. Importantly for my purposes, many of these questions will be political ones. As I have been arguing, human rights morality therefore needs to include specifically political terms of moral assessment.

While my approach is intended to follow the path forged by Buchanan and Sreenivasan in this regard, it departs from the instrumentalism of the arguments they deploy to assess international human rights institutions without relying on a theory of moral human rights. As they have argued, a theory of moral human rights is unnecessary for this purpose because international legal human rights may be morally justified instrumentally, as part of an institutional system that achieves certain morally significant policy goals.[50] As part of this argument, Buchanan and Sreenivasan embrace a conception of law in general, and international human rights law in particular, as "chiefly an instrument, one that serves a diversity of moral purposes."[51] Their own arguments presume a "radical" form of legal instrumentalism that they call "nearly naked instrumentalism," according to which "there is no significant restriction on the purposes that can serve to justify a(n international) legal right. Any morally permissible (but otherwise optional) purpose or combination of purposes is eligible."[52] For example, Buchanan argues that the moral purposes served by a system of ILHRs include a basket of morally desirable ends, from "encouraging and supplementing domestic constitutional bills of rights" to "supplying resources for improving international humanitarian law."[53] In this form of instrumentalism, the morally desirable ends that IHRL serves may or may not be closely connected to the foundational values of human rights morality. In other words, these arguments provide an account of how ILHRs might achieve morally desirable ends that need not have any intrinsic or obvious connection to *human rights morality* in particular.

David Luban has argued that this line of reasoning is problematic because it "decouples ILHRs from their supposed moral foundations."[54] His concern is that international legal human rights need "some connection with moral human rights."[55] Without such a connection, there is (he argues) no basis for violations of international legal human rights to generate the moral outrage that is the currency of human rights discourse in international politics. This is important in turn because international human rights law, lacking its own enforcement mechanisms, relies on moral outrage for its actual influence on international actors. In Luban's view, then, international legal human rights will only be capable of mustering the requisite "mobilization of shame" if they are somehow linked to moral human rights. In sum, "without a connection with moral human rights, ILHRs will fail as legal rights."[56]

Luban's response raises a version of the normativity challenge for (Luban's interpretation of) Buchanan's and Sreenivasan's instrumentalist perspective, arguing that severing the justification of international legal human rights (or the system of IHRL) from a theory of moral human rights "leaves a gap in [the] account of how legalizing (positivizing) and internationalizing human rights is something worth doing."[57] On its face, however, this claim is simply false: instrumentalist arguments about the moral ends that international legal human rights (or the system of IHRL) may serve are precisely designed to show that these things are "worth doing," in a broad sense. Nonetheless, Luban is clearly convinced that instrumentalist arguments justifying international legal human rights are lacking some distinctive, important normative force. I propose that we can better understand Luban's objection if we take him to be looking for a tighter connection between international legal human rights and their moral foundations than instrumentalist arguments permit.

Why might this tighter connection be desirable? Luban's argument articulates an important practical reason: without such a connection, the violation of legal human rights may not generate the moral outrage that serves as "enforcement" for international human rights law. In other words, legal human rights need a moral foundation in order for their violation to inspire outrage. Notice, however, that Luban seems to assume that the "moral foundations" of IHRL are moral human rights. This assumption simply neglects the possibility of providing a political understanding of human rights morality, according to which the point of human rights morality is a direct assessment of international human rights law and practice, rather than producing an account of moral human rights.[58] Such a conception enables us to assess a system of universal legal human rights, which formally assigns equal legal human rights to all persons, as the most immediate political requirement of the value of universal moral equality. In other words, the universal legal equality of IHRL on this view can be seen as a direct political manifestation of the universal moral equality that itself is a foundational political value for human rights morality.

My point here is that legal human rights and international legal institutions may be morally assessed not only in terms of their instrumental value for achieving further morally desirable goals that may be remotely or not at all connected to human rights morality. In addition, when appropriately implemented, they may be morally assessed in terms of how well they institutionalize and promote the foundational values of human rights morality themselves. In this sense, human rights morality, understood as a political morality, provides non-instrumental (or at least much less "nakedly" instrumental) standards for assessing legal human rights and international legal institutions.

This methodology regards as especially important Buchanan's point (mentioned in Chapter 1) that international human rights law, "like law generally, is an institutionalized form of practical reasoning that serves moral values . . . and that has the resources for improving itself over time."[59] I develop a specific interpretation of this point in Chapter 3, paying particular attention to the evolution of moral human rights norms once they are implemented in various aspects of human rights practice. In this regard, it is significant that my project construes human rights practice broadly, to include not only international human rights law, but also at least certain aspects of international criminal law and international humanitarian law. The rationale for this is that some substantive and procedural norms of criminal or humanitarian law may at least share common normative roots with concepts clearly belonging to human rights morality. I will defend this claim more systematically in Chapter 5. For now, however, I simply want to motivate the basic idea by noting that what David Luban calls "human rights thinking" is apparent in the norms of other branches of international law, including in the evolution of protections for individuals in humanitarian law understood "as rights of the protected individuals and not of their states or collectivities."[60] Similarly, as Andrew Clapham has pointed out, the Nuremberg trials struggled to accommodate human rights norms that pulled in different directions, both in the sense that "human rights violations were to be prosecuted as individual crimes," while at the same time accommodating the fact that "[a] human rights principle, later entrenched in human rights treaties, protects the individual from being tried for an offence which was not a crime at the time it was committed (*nullum crimen sine lege*)."[61] The point is that norms of human rights morality are the subject of normative discourse within branches of international law other than international human rights law. In combination with the methodological principle that we can learn about the content of moral norms by attending to how they are understood and evolve over time in practice, this implies that we can learn about human rights morality by attending to claims made in its name within multiple branches of international law, even if their primary legal concern is with subjects other than human rights.

Finally, on the methodology I'm defending, philosophers interested in human rights morality have good reason to attend to the ways in which human rights norms and values evolve in (these aspects of) the practice.[62] Again, the point is the broadly pragmatist one that the normative assessment of social practices should be based on terms that make sense given the goals and normative claims made by the participants in that practice. Human rights practice is itself a particularly normatively rich practice. This does not mean that any claim made by any participant within it is ipso facto normatively authoritative as a standard for assessing the practice as a whole; that would of course be incoherent. The point, rather, is that the standards philosophers use as the basis of a moral assessment of the practice, and for critical reflection on the values of human rights morality in the first place, should be informed by the normative discourses within various aspects of the practice.

NOTES

1. The operative word here is "unreconstructed." Many philosophers have worked on reconstructing canonical views so that they address these and other concerns. For example, for a collection of essays addressing the project of reconstruction of canonical philosophers' views from a specifically feminist perspective, see Louise Antony and Charlotte Witt, eds., *A Mind of One's Own: Feminist Essays on Reason and Objectivity,* 2nd ed. (Boulder, CO: Westview Press, 2002).

2. Scholars of course debate the correct interpretation of this aspect of Aristotle's political theory. For an analysis that suggests that Aristotle is actually critical of the limitations on women in Greek social and political life, see Dana Jalbert Stauffer, "Aristotle's Account of the Subjection of Women," *Journal of Politics* 70, no. 4 (2008).

3. John Rawls, *A Theory of Justice,* rev. ed. (Cambridge: Harvard University Press, 1999), 23.

4. Martha Nussbaum, "Human Capabilities and Female Human Beings," in *Women, Culture, and Development: A Study of Human Capabilities*, ed. Martha Nussbaum and Jonathan Glover (Oxford: Oxford University Press, 1995), 495–551.

5. Rawls, *A Theory of Justice,* 24–30 *passim.*

6. Rawls, *A Theory of Justice,* 25.

7. Thomas Pogge, *World Poverty and Human Rights*, 2nd ed. (Cambridge: Polity Press, 2018), 176 (emphasis original).

8. Pogge, *World Poverty and Human Rights*: 176. As I note below, however, this does not, strictly speaking, apply to Tasioulas's view.

9. Pogge, *World Poverty and Human Rights*, 50–51.

10. Pogge, *World Poverty and Human Rights,* 70.

11. Pogge, *World Poverty and Human Rights*, 71.

12. Pogge, *World Poverty and Human Rights*, 71.

13. Pogge himself "leaves it open whether such [interpersonal] moral wrongs should be considered human-rights violations. A commitment to human rights goes along with interactional moral commitments; but this is no reason to identify the former with the latter." (Pogge, *World Poverty and Human Rights*, 71.) I find it helpful to use the term "human rights violations" to refer to interactional deprivations of the objects of one's human rights, and "human rights fulfillment" to capture the political and institutional obligation to, as Pogge argues, ensure secure enjoyment of the objects of their human rights for all. For the opposite view, see Tasioulas's critique of Pogge: John Tasioulas, "The Moral Reality of Human Rights," in *Freedom from Poverty as a Human Right*, ed. Thomas Pogge (Oxford: Oxford University Press, 2007), 95–97.

14. Tasioulas, "The Moral Reality of Human Rights," 76.

15. Tasioulas, "The Moral Reality of Human Rights," 77.

16. Tasioulas, "The Moral Reality of Human Rights," 76.

17. Tasioulas, "The Moral Reality of Human Rights," 78.

18. Pogge, *World Poverty and Human Rights*, 176.

19. Tasioulas, "The Moral Reality of Human Rights," 100. Quoting James Griffin, "Discrepancies Between the Best Philosophical Account of Human Rights and the International Law of Human Rights," *Proceedings of the Aristotelian Society* 101 (2001): 2.

20. John Tasioulas, "Towards a Philosophy of Human Rights," *Current Legal Problems* 65, no. 1 (2012): 29.

21. Tasioulas, "Towards a Philosophy of Human Rights," 25.

22. John Tasioulas, "Exiting the Hall of Mirrors: Morality and Law in Human Rights," in *Political and Legal Approaches to Human Rights,* ed. Tom Campbell and Kylie Bourne (New York: Routledge, 2017), 79.

23. Allen Buchanan, *The Heart of Human Rights* (Oxford: Oxford University Press, 2013), 68.

24. Tasioulas, "Exiting the Hall of Mirrors," 86.

25. Tasioulas, "Exiting the Hall of Mirrors," 87.

26. Tasioulas, "Exiting the Hall of Mirrors," 86.

27. Tasioulas, "Exiting the Hall of Mirrors," 86.

28. Tasioulas, "Exiting the Hall of Mirrors," 86.

29. Tasioulas, "Exiting the Hall of Mirrors," 80.

30. Tasioulas, "Exiting the Hall of Mirrors," 86.

31. In 2016, then Deputy Attorney General Sally Yates implemented anti-bias training throughout the U.S. Department of Justice, as an "important step in our ongoing efforts to promote fairness, eliminate bias and build the stronger, safer, more just society that all Americans deserve." ("Department of Justice Announces New Department-Wide Implicit Bias Training for Personnel," U.S. Department of Justice, Office of Public Affairs, last modified June 27, 2016, https://www.justice.gov/opa/pr/department-justice-announces-new-department-wide-implicit-bias-training-personnel.)

32. Tasioulas, "Exiting the Hall of Mirrors," 79.

33. As Jean Bethke Elshtain observes, Hannah Arendt defended the maintenance of the private sphere in part because it "is the only space that can shelter children from premature, hence devastating, entry into the public worlds, and burdens, of life." (Jean Bethke Elshtain, "Political Children: Reflections on Hannah Arendt's Distinction between Public and Private Life," in *Reconstructing Political Theory: Feminist Perspectives*, ed. Mary Lyndon Shanley and Uma Narayan [University Park: Pennsylvania State University Press, 1997], 110). However, Elshtain goes on to critique Arendt's public/private distinction as it applies to children.

34. Hilary Charlesworth, Christine Chinkin, and Shelley Wright, "Feminist Approaches to International Law," *American Journal of International Law* 85 (1991): 627.

35. Lucy Ferguson, "Gender, Work, and the Sexual Division of Labor," in *The Oxford Handbook of Gender and Politics*, ed. Georgina Waylen, Karen Celis, Johanna Kantola, and S. Laurel Weldon (Oxford: Oxford University Press, 2013), 337 (italics original). For a related critique of gendered economic definitions of production and "housework," see Elizabeth Anderson, "Pragmatism, Science, and Moral Inquiry," in

In Face of the Facts: Moral Inquiry in American Scholarship, ed. Richard Wightman Fox and Robert Westbrook (Cambridge: Cambridge University Press, 1998), 10–39.

36. Jean Hampton, "The Case for Feminism," in *The Liberation Debate*, ed. Michael Leahy and Dan Cohn-Sherbock (New York: Routledge, 1996), 18.

37. Hampton, "The Case for Feminism," 22.

38. Tasioulas, "Exiting the Hall of Mirrors," 79.

39. Susan Moller Okin, *Justice, Gender, and the Family* (New York: Basic Books, 1989), 175–81 *passim.*

40. John Tasioulas, "On the Nature of Human Rights," in *The Philosophy of Human Rights,* ed. Gerhard Ernst and Jan-Christoph Heilinger (Göttingen: De Gruyter, 2012), 48.

41. Tasioulas, "On the Nature of Human Rights," 48.

42. See Buchanan on "conceptual imperialism" in the philosophy of human rights (Buchanan, *The Heart of Human Rights*, 9–14).

43. This point is powerfully and famously argued by Iris Marion Young, *Justice and the Politics of Difference* (Princeton: Princeton University Press, 1990).

44. See Kate Manne's similar claim about misogyny: "Hostility toward women would simply be an individual quirk or something like a phobia absent a system of patriarchal oppression in the background." (Kate Manne, *Down Girl: The Logic of Misogyny* [Oxford: Oxford University Press, 2018], 67.)

45. Tasioulas, "On the Nature of Human Rights," 26.

46. Tasioulas, "On the Nature of Human Rights," 27.

47. See Tasioulas's characterization of Rawlsian public reason as an attempt to avoid standards of truth in moral argument, for example. (Tasioulas, "Towards a Philosophy of Human Rights," 28.)

48. Allen Buchanan and Gopal Sreenivasan, "Taking International Legality Seriously: A Methodology for Human Rights," in *Human Rights: Moral or Political?,* ed. Adam Etinson (New York: Oxford University Press, 2018), 228.

49. Buchanan, *The Heart of Human Rights.*

50. Gopal Sreenivasan, "A Human Right to Health? Some Inconclusive Skepticism," *Aristotelian Society Supplementary Volume* 86, no. 1 (2012): 239–65; Allen Buchanan, "Why International Legal Human Rights?," in *Philosophical Foundations of Human Rights*, ed. Rowan Cruft, S. Matthew Liao, and Massimo Renzo (Oxford: Oxford University Press, 2015), 244–62; Buchanan and Sreenivasan, "Taking International Legality Seriously."

51. Buchanan and Sreenivasan, "Taking International Legality Seriously," 213.

52. Buchanan and Sreenivasan, "Taking International Legality Seriously," 214. They also discuss a less radical version of instrumentality (which they call "subtle instrumentalism"), according to which "only morally *mandatory* purposes are eligible to ground moral justifications of legal rights." Subtle instrumentalism plays an important role in their critique of the necessity of "a corresponding universal moral right" to justify any particular legal human right; beyond this, the motivation for adopting a narrow instrumentalist view in this sense is opaque to me, so I set it aside here.

53. Buchanan, "Why International Legal Human Rights?," 250–54.

54. David Luban, "Human Rights Pragmatism and Human Dignity," in *Philosophical Foundations of Human Rights*, ed. Rowan Cruft, S. Matthew Liao, and Massimo Renzo (Oxford: Oxford University Press, 2015), 265.

55. Luban, "Human Rights Pragmatism and Human Dignity," 266.

56. Luban, "Human Rights Pragmatism and Human Dignity," 266.

57. Luban, "Human Rights Pragmatism and Human Dignity," 270.

58. In fact, however, the connection that Luban suggests to play the role of the "missing link" in Buchanan's view is itself not actually a philosophical theory of moral human rights *per se* at all. Rather, it is an account of human dignity as a foundational value for moral human rights. Moreover, Luban agrees with Buchanan and Sreenivasan in rejecting the "mirroring view," according to which "the existence of a corresponding universal moral right is necessary to justify any international legal human right" (Buchanan and Sreenivasan, "Taking International Legality Seriously," 214 [emphasis original]). For that reason, we can be sure that he is not presuming that dignity grounds moral human rights, which in turn ground particular legal human rights, since this would be a version of the mirroring view. I think we can therefore conclude that Luban meant to be speaking about "human rights morality" broadly when arguing that Buchanan needed to supply some connection between ILHRs and "moral human rights."

59. Buchanan, *The Heart of Human Rights*, 8.

60. Luban, "Human Rights Pragmatism and Human Dignity," 271.

61. Andrew Clapham, "Human Rights and International Criminal Law," in *The Cambridge Companion to International Criminal Law*, ed. William Schabas (Cambridge: Cambridge University Press, 2016), 12–13.

62. This point may be more continuous with Buchanan's methodology than otherwise. For example, in a broadly pragmatist move, Buchanan refers to "the weight of historical experience concerning what often happens when people are not treated as having equal basic status" as providing a possible reason for shifting the burden of proof in philosophical argument to those who would argue *against* the principle that "all human individuals have the same—and important—basic moral status." (Buchanan, *The Heart of Human Rights*, 135.) For a pragmatist interpretation of Buchanan's account of human rights morality, see Luban, "Human Rights Pragmatism and Human Dignity," 271.

Chapter 3

Structural Equality

The idea of human rights is inherently egalitarian. Because human rights—moral or legal—are universal rights, they belong to all persons regardless of nationality, race, sex, religion, or any other distinguishing characteristic. By itself, this is of course a radical moral idea. But is it not the only way in which human rights may be egalitarian. For example, there may be human rights to certain forms of equality: rights to equal distributive shares or equal opportunity sets, or rights to certain forms of procedural equality (for example, to have one's legal testimony considered as equally reliable to that of others). In this chapter, I argue that another form of equality—*structural equality*—is an important component of human rights morality. Very many systems of social and political inequality rest on deeply entrenched conceptual schemes that make even drastic inequalities seem innocuous, natural, or inevitable, and therefore invisible from the perspective of both theorizing and realizing human rights morality. For this reason, theorizing human rights morality, and realizing it in practice, require identifying and remedying existing forms of social prejudice and bias. Structural equality so understood is therefore an essential foundational value for a political account of human rights morality that aims to explicate and guide human rights practice.

I begin by explaining the sense of structural equality that (I argue) should figure in a political conception of human rights morality. I briefly review three related contrasts that help illuminate this idea. The first is between equal formal legal rights and their effective protection or enforcement. This distinction is helpful for explicating structural inequality insofar as the human rights of some social groups may be insecurely protected if their formally equal legal rights are insufficiently protected in practice. The second and third distinctions both contrast a structural conception of equality, understood as the absence of group-based social and political hierarchies, with two ways of understanding moral equality in a more formal sense: first, the equality of human rights holders as possessors of equal human rights, and second, equality as anti-discrimination.

I then argue that structural social hierarchies constitute both a practical obstacle to the secure fulfillment of human rights and an epistemic obstacle to accurately understanding the requirements of equality in practice (and to some extent in theory as well). This epistemic challenge puts pressure on traditional methods of theorizing human rights morality in terms of a theory of moral human rights insofar as it raises questions about the abilities of those methods to accurately represent many of the real-world social and political contexts in which human rights have their distinctive moral point. By contrast, the methodology I am recommending is useful in response to this kind of epistemic challenge, given that (as I shall argue) international human rights institutions contribute to making such hierarchies visible, by giving authoritative voice to individuals and groups who are fighting the effects of such hierarchies on the realization of their human rights.

In the subsequent section, I show that the Convention on the Rights of Persons with Disabilities (CRPD) explicitly embraces a form of structural equality understood to require the identification and dismantling of existing social and political hierarchies. The CRPD also illustrates the potential of international legal institutions to improve themselves over time specifically by enabling members of marginalized groups to shape the law in ways that better reflect their experiences. The CRPD therefore demonstrates that this value already does play an important and morally progressive role in human rights practice. Given that structural equality is an inherently political concept, the argument in this section therefore supports the claim that any philosophical account of human rights morality that aims to theorize the practice needs to be appropriately institutional, for both theoretical and practical reasons.

Next, I critique orthodox treatments of equality one more time, this time arguing that the conceptual commitments of orthodox theorizing, including their focus on ontological questions about moral human rights, stand in the way of their ability to take structural equality seriously as a possible foundational value for human rights morality. Moreover, while (as I argue earlier) attention to human rights practice would highlight this understanding of equality as a foundational value for human rights morality, orthodox commitments to the disciplinary division of labor discussed in Chapter 1 prevent them from referring to the practice for such moral guidance.

Finally, I critique Beitz's political view for surprisingly similar reasons. While Beitz accurately understands the structural problem for women's human rights, nonetheless the conceptual commitments of his view (in particular, to understanding human rights as existing only when the international community can effectively intervene to ameliorate the problem) complicate Beitz's engagement with the practice. As a result, Beitz's view is unable to endorse the progressive elements of structural equality embraced within human rights practice by the Convention on the Elimination of Discrimination against Women (CEDAW). I conclude the chapter by noting that, if my critiques in this chapter are accurate, the philosophy of human rights is in need of both a more innovative political methodology that enables engagement with human rights practice and an appropriately institutional and political account of human rights morality. I attempt to demonstrate such a methodology in the remaining chapters of this book.

STRUCTURAL EQUALITY

As feminists have long argued, the idea of equality can be deployed in ways that work against our capacity to see and understand oppression. For example, if we understand equal treatment to be morally required only among relevantly similar persons, but we consider gender or race to be a morally relevant difference, then glaring inequalities in law or social practice will not register as morally problematic, but instead as natural and perhaps even unavoidable.[1] Consider the complete complacency with which most modern democratic societies regarded the disenfranchisement of women well into the twentieth century. This is, to contemporary eyes, a massive deprivation of civil and political human rights. And yet, according to the conceptions of equality and gender that were prevalent at the time, this was not a problematic inequality. As this historical example shows, thinking clearly about human rights morality requires careful attention to dominant social concepts or social meanings about social groups, and about what conception of equality is most apt for understanding human rights morality.

In this section, I draw out three different ways of contrasting a formal conception of equality with a more substantive one. The first is the distinction between formal legal protections and their actual effectiveness in reality. In a human rights context, this is the familiar, well-understood point that legal human rights do not on their own secure the objects of those rights for the rights holders. This distinction is helpful for understanding forms of group-based inequality that may be revealed in social contexts where the protection or enforcement of legal rights is systematically ineffective for members of some social groups. This kind of inequality is particularly salient for understanding the structural inequality facing women in many social contexts. Often, a particularly wide gap persists between the legal rights women enjoy on paper and their actual enjoyment of the objects of those rights. One example of this is that Brazil has not been able to reduce its rate of murders of women despite legislation intended to do just that. Brazil reports the seventh-highest rate of femicide in the world, with a rate more than double that of the United States.[2] Referring to a 2006 law which imposed severe sentences for convicted domestic abusers, Maria Laura Canineu, the Brazil director for the international NGO Human Rights Watch, argued that, "In Brazil, we have a very good law. The problem is that it's not being implemented."

Similarly, a 2018 report released by the United Nations Office on Drugs and Crime noted that, statistically speaking, the most dangerous place for women around the world is in the home, given the prevalence of intimate partner and other domestic violence, including dowry disputes and killings related to accusations of witchcraft.[3] The report concluded that, from a global perspective, "[t]angible progress in both protecting and saving the lives of female victims of intimate partner/family-related homicide has not been made in recent years, despite the many programmes developed to eradicate violence against women and the amount of legislation adopted."[4]

Another striking illustration of the wide gap between legislation and substantive protection for women's rights emerges from Hawa Aden Mohamed's recent description of an increase in incidents of rape in Puntland, Somalia, following the passage in 2016 of a law criminalizing sexual violence, which was the first of its kind in the region.[5] The bill was supported by government agencies, women's NGOs, and community leaders. However, not only did rape cases actually increase in the year following the law's passage, but many incidents involved perpetrators from the police or military, some of whom "did not even bother changing out of their uniforms before committing their assaults."[6] As Mohamed argues:

> the lesson from the sad story of Puntland's Sexual Offenses Act is that while formal laws can be vital in influencing attitudes, attitudes and behavior also influence how a law is enforced. The passage of the law was a great start. But what the past year has made clear is that we also need to start changing attitudes in Puntland and the region more broadly, or else these much-celebrated legal advances for women will be rendered meaningless.[7]

The most straightforward implication of this brief discussion is that simply changing the law is not sufficient for securing (to use Thomas Pogge's phrase) "an institutional order and public culture that ensures that all members of society have secure access to the objects of their human rights."[8] But another important implication is that, as Mohamed notes in the Puntland context, "attitudes and behavior also influence how a law is enforced." This means that actually realizing an institutional order that protects human rights equally well for members of all social groups may in many contexts require reforming deeply entrenched patterns of subordination that are rooted in widespread social beliefs and attitudes.

The second distinction highlights the distance between formal equality among persons understood as equal human rights holders (on one hand) and equality understood as the absence of group-based social and political hierarchies (on the other hand). One way to explicate this distinction is via John Rawls's view of human rights, according to which human rights violations provide justification for (or remove an objection to) some form of intervention into the violator state by international actors. Defining human rights as "necessary conditions of any system of social cooperation," Rawls argues that the political function of human rights is to mark the distinction between societies that should be recognized as members in good standing of international society and those that shouldn't. On this view, states that violate human rights have no right to be tolerated on the international stage. This conception of human rights, given its close connection to sovereignty rights and the potential justification of international intervention, puts a very strong downward pressure on the content of human rights. Human rights to life, against slavery, and rights to formal equality ("that similar cases be treated similarly") are included on Rawls's very short list of "human rights proper," but Rawls is explicit that there are no human rights to social or political equality per se, for women or for any other social group. In fact, Rawls's fictional example of Kazanistan, a human-rights respecting, non-liberal but decent people, is deliberately hierarchical in order to make precisely this point.[9] One of the most obviously inegalitarian aspects of Kazanistan is that "only Muslims can hold the upper positions of political authority and influence the government's main decisions and policies, including foreign affairs."[10] Rawls's point is to show that human rights, in his minimalist sense, may at least in theory be adequately protected in non-liberal, hierarchical regimes, which in turn entails that such regimes (if any exist) deserve toleration by liberal societies in international politics. Insofar as the hierarchical structure of Kazanistan society is decidedly opposed to the equal social and political status of its citizens (that is, structural equality) even though they are all equally holders of (Rawlsian minimalist) human rights, this example effectively demonstrates the gap between these two concepts.

Finally, structural equality (understood as the absence of social and political hierarchies) contrasts also with a different substantive understanding of equality as anti-discrimination. The latter was succinctly expressed in a remark by U.S. Supreme Court Chief Justice John Roberts, in support of a white woman's claim that affirmative action in college admissions discriminates against white people: "The way to end discrimination on the basis of race is to stop discriminating on the basis of race."[11] Roberts's claim is embedded in a theory about what the problem of racism is (essentially, making invidious and unjustified distinctions between individuals on the basis of race) and offers a way forward to end racism as he understands it (namely, legally prohibiting invidious and unjustified distinctions between individuals on the basis of race). However, as many scholars of race and racism have argued, Roberts's construal of the problem of racial inequality is itself part of the problem of racial inequality. Indeed, it is no accident that Americans are taught to see the problem of race in the way that Roberts describes it. The version of history implied by Roberts's comment, what Ibram Kendi calls the history of racial progress, blinds us to important parts of our actual racial history—the history of *racist* progress, in which overtly racist agendas have long been pursued via formal law and policy, as well as the more informal perpetuation, legitimation, and teaching of ideas and narratives rooted in ideologies of racial hierarchy.[12] On this latter view, what is necessary to dismantle racism is not "race neutrality," but rather a concerted effort to understand, and actively work to end, the impacts of racist agendas embedded in both ethics and law. As Camisha Russell very aptly puts this point, in order to accurately understand the racial dimensions of any ethical or policy question, what is needed is not a political ideal of neutrality among similarly situated individuals, but rather "a methodical description and analysis of the development and function of the race idea as a political symbol and as constitutive of social realities within specific historical contexts."[13]

Many feminists make an analogous argument regarding women's equality. On this argument, the problem of women's inequality is not adequately captured by describing it as invidious discrimination, as if the problem were that some people make unjustified distinctions on the basis of sex, where individuals should instead be treated identically regardless of sex. While such forms of discrimination do exist and need to be rectified, the deeper problem of women's systemic inequality as a social group results from conceptions of women as inferior (or less than fully human) that are deeply influential in many social, political, and legal contexts as well as in ethics and law (and the histories of both). Indeed, the history of Western philosophy is replete with examples of such thinking about women, in which deeply inegalitarian social and political arrangements are seen to be compatible with formal senses of equality that primarily require treating similar cases similarly.[14] Adequately theorizing women's equality therefore requires, in the first instance, identifying these biased conceptions and the influences they have had on our moral and legal thinking. And actually securing equality for women in the real world will require taking active steps to combat the systemic embodiment of these deeply ingrained biases in both ethical thinking as well as in social, political, and legal institutions. As one legal analysis puts this point: "Sexism is not a legal aberration but a pervasive, structural problem. . . . On this basis, the most productive analysis of inequality is in terms of domination and subordination. Thus, equality is not freedom to be treated without regard to sex but freedom from systematic subordination because of sex."[15]

The point of this section is that the sense of equality that is integral to human rights morality cannot be fully captured by the idea of all persons as equal human rights holders (which Rawls's deliberately hierarchical view satisfies), nor in a sense that can be practically realized by legal reforms (which may or may not be effectively implemented and protected), nor in a sense that simply forbids discrimination on the basis of group membership (which may not only fail to address but also serve to mask the existence of deep structural inequalities). Rather, in order to address persistent group-based inequalities in real-world social and political contexts, equality needs to be understood in a political sense as a property of social groups primarily, rather than a matter of comparing individuals to each other in a way that abstracts from their social and political contexts. Achieving equality in this sense requires actively dismantling the socially constructed inequalities that hide and normalize social and political hierarchies among social groups. Moreover, given that (as I shall argue) this conception of equality animates some of the most progressive elements of international human rights law, any adequate theory of human rights morality, whether orthodox or political, that aims to theorize the conception of human rights within the practice, needs to accommodate (or explicitly repudiate) this conception of equality as a foundational value for human rights morality.

MORAL EPISTEMOLOGY AND HUMAN RIGHTS PRACTICE

One important implication of the discussion thus far is that in social contexts characterized by deeply entrenched group-based hierarchies, even egalitarian-minded human rights reformers may find it difficult to develop an accurate understanding of the requirements of human rights morality. The tendency of deeply entrenched, biased belief systems is to render structural inequalities invisible. From the perspective of those who accept such belief systems, visible inequalities between social groups may appear to be simply the inevitable result of natural differences, rather than the predictable result of deeply intertwined social, legal, and political structures that influence individuals' opportunities and choices. Unfortunately, even for those who are aware of the existence of socially entrenched biases, the very pervasiveness of the underlying belief systems, and their myriad manifestations in so many social, economic, and political contexts, may contribute to the perception that reform is impossible.

Two further points—a practical one and an epistemic one—follow from this. The practical point is the familiar idea that structural inequalities may hamper the realization of moral human rights in practice. The epistemic point is that entrenched group-based hierarchies, especially when they are supported by conceptual schemes that attribute these inequalities to allegedly natural differences, constitute a moral-epistemic challenge to developing accurate understandings of the requirements of human rights morality even in the abstract.

The epistemic and practical points are deeply intertwined: entrenched forms of social group hierarchies constitute substantial obstacles to correctly and fully understanding both human rights morality in the abstract and the real-world requirements of its realization. Awareness of the existence of social hierarchies and their effects on human rights fulfillment in the real world is therefore a component of both a full understanding of human rights morality and of any feasible attempt to implement it in practice.

Moreover, conceptual schemes justifying entrenched social hierarchies, especially when exemplified in laws and norms of governing institutions, have the further (practical) consequence not only of depriving members of subordinated social groups of their basic human rights (to life, to liberty, to physical security, to fair trials, to an adequate standard of living, to equal opportunity, etc.), but also at the same time (epistemically) obscuring the fact that these are deprivations of human rights at all (at least to those within the relevant epistemic community). This argument in turn implies that grasping the epistemic significance of structural equality is necessary for an adequate understanding of human rights morality, which in turn is necessary for the realization and secure protection of basic human rights. Any view that takes basic moral or legal human rights seriously, then, ought also to at least instrumentally prioritize understanding and working to dismantle systemic of inequalities, including their social and epistemic roots in naturalized conceptions of group differences, simply as a means of ensuring, as Pogge argues, that "all members of society have secure access to the objects of their human rights."[16]

However, the flip side of the moral-epistemic difficulties posed by structural inequalities is an important reverse dynamic that may be instrumental to helping to dismantle them in practice. This point builds on Buchanan's claim that the international legal elements of human rights practice constitute "an institutionalized form of practical reasoning that serves moral values . . . and that has the resources for improving itself over time."[17] On one hand, human rights practice, including certain aspects of international criminal law and international human rights law, may unwittingly incorporate and perpetuate social hierarchies via their procedures, norms, and the assumptions made by various actors within the relevant institutions. At the same time, however, these institutions may also provide particularly visible institutional mechanisms and venues (trials at criminal tribunals or treaty body proceedings, for example) whereby deeply entrenched social hierarchies may be productively challenged and upended, not only symbolically, but also in ways that constitute concrete advances toward the realization of status equality and equal human rights. As the case study in Chapter 4 demonstrates, such institutions therefore provide opportunities to improve our understanding of the foundational moral values and implications of human rights morality while also moving toward realizing them in practice. The further implication of this practical dynamic is that it demonstrates the usefulness of opening up philosophical theorizing to human rights practice as a potential source of evidence about human rights morality at a more substantive level than most currently accommodate.

THE CONVENTION ON THE RIGHTS OF PERSONS WITH DISABILITIES

The Convention on the Rights of Persons with Disabilities (CRPD) was the first new human rights treaty of the twenty-first century, having entered into force in May of 2008. The United Nations emphasizes the extreme marginalization of persons with disabilities as one of the most important reasons why a human rights treaty was needed to address their specific challenges:

> Persons with disabilities make up the world's largest and most disadvantaged group. The numbers are damning: an estimated 20 per cent of the world's poorest persons are those with disabilities; 98 percent of children with disabilities in developing countries do not attend school; an estimated 30 percent of the world's street children live with disabilities; and the literacy rate for adults with disabilities is as low as 3 per cent—and, in some countries, down to 1 per cent for women with disabilities.[18]

The CRPD came into existence as the result of concerted efforts to connect existing human rights norms in international law to such lived realities faced by persons with disabilities, whose human rights are often only insecurely protected. The felt need for a treaty specifically addressing the situation of this population reflects the conviction that failing to explicitly address this group's human rights, in a world where those rights are poorly conceptualized, and even frequently violated in ways that are tolerated and expected, risks complicity in a sociopolitical system that does not recognize persons with disabilities as equal human rights holders.

One of the most important innovations of the CRPD was to explicitly involve the participation of civil-society disability advocates at all stages, from the development of the treaty to its implementation. According to one analysis, "[o]ne of the unique attributes of the negotiation process of the

CRPD was the active involvement of civil society institutions, especially disabled people's organisations (DPOs). The negotiation of previous human rights treaties did not engage with civil society institutions in the same systematic manner."[19] Moreover, the CRPD emphasizes the inclusion of DPOs and persons with disabilities in implementing and monitoring the treaty. As another analysis of the treaty argues:

> These features together represent perhaps one of the most progressive developments in human rights law provided by the CRPD (even if stakeholder input is at times informally encouraged by other treaty bodies). It reflects the fundamental principle that the persons most affected have the right to participate in decisions that impact them. In the disability context more specifically, it represents a sharp turn from marginalization and lack of voice in decisional processes.[20]

Another innovation in the CRPD is its assertion of strong and clear duties on states to work proactively to dismantle negative stereotypes about persons with disabilities. As the United Nations emphasizes:

> The Convention follows decades of work by the United Nations to change attitudes and approaches to persons with disabilities. It takes to a new height the movement from viewing persons with disabilities as "objects" of charity, medical treatment and social protection towards viewing persons with disabilities as "subjects" with rights, who are capable of claiming those rights and making decisions for their lives based on their free and informed consent as well as being active members of society.[21]

The key point here is that the same biases that explain the real-world situation of persons with disabilities also explain the widespread failure to recognize them as paradigmatic rights-holders, both by domestic social and political institutions and also within international human rights law prior to the CRPD. The CRPD therefore advances both a fuller abstract understanding about human rights morality *and* practical insight into the real-world situations of persons with disabilities by insisting that respect for their human rights requires actively dismantling both prevalent misconceptions about disability and ideologies that license and tolerate the marginalization or exploitation of persons with disabilities.

One example of the implications of this process is that the CRPD's assertion of the human rights of persons with psychosocial disabilities has fostered extensive subsequent dialogue about whether widely accepted responses to such disabilities, including involuntary detention or treatment, are in fact consistent with the dignity and rights of persons who are subjected to them. Currently, coercive treatment and involuntary detention are often justified on the grounds that they are necessary to protect the well-being of mentally ill individuals themselves, or to protect others from such individuals, and therefore are not regarded as discrimination. According to some disability rights advocates, however, the CRPD and its implementation have prompted a reconsideration of this justification for these measures, on grounds that the CRPD embodies a "human rights model of disability," which "defies the presumption that impairment may hinder human rights capacity."[22] On this reading of the CRPD, status-quo, "medical models" of psychosocial disability are too quick to construe involuntary treatment and detention as "care" rather than taking seriously their potentially rights-violating features.[23] As a result, the CRPD has triggered a rethinking of the legal standard of discrimination, which has been developed by the treaty bodies for the International Convention on Civil and Political Rights, the Convention on the Elimination of Racial Discrimination, and the International Convention on Economic, Social, and Cultural Rights, and which permits differential treatment for members of particular groups as long as that treatment achieves a legitimate aim and is "objectively and reasonably justified."[24]

I do not at all mean to take a side as to which of these views is better justified, all things considered. Instead, I take the commitment to structural equality inherent in the CRPD to support two further points. The first is that these debates show that the careful consideration of human rights norms in context of the lived realities of marginalized or disempowered social groups may necessitate rethinking widely accepted understandings of essential components of human rights morality. The CRPD therefore demonstrates the conceptual gaps or errors that may be hidden in dominant conceptions of human rights. The second is that these gaps can be exposed when marginalized groups are empowered by their equal legal standing as human rights holders under international law to articulate the distance between their current realities and true equality, as they see it. In turn, of course, the practical significance of this point is that these gaps and errors can then be filled and corrected. The embrace of a structural equality framework by the CRPD therefore constitutes an example of the potentially progressive institutional dynamic that I described in the previous section.

EQUALITY AND ORTHODOXY

As the CRPD demonstrates, a commitment to structural equality is not only a component of human rights practice, but there is also a strong argument to make in support of the claim that it functions as an engine of moral progress within the practice. For that reason, a theory of human rights morality that claims to be relevant to and provide normative guidance for the practice has good reason to account for structural equality as a foundational value for human rights morality. In this section, I argue that the conceptual structure of orthodox theories effectively discourages them from doing this.

As noted earlier, whether (and how) equality is a foundational value for human rights morality is a different question from whether there exist human rights to equality in some further, more substantive sense. However, these two questions are closely related in orthodox theorizing, where the foundational values of human rights morality function as the moral grounds of particular human rights. For example, the moral foundation of James Griffin's theory is his account of personhood values, which are understood as "protections of our human standing."[25] At the same time his theory "grounds human rights . . . directly in . . . the values of personhood."[26] Similarly, the foundational values for John Tasioulas's theory (human dignity and universal human interests) function as the grounds for particular moral human rights (albeit not directly, as in Griffin's theory, as we shall see). The fact that the foundational values of human rights morality function as the grounds of moral human rights follows from the orthodox view that the point of philosophical theorizing about moral human rights is to provide a list of justified moral human rights; that is, since the questions their theories are designed to answer are ontological ones, the foundational values of the theories are supposed to provide the basis for answering them. Given this tight connection between foundational values and the grounds of individual moral human rights, orthodox methodology treats any argument for or against a value's being a foundational value of human rights morality as at the same time part of an argument about whether the theory should justify substantive human rights grounded in that value.

For orthodox theorists, equality appears among the foundational values for human rights morality primarily insofar as it is essential to describing the distinctive, equal moral standing of persons. Griffin and Tasioulas both refer to the idea of human dignity as playing this role.[27] Both also take pains to differentiate this sense of equality from more substantive conceptions. In Griffin's view, for example, human dignity does not include any substantive sense of equality beyond the sense in which all human rights holders are equally possessors of the status of personhood. If it did, then (given that human rights are grounded "directly" in substantive values on his view) his theory would conclude that there exist specific moral human rights to equality in that substantive sense. However, as Griffin argues, substantive forms of equality (such as distributive equality) are (generally speaking) the proper business of justice, but are not thereby human rights. This is not a moral "demotion" for egalitarian concerns, Griffin argues, but rather simply a reflection of the way in which "a human right is a quite particular moral consideration."[28] For example, egalitarian distributive justice among persons in a desert island scenario might be a requirement of "equal respect and all that follows from it," but it is not thereby a matter of human rights. As Griffin argues,

> There are forms of distributive justice, for all their importance, that do not bear on our personhood—so long, that is, as the human right to minimum provision is respected. Human rights themselves have distributive implications but ones limited to the protection of personhood. . . . But matters of justice can be highly important in our lives without being matters of human rights.[29]

One important point here is that this reasoning process essentially attempts to establish a kind of reflective equilibrium between Griffin's considered convictions about (on one hand) which moral human rights are reasonable to justify, and (on the other hand) which grounding values seem not only important on their own but also would produce a plausible list of moral human rights. In other words, Griffin's reasoning on this question does not seem entirely foundational (or unidirectional), inferring the existence or non-existence of moral human rights from personhood values. Rather, the reverse reasoning also seems to be in play: from the fact that substantive (say, distributive) equality is not properly a human right, Griffin confirms his rejection of substantive equality as a foundational value in his theory. In this way, pre-theoretical commitments or considered judgments about which human rights plausibly exist put downward pressure on his willingness to expand his theory's foundational values for human rights morality, including by considering more demanding conceptions of equality to play that role.

The only sense of group-based equality that Griffin considers in this discussion is cashed out in terms of human rights against discrimination. On one hand, he argues, it is clearly not a human rights violation if nepotism is the reason that one "top executive of a multinational firm" makes more than another. This example shows that not every form of "objectionable discrimination" is a human rights violation. On the other hand, some forms of group-based discrimination are clearly violations of human rights, as "when the thuggish organs of a government randomly round up members of a hated racial minority and subject them to painful physical abuse."[30] Here the relevant considerations trace back to personhood values: being subject to painful abuse by thuggish government agents would infringe on those values, while the unfairness of being paid less than another executive who happens to be the CEO's relative would not. However, Griffin argues that "[t]he cases of discrimination that exercise us seriously nowadays, mainly racism and sexism, range between these two extremes. In this middle ground it is often hard to tell objectionable from unobjectionable discrimination, the sorts of discrimination that violate human rights and the sorts that do not."[31] To address this uncertainty, he refers again to personhood values to determine whether the kind of discrimination violates human rights, for example, as it might if group-based discrimination has a "destructive effect on an agent's self-image." However, despite in this way noting briefly that group-based inequalities may adversely affect individuals' agency, Griffin does not question more deeply whether a view of equality as non-discrimination adequately captures the egalitarian dimensions of human rights morality.

Four factors therefore seem to insulate Griffin's reasoning process from deep reflection on the particular role of structural equality as a foundational value for human rights morality. The first is the conviction that the point of a philosophical theory of human rights is to produce a plausible list of justifiable moral human rights, which stands in the way of considering more explicitly political values as foundational for human rights morality. The second is the (obviously related) fact that foundational values for orthodox theories serve as the justificatory grounds of particular moral human rights. In turn, this makes considerations about what are proper objects of moral human rights directly relevant to which values might be adequate foundations for the theory. However, structural equality is an inherently political concept, and for this reason it is difficult to express it as the object of a particular moral human right; in turn, this mismatch may have the effect that structural equality simply does not seem apt as a foundational value for human rights morality. The third factor is the strong grip of the conception of group-based equality as anti-discrimination, which in turn prevents theorists from questioning whether their theories have adequately covered issues of group-based inequalities. And finally, the fourth factor is that the reasoning process that attempts to arrive at a reflective equilibrium between foundational values and particular human rights essentially insulates itself from the practice. In other words, there is no obvious impetus within orthodox methodology to refer to the practice for any guidance in this process. As the CRPD example shows (and as the case study in the next chapter will show), reference to how issues of equality and human rights are addressed in human rights practice may well have at least brought the concept of structural equality more directly into consideration.

Tasioulas's view is somewhat more complicated than Griffin's, while still sharing essentially the same structure. As Tasioulas understands his two foundational values, human dignity is a moral status that "relates to the intrinsic value possessed by all human beings simply as members of the human species," while universal human interests "refer to the universal ingredients of human well-being."[32] Demonstrating that a particular human right exists on Tasioulas's view requires showing that a particular interest is "*pro tanto* of sufficient gravity to justify the imposition of duties on others." Dignity (as a foundational value) serves as a justificatory ground for human rights by informing the account of universal interests: "the interests in question [are] generative of human rights in crucial part because they are the interests of human beings who possess equal moral status: human dignity and universal human interests are equally fundamental grounds of human rights, characteristically bound together in their operation."[33] Equality (as part of an interpretation of equal human dignity) therefore plays a foundational role in Tasioulas's account of human rights morality, but its role as a ground for particular moral human rights is filtered through both an account of universal interests and substantive moral reasoning about considerations of "gravity." Nonetheless, the overarching structure of Tasioulas's view is structurally similar to Griffin's in the sense that the foundational values of human rights morality function as the grounds for (or are "generative of") particular moral human rights.

Moreover, like Griffin, Tasioulas also conceptualizes group-based equality in terms of non-discrimination. He describes the sense of equality that he finds inherent in the idea of human dignity, for example, as requiring "moral prohibitions against the discriminatory treatment of various classes of people—women, gays, ethnic and religious minorities, the poor—insofar as it reflects the odious idea that, simply in virtue of belonging to these classes, such people do not 'count' morally as much as others."[34] Interestingly, while Tasioulas expresses this idea in terms of anti-discrimination, there does not seem to be any obvious reason why he could not have interpreted it as a more robust structural equality, requiring the active dismantling of social hierarchies. After all, social hierarchies clearly convey that some people do not count morally as much as others. And, as he emphasizes, the grounding values of particular moral human rights do not necessarily (in his theory) also serve as the *content* of moral human rights. So, even understood as a ground of moral human rights, structural equality might be taken on Tasioulas's view to inform an account of universal human interests according to which every individual has an interest in (say) avoiding social and political patterns of disrespect or social marginalization on the basis of membership in a particular social group, without committing the view to various forms of rights to substantive (for example, distributive) equality. Again, however, structural equality is an inherently political concept, and for this reason it is difficult to express it as the object of a particular moral human right. Tasioulas's commitment to theorizing moral human rights in a non-institutional way (or at least in a way that transcends any particular institutional context) therefore has the further result that references to particular institutional contexts (for example, those relevant to apprehending structural inequalities) are largely absent from the reasoning process about the foundational values of human rights morality. Insofar as structural equality is an inherently institutional concept, then, orthodox theorizing leaves little to no room for it as an interpretation of the sense of equality that might serve as a foundational value for human rights morality.

One further consideration is worth mentioning on this point. I mentioned earlier in this chapter that it is possible to see structural equality as a necessary means of realizing basic human rights in practice. But this point is susceptible to a counterargument that Griffin articulates, arguing that "it is a non sequitur to move from a value's being indispensable in working out [the] implications of human rights to its being foundational to the notion of a human right itself."[35] Here again, however, notice that the terms of argument are already limited by the assumption that the grounding values of human rights morality have one essential function, and that is to ground individual moral human rights. Absent that assumption, there would be no reason to think that we should reject a candidate value as a foundational value of human rights morality if it might directly imply the existence of moral human rights deemed intuitively over-ambitious to properly be the subject of a human rights claim, since that would not (necessarily) be the role of foundational values in a broader, political theory of human rights morality.

My point in this section is that the method that orthodox theorists employ to determine the grounds of human rights essentially insulates them from reconsidering whether they have the correct understanding of equality as it serves as a foundation of human rights morality. In both Tasioulas's and Griffin's methodology, there is no pressure to reconsider the nature of equality as it serves as a foundational value for human rights morality. Importantly, this point connects to the basic aim of orthodox theories: to develop a philosophical theory of moral human rights that can serve to provide normative structure and discipline to human rights law and practice. Because they see their contribution as producing a theory of moral human rights, they are not interested in the ways in which the grounds of human rights might help them theorize the system of international human rights law, or the practice more broadly. So, they do not consider equality as a foundational value for human rights morality other than whether it can serve as the grounds of a plausible list of moral human rights. The point is not that this constitutes a substantive critique of their theories of moral human rights per se. Rather, the point is that simply producing such a theory does not illuminate many broader questions about human rights morality, or about the attempts to realize this morality in law.

Once the scope of philosophical theorizing about human rights morality is expanded to include normative questions about the system of international human rights law and, even more broadly, human rights practice as a whole, the orthodox approach to identifying and interpreting the grounds of human rights morality seems problematically narrow. If, instead of producing a theory of moral human rights, we aim to develop a theory of human rights morality that can inform theorizing about human rights practice, understood appropriately broadly, then we may want to shed the restriction that the foundational values in human rights morality must be, in a more or less direct way, "grounds of moral human rights." Instead, we may want to include foundational values (and interpretations of them) that can (for example) inform judgments about the broader moral purposes that international legal systems may serve, or that provide standards for assessing the procedural justice or the normative legitimacy of international legal institutions, or that help us articulate what counts as moral progress in the development of international legal institutions that aim to advance the social and political equality of all persons.

Importantly for my purposes, a broader account of the foundational values for human rights morality can also enable philosophers to engage with less-abstract questions that emerge from human rights practice itself, and from scholarship in other disciplines. Such questions are often extremely important and even urgent, both morally and practically. However, they are often much more nuanced, and more deeply situated within particular social and political contexts, to be productively addressed by an ontological theory of moral human rights. In their sole focus on producing a philosophical theory of moral human rights, and a general absence of substantive engagement with the practice as a possible source of normative insight, orthodox theorists are essentially insulated from pressure to think more deeply about the social and institutional contexts that animate the moral point of human rights. But it is often in these contexts that we see the great significance for human rights of background conceptual schemes that elevate members of some social groups at the expense of others. Such schemes are relevant not only to apprehending the scope and meaning of existing inequalities, but also to appreciating why legal human rights are needed in real-world contexts and what shape they should take. A prior, methodological question, then, is whether these matters can be adequately addressed by the kinds of abstract, conceptual arguments that orthodox theories invoke to explain and justify their theories of moral human rights, or whether they would be better addressed via a more engaged methodology that looks to human rights practice, and to neighboring academic disciplines, to better understand the practical relevance of background systematic inequalities to human rights morality and law.

BEITZ AND CEDAW

Beitz's political theory of human rights not only rejects orthodox assumptions about the nature and function of foundational values of human rights morality, but also the entire idea that particular human rights need to be justified by some prior account of moral value at all. Instead, Beitz aims to justify human rights claims on the basis of political considerations within human rights practice. Nonetheless, as I argue in this section, his theory's conception of equality (as it surfaces in his consideration of the human rights of women) exhibits (perhaps surprisingly) several of the same defects as orthodox views: first, his view (like orthodox views) is above all concerned to deliver a justified list of human rights; and second, the conceptual limits Beitz's view places on the justification of particular human rights overly restricts his methodology's ability to take up the normative discourse inherent within human rights practice.

Helpfully for our purposes, Beitz explicitly addresses the human rights of women, and in a way that takes seriously the ways in which realizing women's human rights may require dismantling structural inequalities. For example, in explaining why women's human rights might require distinct theoretical attention in the first place, he notes that women's interests may be "more or differently vulnerable" than men's to "threats of abuse that typically occur within the household, such as domestic violence, exploitation of domestic labor, arbitrary deprivation of property, and the subordination of the will and limitation of choice resulting from acceptance of traditional conceptions of the household division of labor."[36] Moreover, Beitz is sensitive to the fact that the threats facing women (as a social group) are structural:

> The human rights of women are properly considered matters of special concern because certain important interests of women are subject to gender-specific forms of abuse. . . . These forms of abuse are patterned in that similar abuses are predictable under relevantly similar circumstances, and they are systematic in that the circumstances in which they occur are embedded in features of societies and cultures which are more-or-less resistant to change.[37]

In keeping with his political theory of human rights, Beitz addresses questions about the egalitarianism of human rights by looking to the practice. In this regard, he notes (correctly) that the Convention on the Elimination of all Forms of Discrimination Against Women (CEDAW) includes equality rights both in the sense of anti-discrimination and in a structural sense that requires dismantling socially embedded gender hierarchies. For example, in Article 5(a), CEDAW ambitiously assigns to states the obligation to "take all appropriate measures to modify the social and cultural patterns of conduct of men and women, with a view to achieving the elimination of prejudices and customary and all other practices which are based on the idea of the inferiority or the superiority of either of the sexes or on stereotyped roles for men and women."[38]

Beitz also notes (again, correctly) that Article 5(a) would require broad social and cultural change to eliminate gendered ideologies and stereotypes that are root causes of women's social and political inequality. This in turn would require "not only large-scale changes in policy and social practice but also in prevailing social norms in some of the world's societies," such that implementing women's human rights will likely run into "conflict between the requirements of human rights doctrine and gendered norms found in the moral outlooks and patterns of social life that prevail in some existing societies."[39] In the effort to implement women's human rights, he argues, "changes in law and administration are unlikely to be successful in securing their objectives without corresponding changes in background beliefs and social practices."[40] For example:

> effective measures to eliminate violence against women in the household would most likely require not only the establishment of criminal penalties for domestic abuse but also changes in law enforcement and in the administration of various social services. Protection against rape would require not only criminal legislation but also the elimination of discriminatory practices in the investigation and prosecution of offenses. The elimination of abuses associated with prostitution would require not only the detection and prosecution of trafficking, debt slavery, and related practices but also measures aimed at changing social norms that justify the treatment of prostitutes as persons undeserving of legal protection.[41]

Given that changes in law and policy in the direction of equality for women seem to require antecedent changes in social norms, Beitz then asks "whether there are any feasible steps open to the international community or its agents that would induce states to adopt policies reasonably likely to accomplish the transformations of cultural belief and practice necessary to secure women's human rights."[42] He thinks that the answer may be no:

> Change in patterns of belief that are well established in a culture, or for that matter in culturally sanctioned habits of legal and administrative practice, is a slow, complex process. It is not well understood, and the epistemic barriers facing outside agents seeking to influence it are substantial. Moreover, the means of influence available may seem crude and not well suited to the task.[43]

Thus, Beitz concludes that "there may be little that any external agent can do to change the conduct of a government that resists adopting measures aimed at inducing comprehensive changes in conventional beliefs. For this reason, human rights doctrine may overreach in embracing an open-ended entitlement to social and cultural change."[44]

It is important to note that Beitz goes on to suggest that the charge of overreach may not be sustainable given other facts about the practice. However, for our purposes, what is more salient is the fact that the structure of Beitz's theory at least presumptively establishes a kind of catch-22 for women's human rights: on his reasoning, the greater the extent that women's structural inequality is deeply entrenched in reform-resistant social ideologies, the less justification may exist for including claims to moral equality as either grounds or objects of the human rights that the theory endorses.

This is a problematic form of theoretical engagement with the practice, for reasons that are strikingly similar to those I noted in my critique of orthodox views in the previous section.[45] First, Beitz's view (like orthodox views) is above all concerned to deliver a justified list of human rights. This has the effect that his approach to CEDAW's Article 5(a) is essentially to ask whether it establishes an "entitlement to social and cultural change," as if this were the object of a human right, rather than a foundational or animating value for human rights practice.

Second, the conceptual limits Beitz's view places on the justification for particular human rights overly restricts his methodology's ability to take up the normative discourse inherent within human rights practice into his substantive account of human rights. In particular, Beitz's commitment to the constraint that human rights exist only when there are effective measures that the international community can take to rectify the situation leads to the conclusion that CEDAW overreaches, rather than to the tantalizingly within-reach opposite conclusion, embraced by many feminists, that women's human rights doctrine within the practice constitutes a promising direction for future development of both international human rights law and (though Beitz does not explicitly think in these terms) human rights morality.

Finally, Beitz concludes much too quickly that there is little the international community can do to reform sexist ideologies in particular social contexts.[46] While Beitz is correct that inegalitarian laws may be rooted in deeply entrenched social expectations and norms, so that merely reforming laws will not change the underlying mores, at the same time the interdependence of laws and mores can be harnessed in the direction of progress toward equality. Changes in law and policy, while insufficient by themselves, may nonetheless both partially constitute steps toward women's substantive equality and initiate other social changes that over time help bring about further shifts in entrenched ideologies. In short, law and policy constitute one significant mechanism of achieving substantive equality. Establishing a social and political commitment to women's human rights to equality in practice, in addition to women's formal status as equal rights holders, is therefore a potentially significant step toward the process of changing deeply entrenched social beliefs about women's inequality.

CONCLUSION

My argument to this point has focused on a critique of dominant methodologies in the philosophy of human rights, and on a sketch for a political methodology that is more sensitive to the effects of structural inequalities on the ability to understand and realize human rights in practice. Earlier in this chapter, I argued that the importance of status equality has already emerged within the practice as well, manifested in efforts to address the human rights of persons with disabilities in the context of deeply rooted social inequalities, and, as we saw in the preceding section, in CEDAW as well. Part of the point of my critique of the overly stark fact/value distinction is to suggest that it would improve philosophical theorizing about human rights if philosophers were more open to learning from the kind of moral progress represented by these elements of human rights practice.

In the remainder of this book, I focus on a case study that functions within my argument as a similar form of moral progress within the practice. The *Akayesu* decision by the International Criminal Tribunal for Rwanda, I will argue, provides a detailed case study that demonstrates how the institutions of international law (in this case, international criminal law) may provide particularly visible institutional mechanisms and venues whereby deeply entrenched social hierarchies may be productively challenged and upended, not only symbolically, but also in ways that constitute concrete advances toward the realization of status equality and equal human rights. These institutions therefore provide opportunities to improve our understanding of the foundational moral values and implications of human rights morality while also moving toward realizing them in practice.

My argument is not that this process constitutes an infallible process of moral discovery. Rather, the argument is that philosophers aiming to theorize human rights morality as it is relevant to human rights practice have good reason to adopt a philosophical methodology that incorporates some mechanism for taking up the substantive contributions of normative discourses within the practice for critical reflection in theory. Unfortunately, as I have argued in this and earlier chapters, traditional philosophical methodology exhibits determined resistance to regarding human rights practice as a potential source of substantive moral insight.

NOTES

1. Catharine MacKinnon, "Difference and Dominance: On Sex Discrimination," in *Feminism Unmodified: Discourses on Life and Law*, ed. Stephen Shute and Susan Hurley (Cambridge, MA: Harvard University Press, 1987); Allen Buchanan, *The Heart of Human Rights* (Oxford: Oxford University Press, 2013).

2. Shasta Darlington, "Domestic Abuse, Shown Blow by Blow, Shocks Brazil," *New York Times*, August 7, 2018, https://www.nytimes.com/2018/08/07/world/americas/domestic-abuse-shown-blow-by-blow-shocks-brazil.html?module=inline.

3. Karen Zraick, "Most Dangerous Place for Women Is the Home, U.N. Report Finds," *New York Times,* November 27, 2018, https://www.nytimes.com/2018/11/27/world/female-homicide-gender-violence.html?action=click&module=Latest&pgtype=Homepage.

4. UN Office on Drugs and Crime, Global Study on Homicide 2018 (Vienna, 2018), 55.

5. Hawa Aden Mohamed, "When Laws Against Rape Aren't Enough," *New York Times*, January 30, 2018, https://www.nytimes.com/2018/01/30/opinion/somalia-rape-laws.html?rref=collection%2Fsectioncollection%2Fopinion&action=click&contentCollection=opinion&region=rank&module=package&version=highlights&contentPlacement=9&pgtype=sectionfront.

6. Mohamed, "When Laws Against Rape Aren't Enough."

7. Mohamed, "When Laws Against Rape Aren't Enough."

8. Thomas Pogge, *World Poverty and Human Rights,* 2nd ed. (Cambridge: Polity Press, 2008), 71.

9. John Rawls, *The Law of Peoples* (Cambridge, MA: Harvard University Press, 1999), 64–65.

10. Rawls, *The Law of Peoples*, 75.

11. Ibram X. Kendi, "Racial Progress Is Real. But So Is Racist Progress," *New York Times*, January 21 2017, https://www.nytimes.com/2017/01/21/opinion/sunday/racial-progress-is-real-but-so-is-racist-progress.html..

12. Kendi, "Racial Progress is Real."

13. Camisha Russell, "The Race Idea in Reproductive Technologies: Beyond Epistemic Scientism and Technological Mastery," *Journal of Bioethical Inquiry* 12, no. 4 (2015): 603.

14. See Susan Moller Okin, *Women in Western Political Thought* (Princeton: Princeton University Press, 1979).

15. Hilary Charlesworth, Christine Chinkin, and Shelley Wright, "Feminist Approaches to International Law," *American Journal of International Law* 85 (1991): 632.

16. Pogge, *World Poverty and Human Rights,* 71.

17. Buchanan, *The Heart of Human Rights*, 8.

18. UN Department of Economic and Social Affairs, Handbook for Parliamentarians on the Convention on the Rights of Persons with Disabilities (Geneva, 2007), 1.

19. Raymond Lang, Maria Kett, Nora Groce, and Jean-Francois Trani, "Implementing the United Nations Convention on the Rights of Persons with Disabilities: Principles, Implications, Practice and Limitations," *Alter* 5, no. 3 (2011): 209.

20. Michael Ashley Stein and Janet E. Lord, "Monitoring the Convention on the Rights of Persons with Disabilities: Innovations, Lost Opportunities, and Future Potential," *Human Rights Quarterly* 32 (2010): 698.

21. "Convention on the Rights of Persons with Disabilities (CRPD)," UN Department of Economic and Social Affairs: Disability, accessed August 12, 2022, https://www.un.org/development/desa/disabilities/convention-on-the-rights-of-persons-with-disabilities.html.

22. Theresia Degener, "A Human Rights Model of Disability," in *Routledge Handbook of Disability Law and Human Rights*, ed. Peter Blanck and Eilionóir Flynn (Routledge, 2016), 35.

23. For an objection to this argument, see Paul S. Applebaum, "Saving the UN Convention on the Rights of Persons with Disabilities—From Itself," *World Psychiatry: Official Journal of the World Psychiatric Association* 18, no. 1 (February 2019).

24. Sándor Gurbai, "Beyond the Pragmatic Definition? The Right to Non-discrimination of Persons with Disabilities in the Context of Coercive Interventions," *Health and Human Rights Journal* 22, no. 1 (May 13 2020): 279.

25. James Griffin, *On Human Rights* (Oxford: Oxford University Press, 2008), 33.

26. Griffin, *On Human Rights*, 34.

27. As does Pablo Gilabert, *Human Dignity and Human Rights* (Oxford: Oxford University Press, 2018).

28. Griffin, *On Human Rights*, 41.

29. Griffin, *On Human Rights*, 41.

30. Griffin, *On Human Rights*, 42.

31. Griffin, *On Human Rights*, 42.

32. John Tasioulas, "Saving Human Rights from Human Rights Law," *Vanderbilt Journal of Transnational Law* 52 (2019): 1181.

33. John Tasioulas, "On the Foundations of Human Rights," in *Philosophical Foundations of Human Rights*, ed. Rowan Cruft, S. Matthew Liao, and Massimo Renzo (Oxford: Oxford University Press, 2015), 56.

34. Tasioulas, "On the Foundations of Human Rights," 56.

35. Griffin, *On Human Rights*, 43.

36. Charles Beitz, *The Idea of Human Rights* (New York: Oxford University Press, 2009), 188.

37. Beitz, *The Idea of Human Rights*, 188.

38. Convention on the Elimination of all Forms of Discrimination Against Women, December 18, 1979, 1249 United Nations Treaty Series 13, Art. 5(a).

39. Beitz, *The Idea of Human Rights*, 190.

40. Beitz, *The Idea of Human Rights*, 194.

41. Beitz, *The Idea of Human Rights*, 194.

42. Beitz, *The Idea of Human Rights*, 191.

43. Beitz, *The Idea of Human Rights*, 194.

44. Beitz, *The Idea of Human Rights*, 194.

45. It is important to ask, first, whether the practice really supports Beitz's claim that moral human rights exist only when action by international actors could feasibly correct a violation; I set this question aside here.

46. I discuss this question in more detail in Kristen Hessler, "Hard Cases: Public Health and Women's Human Rights," *Journal of Value Inquiry* 47, no. 4 (2013).

Chapter 4

Case Study

Prosecutor v. Akayesu

In nearly all legal cultures, gender-based crimes such as rape and other sexual violence against women have historically been (mis-)understood as a property crime against the victim's husband, father, or other male relative, rather than a violent crime against the victim herself.[1] Even when rape and other sexual violence against women is considered a harm to the victim herself, legal and moral codes have struggled to articulate exactly how severe a wrong it is, what exactly is the harm involved, what evidence is required to establish a perpetrator's guilt, and what punishments are appropriate. This social ambiguity surrounding the moral and legal status of sexual violence against women has persisted, making rape and sexual violence notoriously difficult to successfully prosecute. In many national legal systems today, convictions are secured in only a very small percentage of reported incidents of rape. In the United States, for example, only 0.6% of reported rapes from 2010–2014 led to a felony conviction.[2] Indeed, a very low percentage of reported rapes even result in an arrest; according the Bureau of Justice Statistics, "The percentage of reported rape or sexual assault victimizations that resulted in an arrest either at the scene or during a follow-up investigation decreased from 47 percent in 1994–98 to 31 percent in 2005–10."[3] When the fact that many rapes are never reported is factored in, the estimated overall rate of arrest for both reported and unreported rapes in the United States from 2005–2010 drops to only 12 percent.[4]

Under international law, the obstacles to successful prosecution of sexual violence are even more daunting. One study, noting the low rates of conviction for reported rapes in many national jurisdictions, observed that

> [i]f this is the prognosis in states with a relatively high degree of social equality, political stability and a functioning criminal justice system, then the scale of the task facing international prosecutors—exacerbated by cultural stigmatization of

> rape, precarious security conditions and the logistical difficulties inherent in all international criminal investigations—seems almost overwhelming.[5]

International law has historically remained mostly silent in the face of sexual violence in armed conflicts. Even when committed on a massive scale, it has often been tolerated with impunity as an expected consequence of war.[6] Despite the fact that rape has been recognized as a war crime since the early twentieth century, and the Nuremburg and Tokyo trials at the end of World War II were landmarks establishing international legal accountability for war crimes, no defendants at those trials faced charges under international law relating to sexual violence.

Against this historical backdrop, the international tribunals established in the 1990s to prosecute war crimes and violations of international humanitarian law committed in Rwanda and the former Yugoslavia, while deeply flawed and limited in many ways, were nonetheless groundbreaking regarding the prosecution of sexual violence in armed conflict. The *Tadic* case before the International Criminal Tribunal for the Former Yugoslavia (ICTY) was not only the first international war crimes trial since Nuremburg and Tokyo, but also the first international war crimes trial ever to include charges relating to sexual violence.[7] Two other ICTY trials (*Furundžija* and *Kunarac et al.*) focused entirely on charges of sexual violence; these cases also included indictments (and, in *Furundžija*, a conviction) for command responsibility for mass rape committed by the defendants' subordinates.[8] *Kunarac et al.* secured the first conviction under international criminal law for rape as a crime against humanity.[9] While these cases are well known for their exclusive focus on sexual violence, Michelle Jarvis, a former ICTY prosecutor, has argued that a lesser-known case, *Statić*, is even more important insofar as it "is one of the few ICTY cases where sexual violence was found to be an integral component of a common criminal purpose," thus making sexual violence prosecutable as more than merely a "foreseeable consequence" of the armed conflict.[10] And finally, in a case I will discuss extensively below, the ICTY's "sister tribunal," the International Criminal Tribunal for Rwanda (ICTR), overcame notorious initial missteps to set a historical precedent in the successful conviction of Jean Paul Akayesu on charges of rape as a component of genocide.[11]

While the tribunals' champions and critics continue to contest their overall legacies, it is widely agreed that their jurisprudence fundamentally changed the status of sexual violence crimes in international law.[12] I focus on the *Akayesu* case both as a landmark in itself, but also as a single step within larger developments in international law, including other pivotal cases before the tribunals, the subsequent development of both international and national law relating to sexual violence, and the creation of the International Criminal

Court including its self-proclaimed mandate to end impunity for sexual violence. Both *Akayesu* and these larger developments illustrate an intertwined process of legal, moral, and social change that unfolded as a result of the bravery of witnesses and victims, tireless activism on the part of women's advocacy organizations, and the deliberate efforts of individual prosecutors, investigators, and judges to realize gender justice. In turn, all of these efforts took place within the institutional framework provided by the creation of the ad hoc tribunals in the first place.

The connection I draw between these processes in criminal law and human rights morality is the following: ensuring that crimes that disproportionately target a particular social group are both accurately understood for the harm they do to their victims, and that their perpetrators are held accountable by law, is an essential component of realizing both the equal social and political status and the moral and legal human rights of individual members of that group. For this reason, I believe that we can understand international criminal law, including the avenues that these processes furnish for giving voice to grassroots activism, as a part of human rights *practice*, even though as a branch of international law it is (of course) distinct from IHRL. One point, then, is that philosophers who are interested in theorizing human rights morality in a way that is relevant to human rights practice have good reason to attend to the ways in which human rights are addressed in international law and politics beyond IHRL.

The sea-change in legal thinking about sexual violence ushered in by the work of the tribunals would not have been possible without the sustained political and social activism of victims of sexual violence and their allies, mostly but not exclusively other women. Survivors of sexual violence testified as witnesses in national and international courts, and participated in activist movements outside of courts to ensure that women's experiences in armed conflict were taken seriously within their social, political, and legal communities. Explicit efforts on the part of tribunal prosecutors and judges to articulate and adopt a "gender perspective"—in which the work of investigators and prosecutors explicitly recognizes the pervasive social and political subordination of women—were instrumental in revealing the historical tendency to minimize women's voices and experiences in both international and domestic law, and by extension to fail to appreciate the harms done to both women and men (and girls and boys) by sexual violence in armed conflict.[13] Recognizing this history was the first step in developing institutional mechanisms to overcome these institutionalized inequalities. In particular, the ICTY's careful articulation of a gender perspective intended to inform and guide prosecutors, judges, and investigators in sexual violence cases constitutes an important legacy of the tribunals that has enabled courts, social movements, and individuals to transcend these historical limitations to better realize women's humanity and human rights.[14]

These changes highlight the importance of a structural conception of social and political equality to an adequate conception of human rights morality. The progress represented by the work of the tribunals in *Akayesu* and similar cases was not in any straightforward sense an attempt to implement a pre-legal moral conception of human rights. Rather, one of its most important contributions was that it contributed substantively to dismantling aspects of women's deeply rooted and long-standing social and political inequality, making progress toward women seeing themselves (psychologically) and actually functioning within the relevant institutions (socially and politically) as the social and political equals of men. For example, the work of the tribunals featured the testimony of individual women deciding in their own minds that their experiences of sexual violence were not primarily injuries to their "honor" inflicted upon them by neighbors who had "lost control," but rather injuries to their bodies inflicted upon them by men behaving criminally. In other words, these women overcame deeply entrenched, universal norms that have historically ignored and trivialized women's experiences of sexual violence, norms which themselves partly constituted women's unequal social and political status, instead coming to regard themselves as having equal rights to bodily security as men, and equal claims to hold legally accountable the persons who assaulted them. Similarly, women who had experienced sexual violence overcame deep and powerful social taboos against coming forward publicly to tell their stories, supported by other women within their communities who provided safe spaces for them to share their stories in more intimate, healing groups before telling their stories to investigators and ultimately in international courts. In other words, they successfully battled social stigmas that had functioned to keep women from asserting rights against sexual violence. These stories also feature prosecutors who rethought and remade legal categories in a way that enabled them to see sexual violence in armed conflict as a war crime and a crime against humanity, rather than a regrettable side-effect of war; in other words, to see women as the legal equals of men for the institutional purpose of criminal prosecution. And to be successful, these efforts required the presence of women in key legal capacities at all levels, including as investigators, prosecutors, and judges, as a result of the partial erosion of historically pervasive forms of discrimination that had excluded women and girls from securing education, employment, and positions of political power and influence.

Importantly, the dramatic efforts of individual women in all these capacities were required because of the pressure on individual members of subordinated social groups under conditions of inequality. This does not mean that the relevant sense of equality is an atomistic, individualist one. Rather, it is itself a symptom of the injustice of group-based inequality that individuals, in particular but not only women, find themselves shouldering burdens they should not have to bear. Consider, for example, the efforts that individual women judges have undertaken to combat sexist elements of the very law they are empowered to interpret. Justice Bertha Wilson from Canada's highest court, reflecting on whether women judges make a difference in realizing gender justice, argued that it is difficult for judges to do so when "[s]ome aspects of the criminal law in particular cry out for change; they are based on presuppositions about the nature of women and women's sexuality that, in this day and age, are little short of ludicrous."[15] In such cases, the source of the problem in realizing gender justice may actually lie in the law itself. But the existence of such biased systems of law creates a burden on those individuals occupying official capacities within the relevant institutions to reform them. The needed solution is institutional and political, including, in this case, legal reform. In the meantime, however, individual judges find themselves taking on the burden of laboring to change the norms of their profession. The story of *Akayesu* (as I tell it) therefore foregrounds the efforts of individuals, especially women, in a number of roles, whose work was instrumental to bringing about the needed institutional changes, but who (under just conditions) would not have had that individual burden to bear in the first place. However, as will become clearer in Chapter 5, the point of my analysis is not primarily about the efforts of individuals, but about the institutional changes they helped effect.

Finally, I argue that a careful consideration of the legal processes that led to the sea-change in the status of sexual violence in armed conflict in international law, including the essential roles played by individuals and by civil society groups, constitutes a source of insight about human rights morality, and specifically about the role of equality in realizing human rights, that is inaccessible to traditional philosophical methods. Neither orthodox theories, nor political theories in their most familiar versions, can adequately embrace these processes as sources of moral knowledge which are essential to a full understanding of moral human rights, beyond their thinnest and most abstract formulations. This upends philosophers' traditional assumptions about the appropriate division of labor between philosophy (or political theory) on one hand, and practice (including human rights law, criminal law, and activism) on the other, in two ways. First, the division of labor assumed by most philosophical methods regarding human rights locates the process of moral discovery squarely within the work of philosophy as a discipline. However, if my analysis in this chapter is apt, the intertwined processes of law and activism are themselves sources of moral discovery, specifically regarding the egalitarian dimensions of moral human rights. No philosophical method for theorizing moral human rights that subscribes to the traditional division of labor—that is, that distances the process of moral analysis too far from the practice—will have access to the practice as a source of moral discovery. Second, this points to a critique of the kind of moral knowledge claimed on behalf of philosophical theories of moral human rights, according to which the normative content of human rights is specified by philosophy, while the practice specifies the particular empirical contexts in which those norms are to be implemented. Attention to moral progress within human rights practice demonstrates that the inclusion of an abstract norm within a theory of moral human rights does not suffice as an understanding of the full moral content of that norm. Therefore, even if a moral theory of human rights includes a moral human right to bodily security (for example) as an abstract or general principle, this will not suffice to account for the meaning of those abstract moral principles, because it will not have considered the moral force of those principles in the context of existing social norms in deeply inegalitarian contexts. Therefore, abstract moral theorizing about human rights cannot fully understand even abstract moral human rights, especially their egalitarian dimensions and requirements. This is a severe shortcoming for any theory of human rights morality that is intended to serve as a moral guide for human rights activism, law, and practice.

CASE STUDY: *AKAYESU*

The Rwandan genocide (like all genocides) was an intentional, carefully orchestrated, and centrally directed program of state-sponsored political violence, in this case incited by Hutu extremists associated with the slain Rwandan president, General Juvénal Habyarimana, and directed against the minority Tutsi population as part of a broader attempt to hold on to political power.[16] The significance of the social division between Hutu and Tutsi in Rwandan society is (and was at the time of the genocide) contested. "Hutu extremists" promoted the view that "the two are not only different ethnic groups, but different races," while most Tutsi emphasized the political function of the distinction, as well as the common social and political life shared by the two groups in the course of Rwandan history.[17] Most scholarly accounts agree that "'Hutu' and 'Tutsi' identities were defined partly by politics, partly by occupational status, and partly by ancestry," though Belgian colonists exaggerated the racial account of the differences between the groups as part of their system of colonial administration via Tutsi dominance.[18]

Tutsi rule in colonial Rwanda ended in 1959 with a Hutu revolution, supported by Belgium, which killed approximately ten thousand Tutsi and sent many more seeking refuge in neighboring countries. Despite deep social integration between the two groups both before and following the

1959 revolution, animosity between Hutu and Tutsi persisted throughout Habyarimana's twenty-year presidency. Habyarimana's hold on power began to weaken by the late 1980s, and he was at the same time facing increasing pressure from the Rwandan Patriotic Front (RPF), a military force consisting mainly of Tutsi refugees who had fled the 1959 revolution. In 1990, the RPF invaded Rwanda from Uganda, with the stated goals of ousting Habyarimana, repatriating thousands of Rwandan Tutsi refugees living in neighboring countries, and installing a more democratic government in Rwanda.[19] Habyarimana's government exploited the RPF invasion to inflame ethnic tensions within Rwanda, engaging in an extensive campaign of anti-Tutsi propaganda that was widely broadcast via radio and print media, and forming the Interahamwe, a massive "civilian defense force" friendly to the government's anti-Tutsi agenda. Explicit preparations for the genocide included importing weapons; by early 1994, Habyarimana's business associates and political allies had imported machetes in quantities sufficient to arm fully one-third of the male Hutu population of Rwanda.[20]

On April 6, 1994, Habyarimana was killed along with the Hutu prime minister of Burundi, when their plane was hit by a surface-to-air missile as it was returning to Rwanda from a peace conference in Tanzania. The conference was part of the international process attempting to implement a negotiated settlement between the Rwandan government and the RPF. The Rwandan government, without convincing evidence, accused the RPF of responsibility for Habyarimana's assassination, though it may have been the case that Hutu extremists within Rwanda engineered the attack as a means of scapegoating the RPF.[21] The assassination almost instantly ignited the long-planned genocide. The violence unleashed was horrific. Over the next ninety days, upward of half a million (by some estimates as many as 800,000) men, women, and children were brutally murdered. Most were Tutsi, but some victims were Hutu who were mistaken for Tutsi, who attempted to shelter or protect Tutsi friends or neighbors, who refused to take part in the massacres, or who were considered political enemies of the government. Most of the victims were hacked or beaten to death with machetes, knives, and clubs; some victims begged to be shot instead.[22] Others were forced to kill their family members, including their own children, before they were murdered.

Sexual violence was an integral part of the genocidal campaign. Binaifer Nowrojee, who worked in Rwanda for Human Rights Watch immediately following the genocide, has documented how the anti-Tutsi propaganda campaign preceding the genocide specifically portrayed Tutsi women as "calculated seductress-spies bent on dominating and undermining the Hutu," or as "inaccessible to Hutu men whom they allegedly looked down upon and were 'too good' for."[23] Survivors of sexual violence during the genocide consistently reported that their rapists repeated these stereotypes during the sexual assaults. Many women and children were repeatedly raped and sexually tortured before being murdered; many were kidnapped and held as sex slaves by men carrying out the killings (sometimes in arrangements that lasted the full duration of the genocide and even afterward, when victims realized they had no family to return home to); and some women were raped and left alive "to die of sadness" after watching their families murdered. In addition to sadness, many surviving rape victims suffered severe physical harm as a result of the assaults, including HIV infections, genital mutilation inflicted during the rapes, and other injuries from being beaten, often with machetes or clubs. Many survivors had to decide how to handle pregnancies that resulted from rape, and if they chose to keep the children, how to raise them amid conditions of social animosity toward the children, who were sometimes called "children of bad memories" or "children of hate."[24] Many of those children were themselves born with HIV infections, in an environment in which adequate health care was severely lacking.[25] The impact of sexual violence during the genocide was, therefore, far-reaching well beyond the time frame of the genocide itself.

The genocide came to an end with the RPF's military victory over the Rwandan government forces in early July, which in turn precipitated a massive wave of Hutu refugees fleeing both the RPF invasion and possible accountability for the genocide, as well as RPF revenge killings against Hutu. The Hutu exodus from Rwanda was itself a severe humanitarian crisis and a source of continuing instability, as genocidal forces were to some degree able to regroup in exile on Rwanda's borders. Many "genocidal fugitives" found havens in neighboring states where the leaders (like Mobutu Sese Seko in Zaire and Daniel Arap Moi in Kenya) had been associates of Habyarimana.[26]

Immediately following the genocide, prospects for impartial justice for perpetrators and suspects within Rwanda were bleak. The RPF oversaw revenge killings of Hutu numbering in the thousands as it took control of Rwanda from the previous government. The circumstances of justice were therefore compromised, as it was difficult to establish the conditions for impartial trials in Rwanda under RPF control.[27] Moreover, the sheer number of individuals suspected or accused of committing crimes during the genocide was itself an obstacle to successful trials. Violence during the genocide was committed by the Interahamwe, by members of government forces including the police and the military, and by hundreds of thousands of ordinary civilians; as one writer noted, some estimates conclude that as many Rwandans killed as were killed.[28] American journalist Philip Gourevitch visited Rwanda in December 1995, and wrote at the time:

> Nobody knows how many Rwandans it took to butcher as many as a million of their countrymen in three months, and nobody could have known in advance

> how many would be needed. The people were the weapon, and that meant everybody: the entire Hutu population was called upon to kill the entire Tutsi population. In addition to ensuring obvious numerical advantages, this arrangement eliminated any questions of accountability that might arise. If everybody is implicated, then implication becomes meaningless.[29]

In the immediate aftermath of the genocide, nearly eighty thousand individuals suspected of killing during the genocide were imprisoned in Rwanda under wretched conditions.[30] At the same time, Rwanda's institutions badly needed to be rebuilt before they could effectively tackle the task of processing such an enormous volume of cases. As Human Rights Watch reported in 1995:

> Attempting to deliver justice for a genocide could overwhelm even the best organized judiciary. In Rwanda, even before 1994, the judicial system was weak and subject to outside pressures, with relatively few attorneys, magistrates, and police professionally prepared by the study of the law. During the war, many of those persons were killed, themselves committed genocide, or fled the country. Court buildings, few and poorly equipped, were pillaged and in some cases partially or completely destroyed.[31]

At the same time, however, there was ample reason to be skeptical of the possibility of justice via international courts. The International Criminal Tribunal for the Former Yugoslavia (ICTY) had been created by the Security Council Resolution 827 in 1993, following the mass atrocities committed in Croatia and later in Bosnia and Herzegovina.[32] While the Rwandan government initially requested international help in apprehending fugitive leaders of the genocide, they were not necessarily pleased when the Security Council formed the International Criminal Tribunal for Rwanda (ICTR) on November 8, 1994.[33] Because the ICTR shared some staff and offices with the ICTY in The Hague, some Rwandans viewed the ICTR as merely a "satellite" of the ICTY, reflecting the lack of international commitment to justice in Rwanda commensurate with the international community's failure to intervene to prevent or halt the genocide in the first place.[34] The Rwandan government also expressed its dismay that the ICTR, "in accord with growing international practice," would not seek the death penalty, despite the fact that the death penalty was allowable under Rwandan law, and was regarded by many Rwandans as the appropriate punishment for at least some of the genocide's perpetrators. This objection, among others (including the fact that the tribunal's trial chambers would not be located inside Rwanda), led the Rwandan government to cast its vote as a member of the Security Council against the creation of the ICTR, though it did assert its support for an international tribunal in general.[35] Moreover, even supporters of the tribunal, such as Human

Rights Watch, noted the difficulties it faced in getting started on the massive amount of work that needed to be done:

> "At the start, tribunal staff were obliged to spend a great deal of their time dealing with setting up and running offices. Drained by the search for paper clips, pens, and paper, they had little energy left for dealing with the complexities of understanding, investigating, and prosecuting the genocide of at least half a million people."[36]

Given that political and military leaders at the highest levels of Rwanda's national government were involved in organizing and fomenting the violence, it may seem surprising that Jean Paul Akayesu, the bourgremestre (mayor) of Taba, a small rural community near Kigali, became "the international face of the Rwandan genocide."[37] Indeed, the events that took place in Taba, and that ultimately formed the basis of Akayesu's conviction for crimes of genocide, were no different from those that occurred throughout Rwanda during the genocide. Moreover, at the start of the genocide, Akayesu at first prevented violence from breaking out in Taba.[38] This fact was well known both to prosecutors and the trial judges; indeed, the judgment in the case notes that "[m]any witnesses testified to the efforts of the Accused to maintain peace in the commune and that he opposed by force the Interahamwe's attempted incursions into the commune to ensure that the killings which had started in Kigali on 7 April 1994 did not spread to Taba."[39]

As bourgremestre, Akayesu would have been an active and respected authority in the community life of Taba.[40] The prosecutor's case against Akayesu took pains to emphasize the importance of authority figures in Rwandan society, and the social role of the bourgremestre in particular. As the prosecution noted in the indictment against Akayesu, "[i]n Rwanda, the bourgmestre is the most powerful figure in the commune. His de facto authority in the area is significantly greater than that which is conferred upon him de jure."[41] Despite initially using this authority to prevent violence in Taba, however, Akayesu's behavior changed dramatically approximately two weeks after the genocide began, when influential leaders from the interim government, including the prime minister, traveled to the region to stage a political rally as part of their active efforts throughout Rwanda to ensure that as many government officials and ordinary citizens as possible were taking part in the killings. Immediately following that rally, in what prosecutors later alleged was a calculated strategy to advance his own political prospects, Akayesu became an active agitator of the genocide against Tutsi in Taba. He was accused of calling for specific individuals to be murdered, of giving speeches exhorting Hutu to engage in anti-Tutsi violence, and of knowingly tolerating and even encouraging anti-Tutsi violence against the refugees who sought shelter at the bureau communal where his offices were located. There, as in many apparently "safe" places throughout Rwanda during the genocide, including churches and government buildings, refugees who sought shelter found themselves instead trapped in sites of mass rape and murder.[42]

Akayesu was arrested in Zambia on October 10, 1995, over a year after the end of the genocide, with other suspected genocide perpetrators. He was not at the time a target of ICTR prosecutors, so investigators needed to uncover the basic facts regarding Akayesu's involvement in the genocide within the relatively short window before the law required that he be either indicted or released.[43] The prosecutors filed their indictment of Akayesu in February 1996. It did not include any charges relating to sexual violence, because prosecutors maintained that they lacked sufficient evidence to implicate Akayesu in the sexual violence that had taken place in Taba. International women's advocacy groups, however, were vocal in criticizing the absence of sexual violence charges in the indictment.[44] As a response to this criticism, ICTR investigators undertook a follow-up investigation a few months later, in the summer of 1996, to determine whether they should amend the indictment.[45] This investigation concluded in a memo filed in September of that year, that reaffirmed and justified the absence of sexual violence charges in the indictment. According to one summary of it, the memo's justification was that the rapes were essentially not systematic enough to justify sexual violence charges against Akayesu: "the women had been raped in a variety of circumstances by, if you will, a variety of categories of perpetrators: 'ex-FAR [Rwandan armed forces], Interahamwe, and simple peasants who had lost self-control because of the war environment they found themselves in.'"[46]

By this point, however, human rights groups had already begun to document survivors' accounts of sexual violence during the genocide, and these accounts ultimately changed the course of Akayesu's prosecution and trial. Binaifer Nowrojee's report for Human Rights Watch on sexual violence during the genocide was one of the most influential among these efforts. Nowrojee's report was published in September 1996, around the time that the ICTR prosecutors upheld the initial decision not to indict Akayesu on sexual violence charges. Importantly, Nowrojee's report was based in part on interviews with sexual violence survivors from Taba.[47] It is harrowing reading, documenting eyewitness and survivors' accounts of ubiquitous and horrifying sexual violence committed during the genocide. In addition to establishing a public record of widespread sexual violence in Taba during the genocide, the report also called on the Rwandan government, the ICTR, the United Nations field operation in Rwanda, and international donors to ensure that all genocide investigations and ongoing social programs were equipped to recognize and address women's experiences of sexual violence during the genocide and their specific needs in the aftermath of such violence.

Having raised this alarm, however, Nowrojee argued that the ICTR's investigations into sexual violence charges were deeply flawed. For example, prosecutors were unable to overcome predictable factors that make it difficult to investigate rape in many circumstances, including feelings of shame and stigmatization on the part of rape survivors, the well-founded fear of retaliation against witnesses by perpetrators who were still at large in victims' communities, and the reluctance of many rape survivors to tell their stories of sexual violence to male investigators.[48] As Nowrojee reported, the latter reason was over-generalized by ICTR prosecutors to justify their conclusion that it was "nearly impossible to investigate rape" as part of the post-genocide investigation because victims simply would not discuss their experiences of sexual violence at all. Rejecting this conclusion, Nowrojee recommended specific reforms to the investigations, including deploying women as investigators and interpreters, ensuring that investigators were "sensitive to the trauma of rape victims," and implementing appropriate protection for witnesses.[49] Based on these recommendations, the report urged that "existing indictments should be amended, where appropriate, to ensure that rape, sexual slavery, and sexual mutilation charges are brought. If need be further investigation should be conducted by the Tribunal investigators to collect information on sexual violence previously overlooked."[50]

The following month—October 1996—Lisa Pruitt, the ICTR's gender consultant in Rwanda, added her own voice to the call for including sexual violence charges in the *Akayesu* case when she filed a memo arguing that the investigators had "concluded too quickly—and perhaps inaccurately—that Akayesu could not be held responsible for any of the rapes."[51] Pruitt argued that there was no basis for treating the evidentiary standards for charges related to sexual violence any differently than those according to which Akayesu was indicted for other violence committed as part of the genocide. As she noted, "there were indications in the statements that Akayesu knew of rapes and did nothing to stop them."[52] This fact was relevant to Article 6(3) of the ICTR Statute, which establishes criminal responsibility of a superior who knew that a subordinate had committed or was about to commit any acts of genocide, crimes against humanity, or violations of the Geneva Conventions, and failed to either prevent or punish the subordinate.[53] As Pruitt argued,

> There seems to be a mis-perception by some at ICTR that, in order to charge someone with criminal responsibility under Article 6(3) (superior authority), it is necessary to have evidence that he or she ordered or instructed his/her subordinates to commit the criminal acts at issue. Such evidence, or course, is very hard to come by, and it will probably never be available regarding sexual assault crimes.[54]

As Pruitt noted, however, such evidence was not available to support Akayesu's indictment regarding the widespread killings committed in Taba as part of the genocide. Rather, Paragraph 12 of the indictment justified those charges as follows:

> The killings in Taba were openly committed and so widespread that, as bourgremestre, Jean Paul Akayesu must have known about them. Although he had the authority and responsibility to do so, Jean Paul Akayesu never attempted to prevent the killing of Tutsis in the commune in any way or called for assistance from regional or national authorities to quell the violence.[55]

Building on this argument, Pruitt argued that "[t]he same could arguably be said of the rapes that were occurring in Taba. That is, Paragraph 12 might have read: 'The killings and rapes in Taba were openly committed and so widespread. . . . '"

Pruitt also echoed Nowrojee's concerns about how ICTR investigators had interviewed witnesses. The team of investigators whose work led to the initial indictment apparently included no women at all, though Pruitt's memo noted that the team who completed the follow-up investigation leading to the re-affirmation of the decision to exclude sexual violence charges was "reinforced by two female investigators."[56] Perhaps more importantly, the investigators were not members of the Taba community, and there is no evidence that they received any training in interviewing victims of sexual violence. Another of Pruitt's concerns was that statements by victims and witnesses had "provided several leads to additional witnesses, leads on which the team apparently did not follow up."[57] Pruitt also shared Nowrojee's concerns about whether the investigators included enough women and were adequately sensitive to the experiences of sexual violence victims. In particular, the memo notes that the follow-up investigation in 1996, but not the original investigation, had relied on information about the identities of rape survivors given by Godelieve Mukasarasi, herself from Taba, who had begun working with the women of Taba to provide support and healing in the aftermath of the genocide. In Pruitt's estimation, the evidence turned up by the follow-up investigation had much to do with the fact that ICTR investigators had by then "identified themselves with Ms. Mukasarasi," which in turn encouraged the interviewees to open up about their experiences, enabling prosecutors to discover legally relevant testimony and information.[58] However, rather than concluding that the subsequent investigation justified the absence of sexual violence charges, Pruitt suggested that prosecutors ought to have concluded that the initial investigation was so flawed as to be unreliable.

Ultimately, Pruitt's recommendation to amend the indictment was rejected by ICTR prosecutors in The Hague. As far as Pruitt knew at the time, this was the end of her memo's influence, as she soon thereafter left her post as the gender consultant to the ICTR. Akayesu's trial therefore began in January 1997, nearly a year after his indictment, with no charges related to sexual violence. As it happened, however, "the topic of rape entered the room during a witness's testimony."[59] Witness J, testifying in court in response to questions from a prosecutor, mentioned "in an almost offhand way" that her six-year-old daughter had been raped by three Interahamwe soldiers.[60] At this point, the three trial judges who according to ICTR procedures can ask their own questions during a trial, followed up with their own questions about the witnesses' experiences of sexual violence during the genocide.[61]

Witness J testified that ICTR investigators had not asked her about sexual violence, and that while she heard that women and girls were raped at the bureau communal, she did not witness it herself. Beth Van Schaack credits Witness J's testimony, and the judges' responses to it, for opening the door to the Tribunal's reconsideration of sexual violence charges at this key point in the trial. First, she argues, it seems likely that "[i]f J had not offered the fact that her six-year-old daughter had been raped, the existence of sexual violence in Taba may never have made it into the formal record."[62] Second, she adds that "is it noteworthy how few details were solicited from the witnesses, almost as if no one wanted to touch the material or failed to immediately recognize its significance."[63]

The second significant breakthrough came in March 1997, when Witness H, the prosecution's last scheduled witness before a scheduled break in the trial, testified that Akayesu was present at the bureau communal as sexual violence was taking place, and did nothing to stop it.[64] In response to this testimony, an international coalition of women's advocacy groups submitted an amicus brief to the court during the subsequent break in the trial, arguing for a re-investigation of sexual violence in Taba, with the aim of reconsidering the question of indicting Akayesu on sexual violence charges.[65] In June 1997, six months into the trial and a year after the initial prosecutorial investigations during the summer of 1996, the prosecutors requested permission to re-open the investigation into sexual violence charges against Akayesu, though they emphasized that they had come to the conclusion to do so independently of the amicus brief.[66] The trial judges granted the request (but also admonished the prosecutor for the procedural anomaly).[67]

As they pursued their renewed investigation regarding Akayesu's awareness of sexual violence in Taba, investigators rediscovered Lisa Pruitt's memos, which they now found helpful in locating survivors who were willing to testify about their experiences of sexual violence in Taba. In some cases, prosecutors re-interviewed some of the same witnesses. As Patricia Sellers, the ICTR gender consultant in The Hague, later described this period:

> Investigative teams in Rwanda are reconfigured. They go back out to investigate. We took back out Lisa Pruitt's report, and went back to the women and about sexual violence at the mayor's compound. As happens sometimes with sexual violence, when you say that so and so has already testified on the stand and said this and that—it allows spaces for other statements and testimony to be taken. Sometimes testimony fills out evidence where it should have been included earlier.

The testimony of genocide survivor Victoire Mukambanda was particularly pivotal. Pruitt's memo had critiqued the original investigators' dismissal of Mukambanda's testimony as "less than coherent" because she "lost her train of thought." In her memo, Pruitt had noted: "While I understand that a person who loses his/her train of thought and/or is not very coherent does not make the most credible witness, I would not necessarily conclude from this that, in fact, her story is not credible. After all, she has suffered incredibly traumatic events; it is not surprising that her story would be somewhat incoherent."[68]

Returning to interview her again, the reconfigured investigative team found Mukambanda's story, along with that of her sister, Seraphine Mukakinani, to be not only coherent, but also central to establishing "evidence that brought Akayesu even closer to, and consistently in the presence of, the sexual violence."[69] Thanks to the revised procedures, greater sensitivity to the trauma of sexual violence survivors, and the willingness of the survivors to testify about their experiences of sexual violence during the genocide, prosecutors revised the indictment against Akayesu. The revisions were almost exactly those that Pruitt argued for in her memo.[70] The amended indictment added two paragraphs arguing that Akayesu bore command responsibility for failing to prevent or punish the sexual violence that occurred at the bureau communal:

> 12A. While seeking refuge at the bureau communal, female displaced civilians were regularly taken by armed local militia and/or communal police and subjected to sexual violence, and/or beaten on or near the bureau communal premises. Displaced civilians were also murdered frequently on or near the bureau communal premises. Many women were forced to endure multiple acts of sexual violence which were at times committed by more than one assailant. These acts of sexual violence were generally accompanied by explicit threats of death or bodily harm. The female displaced civilians lived in constant fear and their physical and psychological health deteriorated as a result of the sexual violence and beatings and killings.
>
> 12B. Jean Paul Akayesu knew that the acts of sexual violence, beatings and murders were being committed and was at times present during their commission. Jean Paul Akayesu facilitated the commission of the sexual violence, beatings and murders by allowing the sexual violence and beatings and murders to occur

> on or near the bureau communal premises. By virtue of his presence during the commission of the sexual violence, beatings and murders and by failing to prevent the sexual violence, beatings and murders, Jean Paul Akayesu encouraged these activities.[71]

Five rape survivors, including Mukambanda and Mukakinani, testified at Akayesu's trial. They all reported that Akayesu was aware of and even encouraged the sexual violence they experienced at the bureau communal. Mukambanda's testimony as Witness JJ, Mukakinani's testimony as Witness NN, and the testimony of other witnesses and victims, established a terrifying narrative of inescapable sexual violence amid the genocide. As Mukambanda testified, "each time you encountered attackers they would rape you."[72] As the testimony of survivors demonstrated, "attackers" could be Interahamwe, police or other government officials, neighbors, or other men raping opportunistically. While the ubiquity of sexual assault and rape initially complicated the prosecutor's ability to bring charges under international law (because it seemed too difficult to bring charges for sexual assaults that were perpetrated by so many different actors under diverse circumstances throughout the genocide), it is precisely this ubiquity that ultimately secured Akayesu's conviction, for being aware of the rampant sexual violence (including at the bureau communal) yet failing to prevent it.

While it makes for difficult reading, it is worth recounting at least some of the survivors' testimony, if only to demonstrate how strongly it supports Patricia Sellers's later reflection on the initial investigation, that "if the case had been investigated properly, some type of link to him [Akayesu] might have been revealed, because the sexual violence was ubiquitous."[73] Mukakinani testified that their home was attacked and destroyed by Hutu neighbors, who also killed their father and brother. Mukakinani and one of her sisters were subsequently raped at the site of their destroyed home in their mother's presence repeatedly by at least three different groups of neighbors, until "their mother asked her daughters to leave rather than continue to be tortured in front of her."[74] They went into hiding with a relative for about a week and a half, but when they heard rumors that Akayesu had stopped the killings in Taba, they tried to make their way separately to the bureau communal. Two men offered to help Mukakinani along the way, but instead raped her and left her by the road, naked and unable to walk. A group of four men passed by, herding cattle; two of them raped her. Her sister found her and helped attend to her wounds. When she could walk again, they made their way together to the bureau communal.

Mukambanda initially fled to a nearby forest carrying her one-year-old son on her back. She was with her younger sister, who was suffering from machete and axe wounds from the initial attack on their home. She and other refugees, mostly women and children, were pursued through the forest until they sought refuge and protection at the bureau communal. There, officials and Interahamwe beat them and chased them away to fend for themselves against their pursuers. Mukambanda, despite suffering injuries from the beating which left her with permanent disabilities, fled to a field where she spent the night with other refugees. When she left the bureau communal, she left her baby with a Hutu couple who told her they had milk for him. They killed the baby instead. The next day, in despair, she and about ten other refugees returned to the bureau communal and asked Akayesu to shoot them. During the trial, Mukambanda testified that Akayesu "told them that there were no more bullets. . . . He asked his police officer to chase them away and said that even if there were bullets they would not waste them on the refugees."[75]

Finding nowhere safe, many refugees attempted to shelter at or near the *bureau communal*, enduring horrific violence. Interahamwe seized upon the concentration of refugees who attempted to find shelter there in order to murder and rape *en masse*. Women and girls taking refuge at or near the bureau communal were raped and gang-raped repeatedly for days or weeks on end. They were taken in groups to be raped in nearby fields and forests, or, on a day that it was raining, inside a cultural center building on the *bureau communal* compound. Mukambanda's testimony recounted at least eight different specific rapes that she suffered, though as she stated in her testimony, "she could not count the total number of times that she was raped."[76] Some women were held in confinement as sex slaves; for a time, Mukakinani was locked in a house by an Interahamwe who gave the key to other men so they could rape her there as well.

It is impossible to detach the sexual violence from other forms of physical violence that were integral to the genocide. Rape victims were witnessing murders and other assaults and massacres taking place all around them. The sexual violence many victims suffered was itself often lethal, and frequently accompanied by vicious beatings and mutilation; one account describes women and girls being "literally raped to death by perpetrators wielding machetes, sharpened sticks, broken bottles, and other implements."[77] Many women and girls were so injured by horrifically violent sexual assaults and mutilation that they simply died wherever they were left by their attackers. Mukambanda's and Mukakinani sister was one such victim; she died outdoors, having been raped repeatedly, mutilated with a machete, and left "hungry and cold."[78]

Both sisters' testimony, and that of other witnesses, established Akayesu's knowledge of the sexual violence taking place at the bureau communal. Mukakinani testified that Akayesu was at the bureau communal and fully cognizant of the sexual violence occurring there. Mukambanda also testified that Akayesu was present at the bureau communal when rapes were taking place. At one time, she testified, he witnessed Interahamwe transporting her along with a group of women and girls to the cultural center to be raped, and "said loudly to the Interahamwe, 'Never ask me again what a Tutsi woman tastes like,' and 'Tomorrow they will be killed.'"[79]

At trial, Akayesu failed to construct a consistent narrative that could counter the testimony that had accumulated against him.[80] In fact, as the trial went on, his account of his own activities in Taba became incoherent. He had begun the trial arguing, for example, that no one at the political rally he attended a few weeks after the genocide began ever incited violence against Tutsi, and that he never saw a list of names of people in Taba who were alleged to be accomplices of the RPF (which he was accused of reading aloud, thereby inciting the deaths of the named individuals). By the end of the trial, he undermined his earlier story by admitting that he had such a list, but denying that he had read the list aloud. Multiple inconsistencies like this one undermined his credibility in denying the charges against him.

The trial court announced its decision in September 1998, convicting Akayesu, among other things, of command responsibility for the sexual violence committed at the bureau communal as a component of the overall genocide. Akayesu appealed his conviction, in part on grounds that the revision to the indictment in the middle of the trial was unfair. As one commentator argued, there was merit to this claim:

> Today, in light of the "fair notice" jurisprudence established by the ad hoc Tribunals subsequent to the *Akayesu* Judgment, it is highly doubtful that this or any amended indictment containing one or more new charges against a defendant would be allowed five months into the proceedings, and at the close of the Prosecution case. It is also doubtful that the facts in support of the new charges would be considered sufficiently concise to fairly inform a defendant about the nature and cause of the charges or to provide adequate time for the preparation of the case.[81]

Nonetheless, the appeals chamber ruled against Akayesu in 2001. Since then, he has been serving a life sentence in jail in Mali.

EPILOGUE

According to one analysis, "[p]erhaps the least contested element of the ICTR's legacy is the fact that its case law has made significant contributions to doctrinal international criminal law and has demonstrated that individuals in certain positions can be held to account for grave crimes."[82] The *Akayesu* decision was precedent-setting in international criminal law in more than one respect. It was the first-ever conviction for genocide under international law, and the decision provided the first definition of rape and sexual violence under international law, which (as I will discuss in the next chapter) has been influential in efforts to reform rape laws in some domestic contexts as well. Along with other decisions regarding sexual violence before the tribunals, it "helped to modernize the law on sexual violence in [international criminal law]."[83]

The legacy of *Akayesu* extends to its influence on the International Criminal Court's "mandate to end impunity" for sexual violence. As Valerie Oosterveld argues, "[t]he *Akayesu* case, and those that followed, had a profound impact on the drafting of the Rome Statute of the ICC, the ICC's Elements of Crimes and Rules of Procedure and Evidence."[84] Oosterveld argues that the awareness of *Akayesu* among drafters of the Rome Statute led to the intentional inclusion of provisions regarding sexual violence into the Rome Statute, such as an article requiring States parties to consider appointing judges with experience regarding sexual violence. Moreover, the ICC's Elements of Crimes document "adopted wording from the Trial Chamber in the *Akayesu* decision" to include "a specific reference linking sexual violence and torture to the crime of genocide."[85] Moreover, she argues that *Akayesu* and other decisions by the tribunals prompted delegates to decide not only to include the references to rape and enforced prostitution found in the Geneva Conventions, but also to include "[r]ape, sexual slavery, enforced prostitutions, forced pregnancy, enforced sterilization" and other forms of sexual violence as prohibited acts within the provisions on crimes against humanity and war crimes. The delegates deliberately decided to include a "basket" clause—"or any other form of sexual violence"—to ensure that acts such as forced nudity and sexual mutilation, or any other similarly degrading acts invented by perpetrators in the future, could be prosecuted by the ICC as war crimes and crimes against humanity.

Even the missteps in *Akayesu* and other prosecutions for sexual violence before the tribunals influenced the ICC's procedures. What Oosterveld calls the "lack of sensitivity to the elements of gender-based crimes in initial ICTR investigations," as well as an inconsistent prosecutorial strategy at the ICTR regarding sexual violence crimes, "provided negative guidance to those drafting the ICC's governing documents, as well as to the ICC itself."[86] This guidance resulted in the ICC's "taking a wide-ranging approach to ensuring gender-sensitive investigations and prosecutions," as well as the realization that "its Office of the Prosecutor must design a prosecution strategy for sexual violence crimes and apply it from the outset."[87]

The influence of *Akayesu* and other decisions from the ad hoc tribunals did not passively seep into the structure and jurisprudence of the ICC. Rather, as Louise Chappell emphasizes, "feminist activists have been persistent in their efforts to have a gender perspective incorporated into the ICC statute."[88] This was no small accomplishment. As Dianne Luping has argued, "[t]he legal framework of the International Criminal Court reflects significant historical advances made in the investigation and prosecution of sexual and gender-based crimes before international criminal courts."[89] Consider the difference in international law regarding sexual violence before the ad hoc tribunals began their work, compared to today. Recognizing that the great distance between then and now was precipitated by the courage of survivors and witnesses in *Akayesu* and other cases before the tribunals, Catharine MacKinnon argues that

> [t]he fact that the ICC even exists, with its prohibitions on sexual violence, however imperfect, displaying the detail and seriousness they do, is due in no small part to the impetus provided by the ad hoc tribunals, and those who gave them life by believing in them enough to testify before them. The Rome Statute shows that these outrages are more palpable and prominent in international legal thinking today than they ever have been. This legacy, among many others, can never be erased. And *Akayesu's* legs are only beginning to walk over the world.[90]

NOTES

1. Keith Burgess-Jackson, "A History of Rape Law," in *A Most Detestable Crime: New Philosophical Essays on Rape,* ed. Keith Burgess-Jackson (New York: Oxford University Press, 1999), 16–17; Justice Teresa Doherty, "Sexual Violence and the Role of International Courts," *New Zealand Journal of Public and International Law* 11 (2013): 693–705.

2. See Andrew Van Dam, "Less than 1% of rapes lead to felony convictions. At least 89% of victims face emotional and physical consequences," *The Washington Post*, October 6, 2018, https://www.washingtonpost.com/business/2018/10/06/less-than-percent-rapes-lead-felony-convictions-least-percent-victims-face-emotional-physical-consequences/.

3. See "Women Victims of Sexual Violence, 1994–2010," Bureau of Justice Statistics, last modified February 13, 2013, https://www.bjs.gov/content/pub/press/fvsv9410pr.cfm. For an excellent account of the processes at work in police departments and prosecutors' offices that lead to such low numbers in the United States, see Barbara Bradley Hagerty, "An Epidemic of Disbelief," *The Atlantic*, August 2019.

4. Bureau of Justice Statistics, "Women Victims of Sexual Violence."

5. Niamh Hayes, "The Impact of Prosecutorial Strategy on the Investigation and Prosecution of Sexual Violence at International Criminal Tribunals," in *Thematic Prosecution of Sex Crimes,* ed. Morten Bergsmo (Beijing: Torkel Opsahl Academic EPublisher, 2012), 409–39.

6. Exceptions have mostly been isolated cases of individual legal accountability in domestic military courts. See Susan Brownmiller, *Against Our Will: Men, Women,*

and Rape (New York: Fawcett Columbine, 1975), Ch. 3; Doherty, "Sexual Violence," 693–705.

7. Initial Indictment, Tadić (IT-94–1), Prosecutor of the Tribunal, 13 February 1995. For a summary of ICTY cases, see United Nations International Residual Mechanism for Criminal Tribunals: Cases. https://www.irmct.org/en/cases, accessed August 12, 2022.

8. Initial Indictment, Furundžija (IT-95–17/1), Prosecutor of the Tribunal, 2 November 1995. Judgment, Furundžija (IT-95–17/1), Trial Chamber, 10 December 1998.

9. Indictment, Kunarac et al. (IT-96–23 & 23/1), Office of the Prosecutor, 18 June 1996. Trial Judgment, Kunarac et al. (IT-96–23 & 23/1), Trial Chamber, 22 February 2001.

10. Michelle Jarvis, "Overview: The Challenge of Accountability for Conflict-related Sexual Violence Crimes," in *Prosecuting Conflict-Related Sexual Violence at the ICTY*, ed. Serge Brammertz and Michelle Jarvis (Oxford: Oxford University Press, 2016), 7.

11. Trial Judgment, Akayesu, Jean Paul (ICTR-96–4), Chamber 1, 2 September 1998. See also Beth Van Schaack, "Engendering Genocide: The *Akayesu* Case Before the International Criminal Tribunal for Rwanda," in *Human Rights Advocacy Stories*, ed. Deena Hurwitz and Margaret Satterthwaite (New York: Thomson Reuters/Foundation Press, 2009), 193.

12. One commentator noted that "[t]he ruling in the Akayesu case created a new level of accountability for rape in war." Karen Alter, *The New Terrain of International Law* (Princeton, NJ: Princeton University Press, 2014), 321. Kelly Askin, writing in 2000 (and therefore before some of ICTY's key decisions regarding conflict-related sexual violence), referred to the case as "the most important decision rendered thus far in the history of women's jurisprudence." (Kelly Askin, "Women's Issues in International Criminal Law: Recent Developments and the Potential Contribution of the ICC," in *International Crimes, Peace, and Human Rights: The Role of the International Criminal Court*, ed. Dinah Shelton [New York: Transnational Publishers Inc., 2000], 321. Cited in Van Schaack, "Engendering Genocide," 194.) For a critical assessment of the ICTY's legacy, see Marko Milanovic, "The Impact of the ICTY on the Former Yugoslavia: An Anticipatory Postmortem," *American Journal of International Law* 110 (2016): 233–59. The ICTY itself endorses a more celebratory assessment: *ICTY, Achievements—Establishing the Facts*, at http://www.icty.org/en/about/tribunal/achievements.

13. As their work showed, a gender perspective revealed that prosecutors tended to overfocus on the sexual components of sexual violence against women (downplaying their violence), but to overfocus on the violent components of sexual violence against men (downplaying their sexual nature, including in some cases failing to accurately identify male victims of rape as rape victims and to prosecute accordingly). Brammertz and Jarvis (eds.), *Prosecuting Conflict-Related Sexual Violence*, 13.

14. Brammertz and Jarvis (eds.), *Prosecuting Conflict-Related Sexual Violence*.

15. Bertha Wilson, "Will Women Judges Really Make a Difference?" *Osgoode Hall Law Journal* (1990): 515. Quoted in Nienke Grossman, "Sex on the Bench: Do

Women Judges Matter to the Legitimacy of International Courts?" *Chicago Journal of International Law* 12, no. 2 (2012): 659.

16. My main sources for details about the Rwandan genocide are the following: Alison Des Forges, *Leave None to Tell the Story: Genocide in Rwanda* (New York: Human Rights Watch and Fédération Internationale des Ligues des Droits de l'Homme, 1999); African Rights, *Rwanda: Death, Despair, and Defiance* (London: African Rights, 1995); Samantha Power, *A Problem from Hell: America and the Age of Genocide* (New York: Basic Books, 2002); and Gérard Prunier, *The Rwanda Crisis 1959–1994: History of a Genocide* (London: Hurst & Company, 1995). For a helpful analysis of themes in the scholarly literature in the years following the Rwandan genocide, see Peter Uvin, "Reading the Rwandan Genocide," *International Studies Review* 3, no. 3 (Autumn 2001).

17. African Rights, *Rwanda*, 2.

18. African Rights, *Rwanda*, 4. See also Des Forges, *Leave None to Tell the Story*, "The Meaning of 'Hutu,' 'Tutsi,' and 'Twa.'"

19. Des Forges, *Leave None to Tell the Story*.

20. Des Forges, *Leave None to Tell the Story*.

21. Binaifer Nowrojee, *Shattered Lives: Sexual Violence During the Rwandan Genocide and its Aftermath* (New York: Human Rights Watch, 1996).

22. Trial Chamber Judgment, *Akayesu*, Case No. ICTR-96–4-T, at para. 420; Philip Gourevitch, "After the Genocide," *The New Yorker*, December 10, 1995.

23. Nowrojee, *Shattered Lives*.

24. Nowrojee, *Shattered Lives*.

25. For a heartbreaking analysis of the ongoing impacts of the genocide on victims and survivors via HIV infections, see The Sentinel Project, "AIDS Intersects with Genocide," December 1 2013, https://thesentinelproject.org/2013/12/01/aids-intersects-with-genocide/.

26. Gourevitch, "After the Genocide."

27. Des Forges, *Leave None to Tell the Story*.

28. Bill Berkeley, "Judgment Day," *The Washington Post*, October 11, 1998, https://www.washingtonpost.com/archive/lifestyle/magazine/1998/10/11/judgement-day/3ae2490b-c3c7-4c17-b43c-e96bbfc064e5/.

29. Gourevitch, "After the Genocide."

30. See Nowrojee, *Shattered Lives*, 4; Gourevitch, "After the Genocide."

31. Des Forges, *Leave None to Tell the Story*.

32. Security Council Resolution 827, May 25, 1993.

33. See also the discussion in Michael J. Matheson and David Scheffer, "The Creation of the Tribunals," *American Journal of International Law* 110 (2016): 173–90, noting in addition that the Rwandan government opposed including war crimes in the ICTR's jurisdiction, possibly due to their desire "to eliminate the chance that its own military personnel might be accused of having committed such crimes in their struggle to defeat the previous regime" (185).

34. Gary Bass critiqued the ICTY as an "'act of tokenism' by the world community—'The world would prosecute the crimes that it would not prevent.'" (Kathryn Sikkink, *The Justice Cascade: How Human Rights Prosecutions are Changing World*

Politics [New York: W. W. Norton & Co., 2011], 114. Citing Gary Bass, *Stay the Hand of Vengeance* [Princeton: Princeton University Press, 2000], 207.)

35. 3453rd Meeting, 8 November 1994. *United Nations Security Council.* 8 November 1994. pp. 13–16. S/PV.3453, pp. 13–16.

36. Des Forges, *Leave None to Tell the Story*, "Conclusion: Justice and Responsibility."

37. Thierry Cruvellier, in Michele Mitchell and Nick Louvel (directors), *The Uncondemned* (New York: Film at Eleven Media, 2015).

38. Van Schaack, "Engendering Genocide," citing the Trial Chamber Judgment, *Akayesu*, Case No. ICTR-96–4-T, at paras. 187–93.

39. Trial Chamber Judgment, *Akayesu*, Case No. ICTR-96–4-T, at para. 184.

40. My main secondary sources regarding the *Akyesu* case are Van Schaack, "Engendering Genocide," 193–227; Thierry Cruvellier, *Court of Remorse: Inside the International Criminal Tribunal for Rwanda*, trans. Chari Voss (Madison: University of Wisconsin Press, 2010); Mitchell and Louvel (directors), *The Uncondemned.*

41. Indictment, Akayesu, Case No. ICTR-96–4-I, at para. 2.

42. In one case, the church in Nyange was bulldozed, intentionally crushing to death the refugees seeking protection inside. African Rights, *Rwanda*, 410–16.

43. Mitchell and Louvel, *The Uncondemned.*

44. Janet Fleischman and Binaifer Nowrojee, "In Rwanda, Too, Rape Was a War Crime and Must Be Punished," *New York Times,* July 25, 1996, https://www.nytimes.com/1996/07/25/opinion/IHT-in-rwanda-too-rape-was-a-war-crime-and-must-be-punished.html?searchResultPosition=1.

45. Lisa R. Pruitt, "Taba Commune Sexual Assault Evidence Summary: An Analysis of Akayesu's and Kubwimana's Authority and Responsibility," October 25, 1996. Copy on file with the author. As I explain in greater detail below, this memo became influential in guiding the later investigation in response to women's testimony during Akayesu's trial regarding sexual violence in Taba. I am grateful to Professor Pruitt for making a copy of this and other memos available to me.

46. Pruitt, "Taba Commune Sexual Assault Evidence Summary."

47. Nowrojee, *Shattered Lives*.

48. Nowrojee, *Shattered Lives*.

49. Nowrojee, *Shattered Lives*.

50. Nowrojee, *Shattered Lives*.

51. Pruitt, "Taba Commune Sexual Assault Evidence Summary," 2.

52. Pruitt, "Taba Commune Sexual Assault Evidence Summary," 2.

53. Article 6(3): "The fact that any of the acts referred to in Articles 2 to 4 of the present Statute was committed by a subordinate does not relieve his or her superior of criminal responsibility if he or she knew or had reason to know that the subordinate was about to commit such acts or had done so and the superior failed to take the necessary and reasonable measures to prevent such acts or to punish the perpetrators thereof."

54. Pruitt, "Taba Commune Sexual Assault Evidence Summary," 3.

55. Indictment, *Akayesu,* Case No. ICTR-96–4-I, at para. 12.

56. Pruitt, "Taba Commune Sexual Assault Evidence Summary," 1.

57. Pruitt, "Taba Commune Sexual Assault Evidence Summary," 2.

58. Pruitt, "Taba Commune Sexual Assault Evidence Summary," 1.

59. Alter, *The New Terrain of International Law*, 320.

60. For the transcript of this exchange, see Van Schaack, "Engendering Genocide," 6 n. 11, citing *Prosecutor v. Akayesu*, Case No. ICTR-96–4-T, Transcript, at pp. 00101–00102 (27 January 1997).

61. The judges were Judge Laïty Kama, Presiding Judge, from Senegal; Judge Lennart Aspegren, from Sweden; and Judge Navanethem Pillay, from South Africa, the only female judge in the trial.

62. Van Schaack, "Engendering Genocide," 7.

63. Van Schaack, "Engendering Genocide," 7.

64. Van Schaack, "Engendering Genocide," 7. Patricia Sellers reports that the prosecutors knew in advance that Witness H's testimony would indicate Akayesu's presence while sexual violence was being committed at the bureau communal, and were accordingly already anticipating asking for a recess to better investigate sexual violence in Taba with the aim of revising the indictment. The Ad Hoc Tribunals Oral History Project, *Oral History Interview with Patricia Viseur Sellers*, International Center for Ethics, Justice, and Public Life, Brandeis University, 2017, 31.

65. Mitchell and Louvel, *The Uncondemned*. See also Ad Hoc Tribunals Oral History Project, Interview with Patricia Viseur Sellers. The brief itself is available online at ICCWomen.org, at http://www.iccwomen.org/publications/briefs/docs/Prosecutor_v_Akayesu_ICTR.pdf (accessed January 18, 2020).

66. Ad Hoc Tribunals Oral History Project, Interview with Patricia Viseur Sellers; Van Schaack, "Engendering Genocide."

67. "Pierre [Prosper, the trial prosecutor] consults with the Prosecutor who informs him that he should ask for a recess, and request more time to investigate. During the request, the judges are actually admonishing the Prosecutor, as they should have, before granting us the recess to further investigate." Ad Hoc Tribunals Oral History Project, Interview with Patricia Viseur Sellers, 31.

68. Pruitt, "Taba Commune Sexual Assault Evidence Summary," 12.

69. Ad Hoc Tribunals Oral History Project, Interview with Patricia Viseur Sellers, 32.

70. Trial Chamber Judgment, *Akayesu*, Case No. ICTR-96–4-T, at para. 6.

71. Indictment, *Akayesu,* Case No. ICTR-96–4-I, at para. 12.

72. Trial Chamber Judgment, *Akayesu*, Case No. ICTR-96–4-T, at para. 421.

73. Pruitt, "Taba Commune Sexual Assault Evidence Summary," 31.

74. Trial Chamber Judgment, *Akayesu*, Case No. ICTR-96–4-T, at para. 431.

75. Trial Chamber Judgment, *Akayesu*, Case No. ICTR-96–4-T, at para. 420.

76. Trial Chamber Judgment, *Akayesu*, Case No. ICTR-96–4-T, at para. 420.

77. Van Schaack, "Engendering Genocide," 212.

78. Trial Chamber Judgment, *Akayesu*, Case No. ICTR-96–4-T, at para. 434.

79. Trial Chamber Judgment, *Akayesu*, Case No. ICTR-96–4-T, at para. 422.

80. See the account of the trial in Cruvellier, *Court of Remorse*, Chapter 3, "At the First Judgment," 20–31.

81. Suzanne Chenault, "And Since *Akayesu*? The Development of ICTR Jurisprudence on Gender Crimes: A Comparison of *Akayesu* and *Muhimana*," *New England Journal of International and Comparative Law* 14, no. 2 (2008): 221–37.

82. Sara Kendall and Sarah M. H. Nouwen, "Speaking of Legacy: Toward an Ethos of Modesty at the International Criminal Tribunal for Rwanda," *American Journal of International Law* 110 (2016): 218.

83. Darryl Robinson and Gillian MacNeil, "The Tribunals and the Renaissance of International Criminal Law: Three Themes," *American Journal of International Law* 110 (2016): 202.

84. Valerie Oosterveld, "Gender-Sensitive Justice and the International Criminal Tribunal for Rwanda: Lessons Learned for the International Criminal Court," *New England Journal of International and Comparative Law* 12, no. 1 (2005): 121.

85. Oosterveld, "Gender-Sensitive Justice," 123.

86. Oosterveld, "Gender-Sensitive Justice," 125, 125–27 *passim*.

87. Oosterveld, "Gender-Sensitive Justice," 128–29.

88. Louise Chappell, "Women, Gender and International Institutions: Exploring New Opportunities at the International Criminal Court," *Policy and Society* 22 (2003): 14.

89. Dianne Luping, "Investigation and Prosecution of Sexual and Gender-Based Crimes Before the International Criminal Court," *American University Journal of Gender, Social Policy, and the Law* 17 (2009): 433.

90. Catharine MacKinnon, "The ICTR's Legacy on Sexual Violence," *New England Journal of International and Comparative Law* 14 (2008): 211.

Chapter 5

Structural Inequality and Hermeneutical Injustice

Prosecutions at the international tribunals (notably including *Akayesu*) were a watershed in developing effective international legal accountability for sexual violence against women, in response to those women's own accounts of their experiences. By providing an institutional forum that centered the voices of women testifying to their experiences of violence, and demanding that their experiences be regarded as deserving of accountability, *Akayesu* and the broader work of the tribunals elevated the legal status of women survivors of sexual violence in those particular cases and set in motion a process of legal and social reform that has extended into international and even domestic law more broadly. This complex process constituted a form of social moral progress and discovery that illuminates aspects of human rights morality in light of long-ignored realities of women's experiences.

My argument is that the work of the tribunals regarding sexual violence in armed conflict has both methodological and substantive implications for the philosophy of human rights morality. These trials reveal the practical possibility that even a thin and formal realization of universal equality under law—the animating political value of international human rights law—can be leveraged by members of groups whose human rights are insecurely protected in order to press their claims for institutional reforms that improve the protection of their human rights in more substantive ways over time. Regarding philosophical methodology, this practical dynamic in turn demonstrates the value to philosophical inquiry of attending closely to the real-world contexts in which the idea of human rights is deployed, which can orient philosophers toward neglected questions, evidence, arguments, and forms of moral reasoning. For example, without greater representation and empowerment of women in society more broadly, including in the legal profession as judges and prosecutors, the relevant voices would not have been "in the room" to influence the course of the sexual violence prosecutions. This point suggests significant interdependencies among various forms of formal and substantive equality. Moreover, the tribunals' self-reflection on their own initial failure to respond appropriately to sexual violence crimes revealed not only how structural inequalities may distort the prosecution of gendered crimes, but also how these institutions can reform themselves over time and contribute to dismantling structural inequalities within their purview. As a matter of substantive moral reasoning, this bolsters my argument that structural equality is a foundational value for human rights morality, and, more broadly, supports theorizing human rights morality in explicitly institutional and political terms, rather than focusing solely on producing a theory of moral human rights.

In this chapter, I first make the case that, while the activism and advocacy of individuals and groups were essential in influencing the outcome of *Akayesu* and other sexual violence trials at the tribunals, the institutional reforms that these cases precipitated within the tribunals are even more important, as are their effects on the subsequent development of international and domestic law, including the mandate of the International Criminal Court. Importantly for my overall argument, these institutional reforms explicitly grappled with and attempted to overcome the effects of deeply entrenched social beliefs about gender on human rights; they therefore constitute an important example of how international legal institutions may contribute to dismantling structural inequalities. I then argue that these institutional reforms show how *Akayesu* contributed to the rectification of an institutional epistemic injustice, manifested in biased social meanings (in this case, of sexual violence and of the relevant human rights norms) that resulted from the exclusion of women from the process of constructing the relevant shared social meanings. By providing authoritative venues for women to testify about their own experiences of sexual violence, the work of the tribunals contributed to correcting biased understandings that were operative not only within human rights practice, but also in broader social contexts.

In the subsequent section, I explore how the definition of rape used in *Akayesu* has contributed to the subsequent development of international and national law. Catharine MacKinnon has argued extensively that this definition, by incorporating a structural analysis of gender, provides a more accurate understanding of the social reality of rape given its recognition that background conditions may be coercive in ways that obviate the need to include lack of consent among the elements of the crime. However, the attempt to theorize sexual violence in armed conflict from the perspective of "structural feminism" has been extensively critiqued by Karen Engle and Janet Halley, among others. I consider and respond to their critiques in the last two sections: first, I argue that my arguments in this chapter undermine their critique of incorporating a gender framework in international law; then I argue against Halley that feminist values deployed by judges in international courts are not bias but an essential component of objectively good judging in cases where gender justice is at stake. My immediate point in responding to these critics is to defend my use of *Akayesu* as a case study and to bolster my argument that structural equality is a foundational value for human rights morality. But in a broader sense, these discussions also demonstrate the engaged normative work that philosophers can contribute to by theorizing human rights morality at a less-abstract level and by attending to the normative arguments already in play in the practice and in scholarship in other disciplines. Such discussions demonstrate the substantial contributions that a philosophical perspective can make to advancing scholarship in other disciplines while also learning from it.

INSTITUTIONAL REFORM REGARDING SEXUAL VIOLENCE CRIMES

The story of *Akayesu* and other sexual violence trials at the ad hoc tribunals is the story of the process by which sexual violence in armed conflict came to be a successfully prosecutable war crime under international law. Despite the prosecution's inauspicious beginning, when the initial indictment against Akayesu included no charges relating to sexual violence, his ultimate conviction on these charges can be attributed to interventions by individuals and groups advocating for reform of the institutional culture of the tribunals and broader social norms regarding sexual violence. This advocacy included the mobilization of international women's groups, whose efforts included a *New York Times* opinion piece in 1996 specifically about the *Akayesu* case; efforts to educate prosecutors from within the tribunals by Lisa Pruitt, the ICTR's gender consultant; programs developed by Rwandan community activists to provide social and emotional support to women survivors of the genocide and to combat the impacts on survivors of archaic conceptions of sexual violence as shameful to its victims; and those survivors themselves in overcoming traditional but biased social expectations to come forward and testify as witnesses.[1]

Individual women played pivotal and influential roles in this process as witnesses, judges, prosecutors, trial lawyers, and organized advocates for women's issues through nongovernmental organizations and victims' advocacy groups. Importantly, some of these women were in a position to impact this process in part as a result of the relatively recent increase in the representation of women in the relevant professions. Once there, however, they found that there was still significant work to do to combat multiple forms of gender bias within these professions. For example, one way that women lawyers made a difference in the legal processes of the tribunals was by challenging the male-dominated culture of the Office of the Prosecutor. As Dianne Luping has argued, this culture had an impact on the early trials:

> The former Chief Prosecutor of the ICTY and ICTR, Richard Goldstone, said that in the early years of both tribunals he believed that there was a "gender bias" within his office. He referred to the lack of senior female investigators and criticized the attitude among his investigators, stating that "[t]heir culture was not such as to make them concerned about gender-related crime."[2]

The women who served as judges in sexual violence cases at the tribunals have perhaps received the most recognition for their contributions to changing the status of sexual violence as a prosecutable crime. As Luping notes, Goldstone credits women judges, including Judge Odio Benito of the ICTY and Judge Navanethem Pillay of the ICTR for playing a central role in advocating for the importance of rendering sexual violence visible and the need for developing frameworks for legal accountability for sexual violence.[3] Christina Lamb observes that "[i]t surely cannot be a coincidence" that women served as judges in the cases before the tribunals that resulted in convictions for sexual violence.[4] And in her reflections on the changing status of sexual violence in armed conflict, Judge Teresa Doherty of the Special Court of Sierra Leone notes that the presence of women in key roles such as judges helps women's voices be heard in legal proceedings:

> I am not qualified to say why there has been an increase in the prosecution of crimes of sexual and gender-based violence. . . . I am not convinced that the presence of women on the bench is the sole reason for a more progressive view of sexual offending as a crime against humanity. I suggest that these developments also reflect the trend in domestic jurisdictions and the work of groups and civil society to raise awareness of sexual and gender-based violence and the need for action against such violence. We, as judges of international tribunals, were the ones who had the opportunity to actually say what many already believe.[5]

As important as women were in bringing about these changes in the legal culture regarding sexual violence, some men played pivotal roles in fostering these changes and supporting the work of women at all levels and at every stage of the process. Beth Van Schaack argues that while "[i]t is tempting to credit much of the story about the progress of gender justice before the international tribunals to the presence of key women involved in the international criminal process," it is also the case that "male judges and prosecutors were at times equally as enlightened to issues of gender justice as their female counterparts."[6] Men who used their roles to advance the cause of gender justice in *Akayesu* include Richard Goldstone, in his role as lead prosecutor for the tribunals, and Judge Laïty Kama, who joined Judge Navanethem

Pillay in following up on Witness J's testimony about sexual violence in Taba. Patricia Sellers (the Legal Advisor for Gender at the ICTR) also credits Theo van Boven, a former U.N. Special Rapporteur on Torture, who "consciously created human resource structures within the Victims and Witnesses Unit that facilitated the testimony of sexual assault survivors," which created the precedent leading to the development of a "long-term gendered strategy in the Victim and Witnesses Unit."[7]

The problem that all these individuals were addressing in all of these diverse ways was not necessarily that prosecutors and others literally could not see that sexual violence had occurred in Rwanda, and on a massive scale. Rather, the problem was that this violence did not appear to those representing the institutional culture of the tribunals as prosecutable crimes, and therefore as relevant to their understanding of their mission. As Sellers reported, a prevailing attitude among investigators seemed to be that the sexual violence was unrelated to the genocide, so attending to it would distract from their mandate.[8] Importantly for our purposes, the overarching mind-set of prosecutors and investigators was rooted in prevalent shared understandings that confirmed the status quo bias against prosecuting sexual violence in armed conflict. For example, some women who reported having been raped did not appear credible to investigators, partly because the investigators lacked the relevant training and sensitivity in talking to rape survivors. Moreover, there was no widespread legal strategy among prosecutors about the broader social significance of rape and sexual violence that would help them tie it to crimes of genocide and crimes against humanity, and no clear mandate from the highest levels of the tribunals that crimes of sexual violence were to be treated as part of the genocide.

What was missing in this environment, then, was an *institutional* recognition of sexual violence in armed conflict as a prosecutable crime among other crimes of war, leading to the initial failure of the institution itself to respond appropriately to the rights violations that it had a duty of justice to enforce. Guilty verdicts may be prosecutorial victories, but they cannot on their own solve what are essentially failures of institutional capacity. Instead, rectifying the underlying problem requires institutional and systemic reforms.

Such reforms were in fact the primary focus of a self-study of prosecutorial methods for conflict-related sexual violence conducted by the ICTY's Office of the Prosecutor (OTP), before the ICTY officially closed its doors on December 31, 2017.[9] (The ICTR shared the ITCY's OTP in The Hague, though an independent team of prosecutors and investigators was deployed to Rwanda.) The study took an explicitly institutional focus in a number of respects. For example, the ICTY's self-conscious efforts to identify, analyze, and overcome deeply gender-biased stereotypes required constructing and institutionalizing new procedures and expectations regarding sexual violence.

Their report characterizes these accomplishments as improvements to the functioning of the institution as a whole; in the words of its editors (former ICTY prosecutors), "we have established operational procedures, legal precedents, and a new body of expertise that has transformed the justice landscape for conflict-related sexual violence crimes."[10]

One point of these institutional reforms is to reduce reliance on individuals who happen to be sensitive to issues of gender justice to raise such concerns on their own initiative, instead institutionalizing processes and methods that enable the appropriate prosecutorial response to sexual violence crimes. This includes the deliberate attempt to develop an accurate understanding of sexual violence as a crime and better investigative techniques for interviewing survivors of sexual violence, as well as developing a more informed understanding and application of existing international criminal law to crimes of sexual violence. The point of the self-study was, therefore, to institutionalize a better-informed perspective precisely so that responsibility for bringing issues of gender justice to light does not fall solely or primarily on particular individuals within or outside of those institutions, as it did in *Akayesu*. Instead, the reformed institutions should, by default, take issues of gender justice seriously, including by developing the resources to investigate and prosecute sexual violence on the same terms as other crimes.

As noted in retrospect by ICTY prosecutors, given the groundbreaking nature of their work prosecuting sexual violence in armed conflict under international law, it is unsurprising that they initially grappled with missteps and misunderstandings, especially in their earlier cases involving sexual violence indictments.[11] In reflecting on the progress they made in prosecuting sexual violence after these initial missteps, ICTY prosecutors identified several misconceptions about sexual violence that they needed to overcome in their efforts to prosecute sexual violence effectively. Importantly, these misconceptions were not idiosyncratic beliefs held by specific individuals at the ICTY, but rather were rooted in deeply entrenched and widespread social meanings of gender.

One such misconception was based on the traditional view of sexual violence reflected in the 1949 Geneva Conventions, namely, as "attacks on 'honour' that are incompatible with the 'modesty' and 'dignity' of women," rather than as violent crimes.[12] This understanding reflects archaic conceptions of sexual violence as damaging a woman's social value as "chaste" and hence marriageable, or reflecting her family's honor, rather than as a harm to the victim herself.[13] These social meanings of sexual violence were embedded not only in the social communities in which the tribunals worked, but also in the minds of many tribunal investigators, prosecutors, and judges. Uncovering and critiquing these social meanings enabled prosecutors to rethink and better understand the real impacts of sexual violence in armed conflict on victims and their communities, how to think about sexual violence more effectively from a prosecutorial perspective, and how to reform their own procedures and norms for criminal investigations in contexts where sexual violence is a factor. For example, the predictable but misplaced shame that many sexual violence survivors experience came to be seen as an explicit part of the intent behind campaigns of sexual violence in armed conflict by perpetrators (and hence as playing an instrumental role in campaigns of genocide and ethnic cleansing). Perhaps even more importantly, the realization that the conception of sexual violence as damaging to a woman's honor was written into international law via the Geneva Conventions, and was so embedded in "common-sense" thinking about sexual violence that it was likely to be shared by personnel at the tribunals, highlighted for prosecutors the need to reform their own institutional perspective so that they could ensure that the legal process that they represented they did not itself contribute to victims' sense of shame by implicitly communicating that sexual violence was somehow defiling or shameful to the victim.

The second misconception, intricately connected to the first, was that many prosecutors regarded sexual violence as simply less serious than other violent crimes. Tracing the roots of this problem to the structural inequalities common in many societies, Sellers has argued that many investigators at the international tribunals came from domestic legal systems in which "most female detectives worked in what was a family crimes section, where you did some sexual violence, or domestic violence. Female detectives rarely received promotions into upper level detectives ranks. Therefore, most could not be seconded by their governments and sent to the ICTY."[14] In addition to resulting in fewer women as investigators at the tribunals, this phenomenon also contributed to the sense among investigators both that "it was normal for men to be in charge," and that sexual violence was simply not a priority for prosecutors investigating a genocide. As Sellers notes: "To investigate sexual violence would not have given them high prestige and power in their jobs at home."[15] The misconception of sexual violence as primarily a "domestic" issue and not a serious crime in turn supported the belief among prosecutors that sexual violence prosecutions were a distraction from prosecuting genocide-related crimes, rather than integral to it. The ICTY report therefore highlights "the imperative of seeing—and treating—sexual violence prosecutions as core work for any prosecution office addressing conflict-related atrocities."[16]

The third misconception was the perception of sexual violence in armed conflict as an "opportunistic" crime motivated by sexual desire. This perception in turn led prosecutors to "overlook valid connections between these acts and broader patterns of violent crimes unleashed during conflict."[17] For example, the OTP report identified a pattern of cases in which judges expressed a higher degree of skepticism that crimes of sexual violence targeted victims on the basis of their ethnicity, compared to other violent crimes committed during the conflict such as murder or beatings. Such misconceptions about sexual violence made it difficult to prosecute senior officials of command responsibility for sexual violence, since both prosecutors and judges were unprepared to see sexual violence as an inherent part of the overall campaign of violence unleashed in the conflict, instead seeing it as "something separate and apart from the main agenda of the warring parties."[18]

Finally, the fourth misconception (which Lisa Priutt identified and argued against at the time in her memos) is the view that sexual violence should only be prosecuted in international courts if it is "widespread, systematic, or committed pursuant to orders."[19] While such characteristics make it easier to connect sexual violence to the larger campaign of violence, the ICTY prosecutors emphasize that even a small number of rapes (or a single rape) could very well be linked to an overall pattern of violence against a population, as could a small number of beatings, property crimes, or other acts of violence. As they argue, "[a]s with any other crime category, to prosecute sexual violence as a crime against humanity it is sufficient to show that an act of sexual violence formed part of a widespread or systematic attack against the civilian population. It is not necessary to show that sexual violence, viewed in isolation, met these criteria."[20]

As this brief summary shows, the OTP report reflects the tribunals' eventual recognition that an institutional framework capable of apprehending structural inequalities and their resulting biases is essential to their ability to carry out their mission effectively and accurately. Over the long run, then, even more groundbreaking than the early efforts of enlightened individuals that led to precedent-setting verdicts in *Akayesu* and related trials was the fact that the tribunals took up the task of institutionalizing a gender justice perspective, rethinking everything from investigatory procedures and norms to the definitions of crimes in light of prevalent structural inequalities.

HERMENEUTICAL INJUSTICE, REPRESENTATION, AND RECEPTIVITY

In this section I argue that the institutional implementation of a gender justice perspective can be viewed as the rectification of *hermeneutical marginalization*—a form of epistemic injustice that obtains when certain social perspectives have been marginalized in the processes of constructing shared social meanings, with the result that commonly shared vocabularies cannot accurately describe the experiences of marginalized individuals and groups.[21] In the case of international criminal law, the wrong of hermeneutical marginalization is not merely the epistemic disadvantage that it produces for individuals who are deprived of understanding their own experiences and of the language needed to communicate that experience successfully to others. There is also an additional wrong, specific to the institutional context, given that these institutions have an obligation of justice to recognize and respond appropriately to human rights violations. The injustice lies in the fact that the hermeneutical exclusion of marginalized groups may lead to the result that these institutions instead are likely to misunderstand, minimize, or simply overlook severe human rights violations suffered by members of those groups. The work of the tribunals to institutionalize the principles of equal justice for women's human rights violations under international law can therefore be viewed as the rectification of an *institutional hermeneutical injustice*.

Ensuring that members of previously excluded groups are represented in social roles that are relevant to constructing shared social meanings is an important component of overcoming this kind of hermeneutical injustice. At the tribunals, the representation of women at many different junctures and in different roles therefore had an enormous amount to do with this important transition. The presence of women judges, for example, was significant as one role among many in which individual women contributed previously excluded gender-related perspectives at all stages in the process. Even more importantly, women played key roles as witnesses, local community organizers who formed survivor support groups, international activists, prosecutors, investigators, and gender advisors within the ICTY/ICTR, in addition to judges. In fact, the role of women judges in this process can be seen as a response to, and enabled by, the foundational work done by the other actors in bringing sexual violence to the courtroom in the first place. While representation of women was therefore deeply influential to this story, that representation was most significant in terms of the systemic shift that resulted from increased social and economic equality for women in many societies in the late twentieth century, which in turn led to a greater representation of women in professional capacities society more broadly.

However, by itself, the greater representation of women in various influential positions of authority or advocacy by itself cannot rectify hermeneutical injustice. A true case of hermeneutical injustice is characterized by the absence of shared concepts and the associated vocabulary needed to make sense of the experiences of members of marginalized groups. Members of marginalized groups therefore cannot overcome this problem entirely by themselves, because part of the injustice is their inability to communicate the full significance of their experiences in ways that are intelligible to the broader community. Even if they come up with language to describe their experiences, hermeneutical justice in an institutional context requires that this language and associated concepts be taken up by the larger culture or institutions in which group members have an interest in making their experiences understood. In this way, the process of rectifying an institutional hermeneutical injustice requires collaboration from the broader institutional culture, not just activism and consciousness-raising within the marginalized group.

For these reasons, any solution to an institutional hermeneutical injustice needs to be supplemented by an account of what I will call *receptivity*. A politics of receptivity, in contrast to representation, is a politics of responsiveness and openness, more associated with listening than with speaking. Jennifer Nedelsky characterizes receptivity as akin to mindfulness, or coming to see things as they are without our habitual filters.[22] As many human rights activists would argue, the protection and promotion of human rights often requires developing new ways of seeing, in order to transcend socially entrenched views about what constitutes acceptable treatment for vulnerable groups (such as migrants and refugees, or persons with disabilities, for example). Nedelsky attributes to Hannah Arendt the notion that the banality of evil is in some ways a failure of mindful receptivity, noting that "[t]he failure to . . . pay attention to what is really happening and assess it in all its novelty, can be catastrophic."[23]

The reforms to the ICTY's institutional culture and prosecutorial procedures described in the previous section constitute a kind of institutionalization of receptivity, so understood. Again, the point of these institutional reforms is to rely less on the representation of previously marginalized perspectives by specific individuals, and more on institutionalized processes and methods that enable the appropriate institutional response to sexual violence crimes. This dynamic can be seen as the closing of a circle: The original institutional injustice results in part from the marginalization of perspectives characteristic of social groups defined as locations in a particular social structure, and so, at least in its early stages, the rectification of that injustice depends heavily on increasing representation of those perspectives. However, institutional reliance on representation is not enough. Full rectification of an institutional hermeneutical injustice further requires the construction of more inclusive (less exclusionary) shared social meanings, which can in turn be used to identify and work toward institutional reforms that are sensitive to the previously excluded perspectives. Successfully done, this institutionalization can be seen as broadening the receptivity of the institution in a systematic way, thereby changing the broader social reality in the direction of greater inclusivity and improved responsiveness to human rights violations even when the victims are members of marginalized groups.

If this is correct, it supports various components of my larger argument in this book in several ways. First, it supports the notion that structural equality, an inherently institutional concept, is an important foundational value for human rights morality. It therefore also supports my claim that institutional and political concepts are necessary for adequately theorizing human rights morality (and for realizing it in practice). Finally, it demonstrates how attention to human rights practice broadly understood can be normatively instructive for philosophers theorizing human rights morality. It therefore supports a methodology that more closely engages with various aspects of human rights practice, rather than relying solely on traditional philosophical methods of abstract moral reasoning.

DEFINING RAPE IN INTERNATIONAL LAW

According to the ICTY's self-study, their "overarching insight" emphasizes the importance of "situating sexual violence in the gender framework." By this they mean that a full understanding of sexual violence requires an awareness of "the socially constructed roles and identities of males and females in a given society," centrally including "prevalent inequality between males and females, which is often exacerbated during periods of armed conflict."[24] Michelle Jarvis, a former ICTY prosecutor, argues that "understanding the influence of gender is important to ensure that crimes are accurately characterized and that the full nature of the harm inflicted on the victim is recognized in the criminal charges brought and the sentencing submissions made."[25] Applying this lesson to their own role as prosecutors, they argue that

> it is particularly important for investigators and prosecutors to be aware that the distinctive experiences of females in conflict-related situations are much less likely to be inherently recognized, or appropriately addressed, or prioritized than those of males. This reality flows from the structural inequality that persists between males and females around the world, which tends to obscure female voices and results in the adoption of male norms as the standard reference point.[26]

Finally, they emphasize that prosecutors need to be aware of, and engage in self-conscious efforts to combat, deeply rooted gender inequalities in order to effectively realize their own mission:

> In short, understanding the impact of gender is not an esoteric matter that can be left to gender theorists. Unless international criminal law practitioners understand the influence of gender on conflict-related sexual violence, they remain vulnerable to mischaracterizing, overlooking, or under-prioritizing sexual violence and other gendered harms in their work.[27]

Importantly for my larger argument, these reflections demonstrate that the ICTY self-study led to the conclusion that an awareness of structural inequality is essential to adequately understanding harms to members of excluded social groups and to conceptualizing them accurately as crimes. Regarding the successful prosecution of sexual violence in armed conflict, this means ensuring that the institutional perspective is informed by the ways in which gendered social roles, expectations, and meanings relate to crimes like sexual violence.[28]

One of the most important manifestations of this institutionalization of a gender perspective at the tribunals involves the legal definition of rape. The trial chamber in *Akayesu* noted that there was at the time "no commonly accepted definition of this term in international law."[29] The tribunal rejected standard legal definitions of rape, which typically prohibit specific forms of nonconsensual penetration, noting that "the central elements of the crime of rape cannot be captured in a mechanical description of objects and body parts."[30] In support of their approach, the tribunal compared the definition of rape to that of torture, noting that "[t]he Convention against Torture and Other Cruel, Inhuman and Degrading Treatment or Punishment does not catalogue specific acts in its definition of torture, focusing rather on the conceptual framework of state-sanctioned violence."[31] The tribunal therefore adopted a "conceptual framework" definition of rape as "a physical invasion of a sexual nature under circumstances which are coercive."[32] This definition introduces a broader, more context-sensitive notion of sexual violence, and eliminates reference to lack of consent as an element of the crime.

Louise Chappell argues that the definition of rape used in *Akayesu* was a milestone in international law, not least because it was the first definition of rape under international law, but also because it marks a significant departure from existing references to women in international law, which emphasized women's roles as mothers or in relation to men. In particular, many references noted that women are weaker than men and therefore in need of protection, especially as regards their "honor."[33] Against this backdrop, rape had often been construed in international law as a violation of women's honor, rather than a crime of violence. Thus, "[t]he tribunal's definition of rape in the *Akayesu* case . . . represented a breakthrough in terms of recognizing women's experience of this form of violence," thereby moving international law toward a construal of women as "subjects, rather than just objects of the law."[34]

Catharine MacKinnon has argued extensively that the *Akayesu* case's definition of rape was a leap forward in legal definitions of rape that might make it a more successfully prosecutable crime. The central insight captured by this definition, in her view, is that "coercive circumstances may be inherent in certain situations, such as that of armed conflict or the presence of Interahamwe militia among refugee women, and need not be evidenced by a show of physical force."[35] This contrasts with standard legal definitions of rape, which, as MacKinnon notes, "is generally defined in Western countries as sexual intercourse by force or without consent or both."[36] Such definitions, including those in most countries' legal codes, typically revolve around the presence or absence of consent to specific sexual acts, and require proving that penetration was the result of actual force, where absence of force is often taken as evidence that the sex was consensual. MacKinnon critiques the consent standard as a concept, given that it is often understood to include acquiescence or submission even in the face of obvious coercion. On this understanding, consent may appear to be present even in cases of "forced trade-offs"; one example is a case in which a woman was found by a grand jury to have consented to sex because she "insisted that a strange man who climbed through her window brandishing a knife use a condom before he raped her because she feared HIV infection."[37] More saliently for our purposes, however, MacKinnon argues that a consent requirement ignores background gendered inequalities that characterize the conditions under which many instances of rape, and attempts to prosecute them, take place. As MacKinnon argues:

> The *Akayesu* approach and the pattern of outcomes in cases since support the suggestion that rape laws fail because they do not recognize the context of inequality in which they operate, focusing as they so often do on isolated proof of non-consent against a false background presumption of consent in the context of a presumed equality of power that is not socially real.[38]

As Suzanne Chenault notes, the *Akayesu* definition involves two significant innovations in defining rape: "first, lack of the victim's consent is not an element to be proved, or even considered, in coercive circumstances; second, sexual violence may involve acts of a sexual nature which do not involve penetration of the sexual organs or even physical contact, such as forced undressing or forced performance of exercises in the nude."[39]

While this definition arguably facilitated Akayesu's guilty verdict on sexual violence charges, later cases decided by the tribunals reverted to a more standard conception of rape, re-introducing both the salience of consent as well as reference to specific actions and body parts. This was largely in response to a perceived need for a more "specific" definition of rape than the *Akayesu* definition. For example, the ICTY in the *Furundžija* case reverted to a definition of rape as non-consensual penetration, specifying specific prohibited actions. Subsequently, the ICTY (in *Kunarac et al.*) "adopted the mechanical *Furundžija* test and required the Prosecution to prove that the victim did not consent to rape or sexual violence."[40] The consent requirement under this definition of rape was also operative in the ICTR's trial chamber in a later case (*Gacumbitsi*), where the tribunal felt the need to establish that "the utterances made by the Accused to the effect that in case of resistance the victims should be killed in an atrocious manner, and the fact that rape victims were attacked by those they were fleeing from, adequately establish the victims' lack of consent to the rapes."[41] MacKinnon argues that the idea that victims could have consented in any meaningful way under such circumstances, among other factors, eroded the credibility of the tribunals with women victims, and diminished women's willingness to come forward to testify. As an example, in one ICTY trial of a guard at a camp where a group of women was systematically raped, the only indictment of sexual assault charged in the case was a sexual attack against a male victim.[42]

Nonetheless, later decisions show that the tribunals seemed to endorse and develop important aspects of the legacy of the *Akayesu* definition of sexual violence, particularly regarding the element of non-consent, even while adhering to the specifics of the *Furundžija* definition. In *Kunarac*, for example, the ICTY explicitly specified that "[c]onsent . . . must be consent given voluntarily, as a result of the victim's free will, assessed in the context of the surrounding circumstances," thus leaving the door open to consider the inherent coerciveness of certain circumstances. Notably, the ICTY Appeals Chamber in *Kunarac*, noting that the victims were held captive and raped by the armed men guarding them, argued that "[s]uch detentions amount to circumstances that were so coercive as to negate any possibility of consent."[43] Moreover, in the *Muhimana* decision, the ICTR argued that the "the physical elements of rape articulated by the ICTY Appeals Chamber in *Kunarac* simply specify the parameters of what constitutes 'a physical invasion of a sexual nature' amounting to rape"—essentially subsuming the *Kunarac/Furundžija* definition under the umbrella of the *Akayesu* definition (perhaps showing the value of adopting a "conceptual framework" definition in the first place).[44] On this closer reading of subsequent cases, the *Akayesu* definition of rape was more influential for later cases at the tribunals than it might appear on the surface.

While the jurisprudence of the tribunals on the status of sexual violence has been influential in international law, it has also contributed to efforts to reform domestic law regarding sexual violence in national legal contexts as well. Defining rape in a way that makes it a prosecutable crime comparable to other crimes is a major hurdle to the effective prosecution of rape in national jurisdictions the world over. The United States is currently engaged in a widespread effort to revise criminal definitions of various forms of sexual violence, largely in response to the widely recognized fact that such violence, whose victims are disproportionately women and children, is not only difficult to prosecute but difficult to even reliably track. Some of the changes are moving slowly in the direction of the standard that the ICTR used in *Akayesu*, in particular by moving away from proving non-consent and the presence of force, and explicitly recognizing background coercive circumstances. The FBI, for example, only in 2013 revised its long-standing definition of rape as "the carnal knowledge of a female forcibly and against her will."[45] The new definition still emphasizes consent, but removes reference to force. What it doesn't do, which the *Akayesu* definition did, is to recognize that background social conditions can be coercive, including, as many feminists argue, background conditions of women's inequality with men in their social and political communities. However, at the same time, two states, California and Illinois, "incorporating *Akayesu's* insight," have more recently defined criminal rape as "[a] physical intrusion or physical invasion of a sexual nature under coercive conditions,"[46] thereby eliminating lack of consent as an element of the crime to be proven, as well as recognizing that background conditions may be inherently coercive.

FEMINIST CRITIQUE

Some feminists have sharply criticized these developments in international criminal law regarding sexual violence, and the form of feminist theory that supports them. In this section, I consider arguments primarily from Karen Engle and Janet Halley, both of whose work is often cited by critics of feminist advocacy regarding the sexual violence trials at the ad hoc tribunals. In their view, feminists like MacKinnon adopt a problematic account of women's subordination as a pervasive, systemic social structure, and are in the grip of a "hyper attention to sex" as the primary means by which women are subordinated.[47] Engle's and Halley's wide-ranging critiques allege (among other things) that "structural feminism" (so understood), especially when translated into legal rules and procedures, threatens to undermine women's agency, insofar as it renders women legally incapable of consenting to sex under certain circumstances, and may lead to problematic unintended consequences in the form of legal overreach and false convictions. While I don't have space here for a fully detailed assessment of their critiques, I show in this section that my arguments earlier in this chapter suggest that these critiques are not ultimately convincing in several key respects. At the same time, I argue that their critical arguments pose problematic unintended consequences of their own.

Engle has extensively critiqued the tribunals' work on sexual violence cases, especially including feminist advocacy in favor of applying a broad structural approach to examining the criminal elements of sexual violence.

In Engle's view, a structural feminist perspective obscures the fact that some women may have been perpetrators in the relevant conflict, rather than victims, and fails to recognize that some women, even in circumstances of armed conflict, might freely choose to enter into sexual relationships with soldiers from "the other side." She is particularly critical of the tribunals' treatment of consent. As she describes it, the appellate decision in *Kunarac* "uses the fact that women were detained in what it described as 'de facto military headquarters, detention centres and apartments maintained as soldiers' residences' to conclude that these 'amount[ed] to circumstances that were so coercive as to negate any possibility of consent.'"[48] This is problematic, in her view, because it "makes consensual sexual relationships legally impossible in some sets of circumstances."[49] The practical motivation for her concern is that the defendant in the case had claimed that a woman he took from forced detention and had sex with had actually initiated that sexual contact, hence it was not rape. But her larger concern is that she thinks the law, as understood in the *Kunarac* appellate chambers, would legally prohibit women from freely choosing sexual activity under certain circumstances, essentially legally disabling women's sexual agency in the relevant circumstances. Janet Halley also worries about the implications of the same case:

> *Kunarac* inferred nonconsent from the "coercive circumstances" of armed conflict in the Foča region and presumed coercion on the basis of the victims' detention. It's very possible that this holding will be understood just as it is written: detention in large camps constitutes coercive circumstances sufficient to negative the victim's consent. But *none* of the rapes charged in *Kunarac* happened in the large detention centers: *all* of them involved victims taken from such places (and possibly elsewhere) to apartments and homes in the region and raped there.[50]

On their face, the practical import of the specific concerns that Halley and Engle raise about *Kunarac* may seem somewhat remote. For example, Halley does not affirmatively state that the coercive circumstances must have terminated the moment the women were removed from the detention camps, a view that is deeply implausible on its face. Moreover, Engle does not consider the possibility that perhaps it is completely appropriate that humanitarian law should prohibit armed soldiers supervising civilians in forced detention from having sex with those civilians. In fact, there are important normative questions here, regarding (for example) how to balance the risks of wrongful prosecution against the possibility that some circumstances may in fact be inherently coercive. However, given that they do not engage in close normative inquiry about these questions, it seems fair to conclude that the concerns that motivate Engle and Halley lie elsewhere, in particular with their opposition to structural feminism itself. As Janet Halley argues, structural feminists "have long argued that, in rape trials, force, resistance, and consent/nonconsent are the wrong issues because of coercive circumstances. . . . It seems right to conclude that structural feminism will score a victory if it indeed makes nonconsent inferable from the coercive circumstances of armed conflict."[51] However, Halley also argues that this victory would be Pyrrhic at best for structural feminists, since their animating concern is that "the relevant coercive circumstance [is] male dominance." As Halley understands the logic of structural feminism, consent should be considered irrelevant to establishing rape under any conditions characterized by male dominance. However, the specific result of the appellate decision in *Kunarac* would be to make "meaningful consent" impossible in only certain circumstances involving armed conflict. This would at the same time "implicitly confirm the possibility of 'meaningful consent' in most non-war (and non-prison) settings. Structural/radical feminism would then have won a battle but lost the war."[52]

The "war" for structural feminists (as Halley sees it) is to get their preferred understanding of structural equality incorporated broadly in law, including rape law domestically and internationally. Halley's concern about this agenda is that, in her view, a slippery slope exists from the expansive conception of rape deployed in *Akayesu* or *Kunarac* to a pervasive structural feminist agenda whereby all heterosexual intercourse in war or peace is considered legally coercive, and therefore rape, due to background structural inequalities along gender lines. The reasoning would be that structural inequalities in the form of gender hierarchies create ubiquitous background circumstances that are coercive, akin to women being held in rape camps by armed guards. In this dystopian legal realm, women would be legally disempowered from freely choosing to have sex with men, because all heterosexual sex would count as rape.

Halley is also concerned about "vacating consent" in proving rape allegations because she believes that structural feminism is predisposed to focus narrowly on sexual violence and is "pretty consistently punishment-oriented," leading to a bias in structural feminist thinking toward over-criminalizing sexual encounters. However, Halley argues that rape laws cannot be made more protective of women other than by "[e]xpanding the definition of rape, subjecting it to lower burdens of proof, eliminating forms of evidence that can be used to persuade juries to acquit, taking away discretion in sentencing, [or] allowing the death penalty for rape." The predictable consequences of this are "more false positives: innocent men in jail." And, in her view, the structural feminist response to this would be: "Why should feminists care about this? The cost falls on men, and all men benefit from male privilege. Let them be afraid of being charged with and convicted of crimes that they did not commit: we'll get even more deterrence and more safety and freedom for women."[53]

However, Halley's and Engle's arguments elide the difference between two distinct ways of eliminating lack of consent from the elements of rape as a crime. The one that Halley and Engle seem to have in mind is to legally define all sex in conditions of background gender (or other) inequality as rape—but this is not MacKinnon's view. Rather, MacKinnon argues that the *Akayesu* definition of rape (which she also proposes as the basis of a standard for domestic criminal law) leaves room for elements *other than* consent for differentiating welcome sex from rape, even though she does think that most societies exist under conditions of male dominance. In MacKinnon's view, background inequalities by themselves do not constitute conditions under which all sex is rape; as she argues, "[d]espite gender being an inequality, not all sex acts under conditions of this inequality are unequal on the basis of gender, just as despite race being an inequality, friendship—an intrinsically equal concept—is possible with conscious work, however complex or fraught, across racial lines."[54] Instead, the element that differentiates welcome sex from rape, even under conditions of inequality, is whether those background inequalities were leveraged, or deployed, or taken advantage of, to facilitate the assault. This approach highlights the structural inequalities along gender lines that often make rape difficult to prosecute, but those inequalities do not by themselves constitute an element of criminal rape. The point of background inequalities for MacKinnon is not, then, that their presence makes sex (legally or morally) impermissible, but that attending to them enables a more accurate understanding of the crime itself: "To those concerned with potential overbreadth in this proposal, its goal is not to define more acts of sex as rape, but to redefine the fundamental crime in terms of the actual forces it draws upon for its realization, and to recognize the real injuries it inflicts to individuals and communities, as well as to society as a whole."[55]

MacKinnon's understanding of the practical import of the *Akayesu* definition, combined with the arguments I made earlier in this chapter, also challenge Halley's schematic perception of reforming rape law as simply raising or lowering existing standards of evidence and the ease of successful prosecution. As the *Akayesu* case study and the subsequent institutional reform of the ICTY demonstrate, reform of rape law may instead involve uncovering deeply rooted misconceptions about gender and sexual violence in society at large and in criminal law in particular. As the ICTY self-study shows, addressing such misconceptions is not a simple matter of raising or lowering evidentiary burdens. Instead, that process focuses on developing an *accurate* legal understanding of rape as a harm to its victims, which in turn requires clear-eyed assessments of actual harms suffered by real people, which may be distorted or trivialized by prevalent conceptual biases when the victims attempt to secure justice or protection under the law. In other words, reforming rape law is better characterized as a process of uncovering the previously unnoticed operation of biases (for example, about how seriously sexual violence harms its victims, or about how rape victims are expected to behave) or simple ignorance (about the social effects of the stigma of rape, for example) that are themselves traceable to structural inequalities and that may adversely affect the ability of legal institutions to fairly and equally pursue prosecutions for human rights violations. These forms of bias or ignorance can distort the functioning of entire institutions for entire populations. The injustice is magnified when those institutions are tasked with duties of justice to respond appropriately to such crimes and to uphold the equality of all as equal rights holders. Making rape more effectively prosecutable is therefore not simply a matter of lowering evidentiary standards in order to increase convictions, and does not necessarily involve "more innocent men in jail."

In fact, there is a potentially serious social cost to characterizing the reform of rape laws in the way that Halley does: it risks encouraging complacency about a severely inegalitarian status quo in which violations of women's human rights are less likely to be recognized and protected. Halley's characterization of attempts to reform this reality as simply lowering evidentiary standards, with the inevitable cost of putting innocent men in jail, implies that no changes can be made to this system without serious moral costs in the form of the violations of the rights of innocent, wrongly accused men. Refusing to go along with such reform may then seem like a taking principled stand against an illiberal feminist agenda. However, if this conclusion is based on an inaccurate caricature of the feminist agenda in the first place, as I am arguing, then the resulting erosion of support for rape law reform is in fact a moral cost with no redeeming value.

One final point on this issue. There is an important sense in which Halley's implication that the structural feminist platform for rape law reform will result in more innocent men in jail ignores an element of MacKinnon's proposal that in fact pulls in the opposite direction. As MacKinnon argues, her proposal helps to avoid the perceived need for legal "categorical prohibitions" on sex between individuals who are unequally situated in some respect. Such prohibitions may be seen as necessary to protect parties who are vulnerable due to inequality, but they may have the result that genuinely wanted sex between unequal parties is categorically criminalized. However, on MacKinnon's view, the standard for proving rape is not the mere existence of inequality, but rather whether those inequalities were leveraged by one party to coerce the other. This strategy at least theoretically obviates the need for legal prohibitions on sex between partners who may be unequal partners, for example, because one is above and the other below the age of 18.[56] In this way, the proposal in at least one respect may remove some risk of criminalizing what is in fact wanted sex. This element of MacKinnon's proposal therefore seems entirely in keeping with Halley's general orientation toward preserving sexual agency and avoiding overcriminalization of sexual activity. If this is correct, then Halley's overly broad arguments against structural feminism's influence on rape law in fact works against her own agenda. Again, the point is that casting all rape reform recommended by structural feminism as entailing unavoidable rights violations has unintended consequences of its own.

One strategy that critical theorists like Engle and Halley employ is to argue, sensibly, that a focus on a particular issue distracts from other important issues. In this vein, Engle has argued that the efforts of human rights advocates on cases like *Akayesu* are misguided because they encourage a narrow focus of attention, time, and resources on crisis situations rather than on "everyday" injustices. Her concern here is both the feminist focus on genocidal rape in particular, which she argues distracts from everyday injustices, including non-genocidal rape, and the feminist focus on criminal law in general, which she argues contributes to "carceral" solutions to social problems.[57] As Aziza Ahmed describes Engle's thesis on this point, "attention to questions of individual accountability distracts from the larger structural challenges human rights advocates care about."[58] But as I have been arguing, a focus on the "larger structural challenges human rights advocates care about" may in fact have a deep and morally significant connection to criminal legal reform. In some cases, as we have seen, attention to questions of individual accountability, including the social determination of what individuals should be held accountable for in the first place, may require careful consideration of entrenched structural inequalities, and even may require rectifying such inequalities in practice. Indeed, this is one point of the hermeneutical injustice argument I made earlier: if hermeneutical exclusion leads to epistemic injustice, which in turn leads to a misunderstanding or trivialization of the human rights of members of excluded social groups, then justice and human rights advocacy require addressing deep structural issues in the attempt to better conceptualize and institutionalize the protection of human rights equally for all. If that is correct, then it is misleading to posit that attention to criminal legal reform is necessarily in competition with structural issues, as if the attention economy of feminist and human rights activism is a zero-sum game.

Finally, Engle claims that feminist advocacy for prosecuting rape during armed conflict at the tribunals has contributed to a problematic obsession with humanitarian intervention in international politics. In her view, feminist activists and theorists who argued that mass rape in the former Yugoslavia, Rwanda, or Darfur was a form of genocide "both capitalized on emerging trends toward humanitarian intervention and furthered those trends."[59] Engle understandably objects to the overuse of humanitarian intervention due to its frequently high humanitarian costs, the possibility of "humanitarian" intervention being a cover for less well-motivated interventions, and the possibility that any particular humanitarian intervention may be counterproductive, causing further crisis, suffering, and harm.[60] However, given that there is an extensive literature about the morality of humanitarian intervention, it is surprising that Engle does not clearly defend any substantive proposal of her own regarding whether humanitarian intervention is ever permissible, despite its obvious moral and human costs, and if so, under what circumstances, or whether she is completely opposed to it under all circumstances. Unfortunately, her avoiding taking any definite position on the difficult ethical issues involved creates the impression that she is primarily interested in criticizing views that endorse intervention in any way, without taking on the argumentative burden of discerning which interventions might be justifiable and which not, or providing any grounds for thinking that they are all unjustifiable.

This emphasis on critique over offering a substantive normative position as a constructive way forward itself, again, may have severely problematic unintended consequences. As Philip Alston has argued, some strands of critical scholarship "disparage human rights by accentuating in dramatic and sometimes destructive ways the undoubted shortcomings of international human rights norms and institutions."[61] The trouble with this critical focus is not that it is critical, but that it avoids doing the work of defending a substantive normative position about what directions of reform might constitute an improvement to the status quo. For example, in her conclusion to a paper criticizing "the human rights movement's attachment to the fight against impunity and its uses of criminal law in the process," Engle notes that "[b]eing against anti-impunity is not the same as being for impunity." Instead, she describes her view as an "anti anti-impunity stance."[62] Again, this move appears to absolve her of any accountability to specify a position somewhere between anti-impunity and "being for impunity," leaving her free to offer critical analysis without defending any relevant alternatives. Indeed, nowhere in her paper does she spell out the moral costs of impunity itself, which David Luban (for one) has described eloquently (in the context of the International Criminal Court):

> the alternatives to trying murderous generals and politicians are summary punishment or impunity, each of which, in its own way, is a backhanded admission that *raison d'etat* and *Kriegsraison* are a legitimate part of public morality. Only trials can communicate the inherent criminality of political violence against the innocent. The decision not to stage criminal trials is no less an expressive act than the creation of tribunals; and the expressive contents associated with

> impunity or summary punishment are unacceptable: both are assertions that political crime lies outside the law.[63]

The larger point here is that institutions may have multiple flaws, and may be instruments of justice or injustice in more than one way. This means that attempts to reform an institution in one respect may be complicit in contributing to injustice in another. At the same time, reform may be possible along one dimension even while an institution remains flawed in other ways. For any argument purporting to assess directions of institutional reform, then, it is important to be clear about the scope and limits of criticism and its practical implications. Unfortunately, Halley and Engle largely fail to clarify the practical import of their critiques in this way. Moreover, by avoiding defending substantive normative alternatives to the views they critique, they seem to be attempting to insulate their critiques from criticism. Ultimately, then, these critiques run the risk of failing to provide clear normative guidance or assessment for feminist or human rights activists.

GENDER JUSTICE AS JUDICIAL BIAS

Beth Van Schaack argues that an important contributing factor to *Akayesu's* outcome was the fact that the trial judges were "enlightened to issues of gender justice."[64] However, some defendants before the International Tribunals argued that what may look (to feminists) like "enlightenment to gender justice" is actually a form of bias, which in turn clouds the courts' ability to conduct fair trials. Akayesu himself during his trial "suggested that the indictment had been amended because of pressure from the women's movement and that the testimony was fabricated: 'There have been some amicus curiae. There have been activities. Akayesu must be accused of rape. People, women are agitated in Rwanda. They are awakened. They are worked up to agree that they have been raped.'"[65] In another instance, the appeal in ICTY's *Furundzija* case argued for overturning the trial judgment on the grounds that Judge Florence Mumba had failed to disclose that she had served on the United Nations' Commission on the Status of Women, which had been actively involved in condemning and seeking prosecutions for the sexual violence in the Yugoslav wars. The accused moved to have Judge Mumba disqualified because "[s]he had been a member of the U.N. Commission on the Status of Women during the Yugoslav war and had participated in its work on allegations that mass rapes were occurring there."[66] As Kelly Askin notes: "The defense clearly insinuated that women judges, particularly women who have attempted to redress human rights violations against women, cannot be impartial because they are predisposed to promote a feminist agenda, and therefore they should be recused from adjudicating any cases involving crimes against women."[67]

The Appeals Chamber took the opposite view in deciding against the appeal; as they argued, "Judge Mumba's membership of the UNCSW and her general experience in the field were, by their very nature, an integral part of her qualifications for nomination as judge of the ICTY."[68] At least some scholarly commentary on this case demonstrates that it is not only criminal defendants who might find it problematic for judges to take up explicitly feminist conceptual frameworks in their work as judges. For example, responding to the appellate judgment's claim that Judge Mumba's prior work on cases involving human rights violations against women was a qualification rather than a bias, Janet Halley remarked dryly: "Feminism *as* neutrality. This is going to be hard to study."[69]

Halley appears to be assuming that deploying feminist values in judging is incompatible with judicial neutrality. This is misguided. Explaining why requires careful thinking about whether and how judicial practice may legitimately embrace moral values, a question on which philosophy has much to contribute. We can turn to the philosophy of science for guidance on analogous questions about the legitimate role of values in empirical inquiry. Feminist and pragmatist philosophers of science have long argued that scientific inquiry is unavoidably structured in a variety of respects by contextual values that "belong to the social and cultural context in which science is done."[70] The idea is that the move from empirical data to a theory that explains the data is never a purely logical inference, but rather requires "assumptions that make or imply substantive claims about the field over which one theorizes."[71] Such assumptions, which themselves may be influenced by contextual value judgments, are an ineliminable component of scientific reasoning. In this way, value judgments may figure in to entirely legitimate scientific reasoning.

Moreover, Elizabeth Anderson has argued that it may be not only legitimate but epistemically beneficial for specifically feminist contextual values to inform some empirical inquiries.[72] It is, of course, epistemically illegitimate to deploy contextual values (feminist or otherwise) in a way that drives the inquiry to a pre-determined conclusion. However, consulting specifically feminist values may in fact open up avenues for inquiry, sources of data, or hypotheses that may be obscured by status quo, non-feminist values. Anderson's example is feminist research on divorce, which understands divorce not as a necessarily negative event (the destruction of a family, with predictably negative consequences on family members) but also (at least for some people) potentially a sought-after event that liberates family members from an unhappy situation. This possibility suggests that divorce may at least sometimes have welcome or positive impacts on family members, including children. Specifically feminist contextual values may therefore point toward novel research questions and a richer array of sources of data, as well as uncovering a wider range of real-world impacts of divorce. In this way, feminist values may be more epistemically fruitful as a guide to empirical inquiry than non-feminist values.

A parallel analysis is possible for the legitimate role of feminist contextual values in judging, especially in cases involving issues of gender justice, where feminist values may help judicial reasoning overcome biases inherent in status quo interpretations of law. If reliance on contextual values is an ineliminable part of *scientific* reasoning, it is likely to play an even greater legitimate role in *judicial* reasoning. Following Anderson, we can expect that feminist values may be advantageous in structuring judicial reasoning in cases where gender justice is at issue. In this case, feminist judges would not only be permitted by the norms of good judging to deploy those values in their decisions, but more importantly, their doing so would lead to objectively better (more just) decisions than those made by non-feminist judges. Importantly, this would not be bias, but rather a question of which contextual values help judges to accurately see the issues of gender justice before them. On this analysis, skepticism (like Halley's) about whether feminist judges can be fair and unbiased rests on an overly simplistic conception of the kind of objectivity or impartiality that characterizes good judging. Calling for judges to be sensitive to issues of gender justice, including awareness of structural inequalities and their impacts in society and in law, is calling for judges to examine the contextual values they inevitably bring to the bench, and to ensure that those values enable them to be appropriately responsive to women's rights and interests.[73]

Akayesu provides an illustration of the moral and legal progress that can be made when judges adopt feminist contextual values (or a gender perspective) and prioritize a commitment to gender justice. As described earlier in this chapter, this progress includes an enhanced understanding of the legal frameworks and definitions relevant for conceptualizing sexual violence as a violation of women's rights. In this vein, the reflections of the Office of the Prosecutor (OTP) for the Yugoslav Tribunal included the observation that

> opening our minds to the possibility of charging sexual violence as an underlying act of genocide helped us move towards a more accurate approach to the legal definition of this crime. In particular, it helped us to identify misconceptions leading to an over-focus on killings as the *sine qua non* of genocide, even though the terms of the Genocide Convention (as reflected in the ICTY statute) are indisputably broader.[74]

Thus, an institutional framework committed to gender equality may in some cases provide more insight into both the morality and law of human rights than a framework reflecting non-feminist, status quo values, or a non-institutional framework incapable of theorizing systemic inequalities.

CONCLUSION

The overall point of the arguments in this chapter is to demonstrate the importance of an appropriately institutional and political perspective for understanding human rights morality, in particular by further supporting the centrality of structural equality as part of the political morality of human rights and as a significant element of human rights practice. It is only with an institutional focus that the impacts of deeply entrenched forms of bias can become apparent. This is one reason why it is important for philosophers to attend to the institutions of international law, since these institutions provide authoritative venues that help to both reveal and begin to rectify structural injustices, especially when they manifest as substantive (if not formal) legal inequalities. My responses to Halley and Engle are a significant component of this overall argument given that their arguments at times oppose structural forms of analysis in feminist legal theory, and at other times simply misread the implications of such analysis. Overall, then, the emphasis of my arguments in this chapter is on the institutional significance of *Akayesu* and its impacts, including both rectifying an institutional hermeneutical injustice in international criminal law and contributing to reform of rape law both domestically and internationally. My further point is that attention to these dimensions of the actual case study is instructive for theorizing human rights morality. Traditional philosophical methods of abstract reasoning cannot, on their own, identify the institutional mechanisms by which structural inequalities in fact impact the enjoyment of human rights or provide avenues for rectifying them. Studying the practice therefore points toward important moral facts within the practice that are essential to an accurate description of the practice and informed moral theorizing about it.

NOTES

1. Janet Fleischman and Binaifer Nowrojee, "In Rwanda, Too, Rape Was a War Crime and Must Be Punished," *New York Times,* July 25, 1996, https://www.nytimes.com/1996/07/25/opinion/IHT-in-rwanda-too-rape-was-a-war-crime-and-must-be-punished.html?searchResultPosition=1.

2. Dianne Luping, "Investigation and Prosecution of Sexual and Gender-Based Crimes Before the International Criminal Court," *American University Journal of Gender, Social Policy, and the Law* 17 (2009): 445.

3. Luping, "Investigation and Prosecution of Sexual and Gender-Based Crimes," 446.

4. Judith Matloff, "The War Crime No One Wants to Talk About," *New York Times,* September 22, 2020, https://www.nytimes.com/2020/09/22/books/review/our-bodies-their-battlefields-christina-lamb.html.

5. Justice Teresa Doherty, "Sexual Violence and the Role of International Courts," *New Zealand Journal of Public and International Law* 11 (2013): 693–705.

6. Beth Van Schaack, "Engendering Genocide: The *Akayesu* Case Before the International Criminal Tribunal for Rwanda," in *Human Rights Advocacy Stories,* ed. Deena Hurwitz and Margaret Satterthwaite (New York: Thomson Reuters/Foundation Press, 2009), 193–227.

7. Patricia Viseur Sellers, "Gender Strategy Is Not Luxury for International Courts Symposium: Prosecuting Sexual and Gender-Based Crimes Before International/ized Criminal Courts," *American University Journal of Gender, Social Policy and the Law* 17, no. 2 (2009).

8. Michele Mitchell and Nick Louvel (directors), *The Uncondemned* (New York: Film at Eleven Media, 2015); The Ad Hoc History Project: An Interview with Patricia Viseur Sellers (International Center for Ethics, Justice, and Public Life at Brandeis University, 2017); Sellers, "Gender Strategy Is Not Luxury."

9. Serge Brammertz and Michelle Jarvis (eds.), *Prosecuting Conflict-Related Sexual Violence at the ICTY* (Oxford: Oxford University Press, 2016).

10. Brammertz and Jarvis, *Prosecuting*, 4.

11. Brammertz and Jarvis, *Prosecuting*, 4.

12. Michelle Jarvis and Kate Vigneswaran, "Challenges to Successful Outcomes in Sexual Violence Cases," in Brammertz and Jarvis, *Prosecuting*, 36. The authors also note that this misconception about sexual violence is "reflected in legal frameworks governing national rape prosecutions, which result in notoriously low rates of conviction."

13. Keith Burgess-Jackson, "A History of Rape Law," in Keith Burgess-Jackson (ed.), *A Most Detestable Crime: New Philosophical Essays on Rape* (New York: Oxford University Press, 1999).

14. The Ad Hoc Tribunals Oral History Project, *Oral History Interview with Patricia Viseur Sellers* (International Center for Ethics, Justice, and Public Life, Brandeis University, 2017), 20.

15. Ad Hoc Tribunals Oral History Project, *Interview with Patricia Viseur Sellers*, 21.

16. Brammertz and Jarvis, *Prosecuting*, 5.

17. Jarvis and Vigneswaran, "Challenges," 37.

18. Jarvis and Vigneswaran, "Challenges," 39.

19. Jarvis and Vigneswaran, "Challenges," 40.

20. Brammertz and Jarvis, *Prosecuting*, 6.

21. Miranda Fricker, *Epistemic Injustice: Power and the Ethics of Knowing* (Oxford: Oxford University Press, 2007), Ch. 7, "Hermeneutical Injustice."

22. Jennifer Nedelsky, "Receptivity and Judgment," *Ethics and Global Politics* 4, no. 4 (2011): 231–54. DOI: 10.3402/egp.v4i4.15116

23. Nedelsky, "Receptivity," 237.

24. Brammertz and Jarvis, *Prosecuting*, 10–11.

25. Michelle Jarvis, "Overview: The Challenge of Accountability for Conflict-related Sexual Violence Crimes," in Brammertz and Jarvis, *Prosecuting*, 11–12.

26. Jarvis, "Overview," 12.

27. Jarvis, "Overview," 13.

28. Importantly, a gender perspective is not just a women's perspective. The ICTY self-study showed that a failure to apprehend the social meanings of sexual violence led to a failure to understand and appropriately respond to sexual violence when men were the victims, although in a different way than when women were victims.

29. Trial Chamber Judgment, *Akayesu*, Case No. ICTR-96–4-T, at para. 596.

30. Trial Chamber Judgment, *Akayesu*, Case No. ICTR-96–4-T, at para. 597.

31. Trial Chamber Judgment, *Akayesu*, Case No. ICTR-96–4-T, at para. 597.

32. Trial Chamber Judgment, *Akayesu*, Case No. ICTR-96–4-T, at para. 598.

33. For example, the Universal Declaration of Human Rights discusses the equal rights of men and women in the Preamble and regarding marriage rights, but discusses women specifically only in Article 25(2), asserting that "[m]otherhood and childhood are entitled to special care and assistance." (Louise Chappell, "Women, Gender, and International Institutions: Exploring New Opportunities at the International Criminal Court," *Policy and Society* 22, no. 1 [2003]: 5–8.)

34. Chappell, "Women, Gender, and International Institutions," 11.

35. Suzanne Chenault, "And since *Akayesu*? The Development of ICTR Jurisprudence on Gender Crimes: A Comparison of *Akayesu* and *Muhimana*," *New England Journal of International and Comparative Law* 14, no. 2 (2008): 225.

36. Catharine MacKinnon, "Rape Redefined," *Harvard Law and Policy Review* 10 (2016): 431.

37. MacKinnon, "Rape Redefined," 447.

38. Catharine MacKinnon, "Defining Rape Internationally: A Comment on Akayesu," *Columbia Journal of Transnational Law* 44 (2006): 955.

39. Chenault, "And since *Akayesu*?," 225.

40. Alex Obote-Odora, "Rape and Sexual Violence in International Law: ICTR Contribution," *New England Journal of International and Comparative Law* 12, no. 1 (2005): 152.

41. Obote-Odora, "Rape and Sexual Violence in International Law," 154. Citing *Gacumbitsi*, ICTR 2001–64-T, Judgment at paragraph 325.

42. MacKinnon, "Defining Rape Internationally," 947.

43. MacKinnon, "Defining Rape Internationally," 951.

44. Chenault, "And since *Akayesu*?," 232.

45. The new definition is as follows: "Penetration, no matter how slight, of the vagina or anus with any body part or object, or oral penetration by a sex organ of another person, without the consent of the victim," https://www.fbi.gov/about-us/cjis/ucr/recent-program-updates/new-rape-definition-frequently-asked-questions (accessed May 25, 2016).

46. MacKinnon, "Defining Rape Internationally," 956 n.74.

47. Karen Engle, "Feminist Legacies," *American Journal of International Law Unbound* 110 (2016): 220.

48. Karen Engle, "Feminism and Its (Dis)Contents: Criminalizing Wartime Rape in Bosnia and Herzegovina," *American Journal of International Law* 99 (2005): 804.

49. Engle, "Feminism and Its (Dis)Contents," 804.

50. Janet Halley, Prabha Kotiswaran, Hila Shamir, and Chantal Thomas, "From the International to the Local in Feminist Legal Responses to Rape, Prostitution/Sex Work, and Sex Trafficking: Four Studies in Contemporary Governance Feminism," *Harvard Journal of Law and Gender* 29 (2006): 380 (emphasis original).

51. Halley et al., "From the International to the Local," 380–81.

52. Halley et al., "From the International to the Local," 381.

53. Aziz Ahmed, "Janet Halley in Conversation with Aziz Ahmed: Interview," in *Beyond Virtue and Vice: Rethinking Human Rights and Criminal Law*, ed. Alice Miller and Mindy Roseman (Philadelphia: University of Pennsylvania Press, 2019), 29–30.

54. MacKinnon, "Rape Redefined," 471.

55. MacKinnon, "Rape Redefined," 477.

56. MacKinnon, "Rape Redefined," 471.

57. Karen Engle, "Anti-Impunity and the Turn to Criminal Law in Human Rights," *Cornell Law Review* 200, no. 5 (2015): 1069–127.

58. Aziza Ahmed, "Women's Rights, Human Rights and the Criminal Law, or, Feminist Debates and Responses to [De]Criminalization and Sexual and Reproductive Health," *American Society of International Law Proceedings* (2018): 88.

59. Karen Engle, "'Calling in the Troops': The Uneasy Relationship Among Women's Rights, Human Rights, and Humanitarian Intervention," *Harvard Human Rights Journal* 20 (2007): 190.

60. "I am uneasy with the idea that destroying life and infrastructure is a way to demonstrate concern for a particular place or situation, especially when most of history has shown that such intervention—regardless of motivation—rarely improves the lives of the individuals who are the stated subjects of intervention." (Engle, "Calling in the Troops," 190.)

61. Philip Alston, "The Populist Challenge to Human Rights," *Journal of Human Rights Practice* 9 (2017): 13.

62. Engle, "Anti-Impunity," 1127.

63. David Luban, "Fairness to Rightness: Jurisdiction, Legality, and the Legitimacy of International Criminal Law," in *The Philosophy of International Law,* ed. Samantha Besson and John Tasioulas (Oxford: Oxford University Press, 2010), 576.

64. Van Schaack, "Engendering Genocide," 227.

65. Van Schaack, "Engendering Genocide," 207–8.

66. Halley et al., "From the International to the Local," 336–423.

67. Kelly Askin, "Women's Issues in International Criminal Law: Recent Developments and the Potential Contribution of the ICC," in *International Crimes, Peace, and Human Rights: The Role of the International Criminal Court,* ed. Dinah Shelton (New York: Transnational Publishers, Inc., 2000), 57.

68. Halley et al., "From the International to the Local," 345.

69. Halley et al., "From the International to the Local," 345.

70. Helen Longino, "Can There Be a Feminist Science?" *Hypatia* 2, no. 3 (1987): 54.

71. Longino, "Can There Be a Feminist Science?," 55.

72. Elizabeth Anderson, "Uses of Value Judgments in Science: A General Argument, with Lessons from a Case Study of Feminist Research on Divorce," *Hypatia* 19, no. 1 (2004).

73. I discuss this argument at greater length in Kristen Hessler, "Women Judges or Feminist Judges?: Gender Representation and Feminist Values in International Courts," *Journal of Social Philosophy* 52, no. 4 (2021): 459–72.

74. Brammertz and Jarvis, *Prosecuting*, 9–10.

Chapter 6

Engaged Moral Inquiry

My main goal in this chapter is to further develop a few of the implications of my overall argument, and to respond to several objections to it. After summarizing the argument of the book in the first section, I then turn to a moral evaluation of the overall legacy of the ad hoc tribunals. I argue that it is important to attend to the broader social functions of the tribunals in an overall assessment of their accomplishments. On this broader accounting, while their achievement of some goals may be contested, there are also important and concrete ways in which they have contributed to both a better public understanding of human rights morality and constitute an important component of women's equal standing. In the following section, I emphasize various ways in which the potential for morally progressive development in international law enabled feminist advocacy to play a significant role in the development of the international criminal tribunals, and later the ICC. The larger point of this argument is that the aims and goals of participants in the practice should inform the moral standards used for assessment and evaluation of the resulting institutions. I then argue that a practice-based approach provides novel ways for thinking about the standards of normative legitimacy for international institutions. Next, I consider and respond to an objection to my view that sees it as merely advancing a practical understanding of how to implement human rights morality, but that does not illuminate the philosophical project of theorizing human rights. My response argues that the objection itself betrays the grip of the overly stark version of the distinction between facts and values that I critiqued in Chapter 1. Finally, I address two concerns about my reliance on international criminal law in my case study. The first is that it has no clear connection to human rights morality, and the second is that this focus is in tension with feminist critiques of criminal law.

THE ARGUMENT

The point of my argument in this book has been to sketch the outlines of a methodology for a feminist political philosophy of human rights. This approach starts with the conviction that deeply rooted, systemic inequalities make it difficult not only to realize women's human rights but also to adequately understand their requirements even in the abstract. Therefore, a feminist approach needs to deploy explicitly institutional and political concepts, in order to adequately account for the practical and epistemic challenges posed by structural inequalities.

For that reason, this approach is, of necessity, a political account of human rights morality understood in a broad sense, rather than an account of which moral human rights exist and how they are to be justified. A political morality specifies grounding values that can be used to assess the functioning of these institutions over time, including directions for their reform and future development. This is the first sense in which the account is political: that is, in utilizing explicitly political terms of theorizing to assess a range of social and political realities, including the functioning of institutions of international law.

At the same time, I have emphasized the potential for human rights practice to improve its own understanding of its grounding values over time, as well as their realization in practice. Awareness of the existence of social hierarchies and their effects on human rights fulfillment in the real world is therefore a component of both a full understanding of human rights morality and of any feasible attempt to implement moral human rights in practice. These institutions also provide particularly visible mechanisms and venues (trials at criminal tribunals or treaty body proceedings, for example) whereby deeply entrenched social hierarchies may be productively challenged and upended, not only symbolically, but also in ways that constitute concrete advances toward the realization of status equality and equal human rights. This indicates a second sense in which the approach I'm recommending is political and institutional: that is, it looks to the actual functioning of legal and political institutions over time for evidence that is salient to a full understanding of human rights morality.

One implication of this form of political approach is that it gives the foundational values of human rights morality a distinctively *political* role in justifying or critiquing legal human rights (or other aspects of human rights law and practice). This route situates the grounding values of human rights morality within an account of the political morality of the relevant institutions. Those values therefore play a direct role in assessing and guiding how those institutions (should) function, together with the appropriate political considerations inherent to the institutions (such as, for example, on whom they have the authority to impose legal duties of various kinds). Rather than conceptualizing IHRL as giving effect to moral human rights, then, a political account may instead conceptualize IHRL as giving institutional effect to the values of status equality and protection of individuals' interests via a system of uniform legal rights for all persons.

The critical argument I have made in this book is that neither orthodox theories, nor political theories in their most familiar versions, can adequately recognize international institutions and practices as sources of moral knowledge which are essential to a full understanding moral human rights, beyond their thinnest and most abstract formulations. Orthodox methods in particular subscribe to an overly stark version of the distinction between facts and values, and (in turn) to a disciplinary division of labor that locates processes of moral discovery solely in abstract philosophical reasoning. Their Achilles' heel, therefore, is the question of their relevance to human rights practice. Existing political theories, while clearly relevant to the practice (or at least to a particular interpretation of it) struggle to explain the normativity of their views, and why they are not simply positivist descriptions of the practice. To solve this problem, the methodology I have suggested draws on the pragmatist insight that social practices are themselves sources of normativity that philosophers have good reason to take up into their theorizing as evidence regarding the truth of our moral claims, and about whether they are apt for the social and political contexts in which they operate. Human rights practice in particular is suffused with explicitly normative aims and self-justifications. An appropriately political philosophy of human rights morality, one that engages in critical reflection on the moral insights and debates within the practice, can stake a clear claim to be relevant to the practice and to provide normative guidance for it. The standards philosophers use as the basis of a moral assessment of the practice, and for critical reflection on the values of human rights morality in the first place, should be informed by the normative discourses within various aspects of the practice.

One result of this move is greater engagement with less-abstract normative questions that emerge from the practice itself. Orthodox and existing political theories generally aim to assess or critique the practice from a distance and at a high level of abstraction. The methodology I'm suggesting focuses on moral questions that emerge from the practice itself, and its assessments of the practice are intended to be in terms that are at least closer to those that competent participants in the practice would recognize as deeply relevant to its animating moral concerns. Closer attention to these concerns can reveal possibilities that do not fit the existing conceptual commitments of even practical theories of human rights (like Charles Beitz's). Philosophy done in these terms, as I hope my case study shows, may focus on more concrete and less abstract moral questions and issues, which are often fascinating and sometimes morally inspiring in their own right.

ASSESSING THE TRIBUNALS

The primary goal of criminal trials is to assess the guilt or innocence of the accused. In practice, however, they often have much broader social or political significance and serve larger social and political functions. For example, in international criminal law, as David Luban notes, the goals of trials include "promoting social reconciliation, giving victims a voice, or making a historical record of mass atrocities to help secure the past against deniers and revisionists."[1] In this section, I consider the extent to which the tribunals have achieved such broader goals. Highlighting the fact that the tribunals were in fact deeply flawed, I argue that they can nonetheless be seen as part of a morally welcome trajectory in several ways. Moreover, I argue that the broader moral functions of these criminal trials need to be considered as part of an overall moral assessment specifically regarding the sexual violence jurisprudence, including *Akayesu*.

In the aftermath of the violence in Rwanda and the former Yugoslavia, it was hoped that the trials at the ICTY and ICTR would help to ensure criminal accountability of the guilty, but also "to deter the repetition of such crimes, to remove the perpetrators from positions of power and influence, to give victims and victim groups a sense of justice, to encourage reconciliation, and to demonstrate the determined opposition of the international community to atrocity crimes."[2] The president of the ICTR, in a 2014 speech commemorating the twentieth anniversary of the 1994 founding of the tribunal, claimed that the ICTR helped to reaffirm and publicize norms of justice and accountability:

> In 1998, the ICTR became the first international tribunal since Nuremberg and Tokyo to issue a judgement against a former head of government and demonstrated that in the fight against impunity no person is immune from accountability. The Tribunal also rendered the first judgement examining the role of the media with respect to direct and public incitement to commit genocide. It is now recognised that civilians can also be prosecuted for international crimes when they participate in hostilities.[3]

Similarly, a statement on the ICTY's website maintains that one of its legacies has been to establish a historical record, thereby contributing to stability and justice in the former Yugoslavia:

> The Tribunal has established beyond a reasonable doubt crucial facts related to crimes committed in the former Yugoslavia. In doing so, the Tribunal's judges have carefully reviewed testimonies of eyewitnesses, survivors and perpetrators, forensic data and often previously unseen documentary and video evidence. The Tribunal's judgments have contributed to creating a historical record, combatting denial and preventing attempts at revisionism and providing the basis for future transitional justice initiatives in the region.[4]

These are indeed important post-conflict objectives, and it seems reasonable to expect that criminal trials for those responsible for atrocities during armed conflict would contribute to achieving them. However, some observers argue that the ad hoc tribunals may not have contributed as much as might be desired to the goals of reconciliation and establishing an authoritative historical record in the societies attempting to move on after the conflicts. Regarding the ICTY, for example, Marko Milanovic reports that, according to public opinion surveys conducted in the countries of the former Yugoslavia, "denialism and revisionism are not just alive and well in the former Yugoslavia—they are thriving."[5] Particularly discouraging are the findings that in Serbia, Croatia, Bosnia and Herzegovina, and Kosovo, people's confidence in the ICTY, and their beliefs about which ethnic groups committed or suffered crimes during the conflicts of the 1990s, are strongly influenced by their ethnic group membership. Regarding crimes like the massacre of Muslim men and boys in Srebrenica, for example, Milanovic reports that "twenty years on, barely one-fifth of the Bosnian Serb population believe that any crime (let alone genocide) happened in Srebrenica, while two-fifths say that they had never even heard of any such crime."[6] But it was not only Serbs whose ethnic identity colored their view of what actually occurred. Each ethnic group was much more likely to have heard of crimes committed by other ethnic groups, and to rank their own ethnic group as the one that suffered the most during the conflicts. According to Milanovic:

> The surveys thus show that victimhood narratives, in which one's own group is seen as the principal victim of crimes, and others as the principal perpetrators, are thriving in the Balkans. . . . [T]he surveys clearly show that the different ethnic communities in the former Yugoslavia are (still) engaged in competitive victimhood, which is a major impediment to mutual forgiveness and reconciliation.[7]

The ability of the ICTR to establish an authoritative historical record that can contribute to reconciliation within Rwanda may also be similarly compromised. One analysis points out that "[t]he extent to which the Tribunal's historical record will be accepted in Rwanda will be shaped by the political context within which it is received."[8] This context is one in which "the country's official history is written by the government, with little space for critical engagement."[9] Consequently, supporters of the government may simply endorse the government's praise for ICTR convictions and criticize acquittals, while government opponents may reject the legitimacy of the court and its legacy entirely. This evidence shows that while reconciliation and a common understanding of the past might be most needed in deeply divided communities in the aftermath of armed conflict, this is also precisely where they are also most difficult to come by. The deep and enduring social and political divisions in post-conflict societies may undermine the potential for conflict-related criminal trials to achieve more ambitious social aims, or even their prospects of being regarded as legitimate or authoritative in the first place.

It is also important to acknowledge that criminal tribunals, and criminal law generally, cannot by themselves achieve full justice: they (of course) cannot undo crimes, bring back the dead, restore the injured to health, or reinstate the pre-conflict status quo. Criminal trials also cannot rectify larger social and political injustices that may have contributed to sparking the conflict in the first place, or to the prevalence of particular forms of violence within it. As Kirsten Campbell has pointed out, "international prosecutions of sexual violence alone do not provide gender justice, whether in terms of addressing the individual material and social needs of survivors, or the broader collective challenge of transforming gendered inequalities."[10]

Indeed, the tribunals' successful prosecutions for sexual violence have not necessarily been followed by similar successes regarding more recent armed conflicts. Simply developing the conceptual and prosecutorial tools in international law to prosecute sexual violence in armed conflict does not mean that it will in fact be prosecuted. One proof of this is the fact that, while the ICC's mandate makes sexual violence prosecutable as both a war crime and a crime against humanity, and despite the persistence of sexual violence in armed conflict, the ICC has yielded exactly one sexual violence conviction, issued in 2019, since it began work in 2002.[11] As Victoire Mukambanda argued, years after she testified as a rape survivor in the *Akayesu* trial at the ICTR:

> much still remains to be done. There are so many others like me—the Yezidi victims of ISIS, the women of San Salvador Atenco in Mexico who were raped by security forces, my neighbors in the Democratic Republic of the Congo who have endured systematic rapes, girls forced into marriage by militants in Mali—who have struggled to find justice and whose voices have not been heard. I hope that my case shows them you can to make a difference, that justice is a possibility.[12]

It is therefore important to nurture a healthy awareness of the limits, ambiguities, and shortcomings of the tribunals' accomplishments. However, as Mukambanda's statement emphasizes, it is at the same time important to consider the tribunals significant innovations and successes alongside their shortcomings.

One significant element of the moral significance of the tribunals' jurisprudence on sexual violence is that, while trials and legal verdicts do not alone transform gendered inequalities, they may nonetheless constitute an important step toward achieving gender equality. As was apparent in *Akayesu*, many observable gendered inequalities are partially constituted by women's *de facto* lesser legal and social status. This has the effect that distinctively gendered harms suffered disproportionately by women are not commonly understood nor legally regarded as the human rights violations that they are, which in turn supports the continuation of a status quo in which women's rights, even basic rights to bodily security, do not receive equal legal or social recognition and protection. The *Akayesu* case, and the further developments it helped to trigger in both international law and some domestic jurisdictions, facilitated the reconceptualization of sexual violence as a human rights violation that should be prosecuted according to the same principles as other kinds of physical violence. As such, it has contributed in a significant and substantive way in transforming some particularly problematic forms of gendered inequality.

Moreover, in addition to constituting a public manifestation of women's equal standing, the trials also played an important educative function regarding human rights morality. Allowing sexual violence to go unremarked in legal adjudication of the genocide would have sent a powerful message about the relative severity of the harms inflicted by such violence and a commentary on the legal standing of the victims of such violence. The successful prosecution of such crimes plays an important educative function by emphasizing in a public legal forum that this kind of violence constitutes a violation of human rights. In turn, this can further contribute to reforming women's social and legal standing by shifting public perception and attitudes.[13] As Catharine MacKinnon argues, "[t]he real point of law is not incarceration or damage awards anyway but voluntary compliance, otherwise known as legal socialization or education."[14] As an example of this kind of effect of criminal trials, Kathryn Sikkink, writing about the trials of deposed military leaders in Argentina in the 1980s, argues that they played an important role in convincing the broader population that the military regime was responsible for disappearances, torture, and other crimes. Many in Argentina had supported the military coup, and did not accept that the military would have committed such crimes. Against this background, " . . . the trials were a national event, a public spectacle that had the purpose of punishing the guilty, reaffirming certain norms, and creating a national understanding of the past."[15] In Sikkink's view, such trials can also function as a deterrent to backsliding into another criminal regime. As she argues: "If the trials prevent future human rights violations . . . it will not only be because they punish the perpetrators. It is also because the ritual or symbolism of a trial, the evidence presented, and the apparent neutrality of the process convinces broader parts of society that the perpetrators deserve punishment."[16]

Another further impact of the trials is their public demonstration to the victims that their social and legal communities utterly condemned the violence they suffered and were willing to punish the perpetrators. Indeed, the women who testified at Akayesu's trial expressed after the guilty verdict that, while nothing could undo the harms they had suffered, the feeling of being vindicated by law at the very least constituted a form of social confirmation of their own humanity.

Finally, beyond punishing the perpetrators, an important goal of criminal law is, as MacKinnon argues, to make the criminalized conduct "exceptional, then extinct."[17] Of course, simply changing laws, by itself, cannot change behavior. But law plays an important social role over time including via socialization, education, and as a manifestation of social values and the equal standing of all persons before the law, in addition to the bare purpose of punishment. None of this implies that the tribunals' virtues outweighed their flaws, all things considered. But these further ends served by the sexual violence trials must be considered as part of an overall moral assessment of them.

INTERNATIONAL COURTS AS A VENUE FOR LEGAL INNOVATION AND FEMINIST ADVOCACY

The innovations of the *Akayesu* decision were possible in no small part due to the fact that the case was heard before an international court. A further dimension of an overall moral assessment of the tribunals' jurisprudence on sexual violence is that they represent the conscious efforts of activists to harness the potential of international legal forums for development of law and international institutions in a progressive direction. International legal institutions may provide novel opportunities for victims' voices to be heard, to provide fertile ground for grasping the human rights significance of victims' testimony, and to create actionable remedies for existing human rights violations that may not be possible to achieve at the national level.

As Louise Chappell has emphasized, the dynamic nature of international law has enabled mobilized women's groups to influence the structure of international institutions and the norms they deploy. As Chappell argues,

> the law, as with other institutions, is not fixed but dynamic and open to challenge. Opportunities to contest gender assumptions can arise periodically either through the development of case law or from the creation of new institutions. When the two occur simultaneously—such as with the development of jurisprudence at the International Criminal Tribunals for Yugoslavia and for Rwanda and the creation of the ICC—a window of opportunity emerges and the chances of challenging existing assumptions appear all the greater.[18]

Chappell's point is in broad alignment with Kathryn Sikkink's argument that civil society activism has been one of the main drivers of the movement to develop norms of individual accountability for human rights violations, including in the processes leading to the creation of the International Criminal Court. Following the Nuremburg and Tokyo tribunals after World War II, Sikkink argues that individual accountability for human rights violations in international law developed out of intertwined processes at both the national and international levels.[19] Within states that had experienced disappearances and torture under dictatorial regimes, such as in Greece, Argentina, and Uruguay, activists and lawyers led efforts to establish domestic accountability for human rights violations. At the same time, these activists were also participants in international networks working to develop international human rights standards and mechanisms of accountability, including new international conventions on torture and apartheid, and eventually working toward the establishment of the ICC. Many of these activists regarded such international efforts as essential for backing up and enforcing domestic efforts toward individual accountability for widespread human rights abuses.[20] Importantly, in post-conflict societies where securing internal accountability for crimes may be most problematic, international avenues of achieving accountability will generally be most useful.

Like Chappell, Sikkink emphasizes the human effort and activism involved in bringing about the development of norms of criminal accountability for human rights abuses in international law. International courts, treaties, and legal norms were the result of political agitation by victims, their families and their allies, who refused to simply forget the human rights abuses they had suffered. Describing the development of mechanisms and venues to pursue criminal accountability for human rights abuses as a "justice cascade," Sikkink argues that, "at each stage of the cascade, real people are deeply involved in pressing for change."[21] As she argues,

> *the political world is not static.* Human agency has the capacity to transform the conditions within which political action takes place. . . . The early cases of prosecutions altered people's expectations about the effects of trials; by altering such expectations, they made it more likely that citizens would be less fearful and more emboldened to demand justice.[22]

Activism by women's organizations in the *Akayesu* case is one example of the potential legal impact of this kind of transformative human agency. Indeed, the creation of the international tribunals in the first place was partly the result of women's activism. Julie Mertus has argued that the wars in the former Yugoslavia helped mobilize women's activism internationally in the early 1990s, which in turn helped provide the impetus to create the tribunals. As Mertus notes:

> Although the 1993 U.N. Conference on Human Rights in Vienna provided a focus and opportunity for the advocates seeking to draw attention to sexual violence in the Balkan wars, the groundwork for the advocacy campaign began before (and reached far beyond) the Vienna meeting. Transnational networks in solidarity with the women of Yugoslavia provided the backbone for the campaign, which emerged in 1992 under various banners, including the influential New York–based Women's Coalition Against Crimes Against Women in the Former Yugoslavia.[23]

As reports of sexual violence in the armed conflicts in the former Yugoslavia garnered unprecedented international attention, media reports amplified international calls for accountability.[24] In the process, "[w]omen's groups, in particular, played a pivotal role in the ICTY's establishment, through their 'mobilizing, strategizing, and lobbying efforts on behalf of prosecuting gender-based violence.'"[25]

Karen Alter applies a similar analysis to *Akayesu* in particular, arguing that "[t]he *Akayesu* case shows how delegation to [international courts] creates new opportunities for mobilized actors, in this case women's groups who were able to leverage opportunities created in court into actionable strategies, influencing legal outcomes in real time and building legal precedents that can be invoked in the future."[26] Indeed, in Alter's analysis, international courts can be expected to function in a progressive way on a wide variety of issues. As she argues: "To create an [international court] is to introduce the possibility of a legal remedy. Not only does the existence of this remedy instantiate the legal right, making it meaningful, the prospect of the remedy also mobilizes stakeholders to claim their rights."[27]

However specific cases are decided in courts, Alter argues that international courts are "part of a forward-looking project."[28] According to her dynamic view, the processes of international law progressively affect the content of international law: "Rights claimers of the future can draw inspiration, future litigants can invoke legal precedent, expectations can shift, and in the next iteration litigants, advocates, and judges can ask for more."[29] In Alter's analysis, *Akayesu* provided an opportunity for women's advocacy groups to press for accountability for gender-based crimes, and ultimately the adoption of a gender perspective in international courts, partly because of the new opportunities opened up by the international nature of the ICTR.

In addition, once they exist, international courts provide venues where establishing accountability for human rights violations may be more easily effected than in domestic courts, for several reasons. International courts may enjoy greater perceived legitimacy and neutrality than domestic courts in the aftermath of armed conflict, even when the conflict itself is not an international one. They may be more likely than domestic parties to apply criminal norms impartially due to their relative immunity to domestic political forces. Moreover, the actors involved in an international court can help to transcend the limits of what is conceivable within a particular society in terms of how to interpret and apply relevant legal norms, partly because international actors may bring to legal processes more diverse ways of conceptualizing crimes like sexual violence. Again, the ability of international courts to achieve these ends may be incomplete, especially in divisive social climates (as in the former Yugoslavia), and their legitimacy may be contested (as in Rwanda). Even so, the larger point is that international legal processes may present significant opportunities to innovate in the direction of recognizing previously unappreciated aspects of human rights and legal mechanisms for their protection.

Finally, international courts may have legal norms at their disposal that are not available in domestic courts. One important development made possible by the specifically international aspect of the tribunals was their ability to address "command responsibility" for sexual assault, which was key to Akayesu's conviction. Command responsibility "can be used to hold superiors liable when they do not do enough to detect, restrain, and punish criminality by subordinates, even if it is the subordinates, not the superiors, who instigate the crimes."[30] The legal provenance of this doctrine is distinct to international law: "Unlike the other modes of liability, which were inspired by, and transplanted from, domestic analogues, command responsibility has a distinct pedigree: it is indigenous to international law. The ICL doctrine of command responsibility is derived from the duties of commanders established in international humanitarian law."[31]

While I have been arguing that international law provides doctrines, processes, and venues that may provide the necessary conditions to innovate in a progressive direction, I do not mean to suggest that any international legal ruling will necessarily be progressive on matters of human rights. What matters is how well the procedures in place are able to respond to advocacy on behalf of human rights that may not get a hearing in other contexts, including in domestic political or legal contexts. Thus, my claim in this section is not that international courts are necessarily progressive venues for advancing women's human rights, or even for contributing to our understanding of what human rights require. Rather, the argument, following Karen Alter and Louise Chappell, is that international courts at least *may* play a uniquely progressive role in articulating and protecting women's human rights, *if* women themselves are adequately mobilized and can make themselves heard in these venues. At the same time, international courts may generate new possibilities for international coalitions of activists to influence the development of law that are not necessarily available in national courts or other contexts. These intentions on the part of agents within the practice should play a role in the overall moral assessment of the institutions themselves.

LEGITIMACY

While I have argued that the moral reasoning embedded in the institutions of international law may be instructive for philosophical theorizing, I have not provided a general account of the normative political legitimacy of those institutions. This may seem a grave omission. After all, the function of a theory of normative political legitimacy is precisely to provide an account of when the decisions or workings of an institution should be regarded as normatively authoritative. Helping myself to the assumption that philosophers should so regard the processes and decisions of various international legal institutions may therefore seem like putting the cart before the horse. Just because international court has reached a particular verdict, or just because (as Beitz notes) CEDAW "embrac[es] an open-ended entitlement to social and cultural change" specifically on behalf of women's equality, does not mean that it should have done so.[32] As Karen Alter recognizes, even apparently progressive innovations by international courts (such as the *Akayesu* verdict) may stretch or exceed the bounds of their perceived legitimacy among international actors, provoking resistance on the part of states or other international actors to their rulings.[33] As Alter notes:

> The contentious notion that international courts can be seen as constitutional bodies enforcing higher order international laws against strongly legitimated domestic actors has generated active debate. Critics of the constitutional analogy question whether treaties can or should create higher order legal obligations, whether one can have an international constitution without a corresponding *demos* that supports it, and whether international legal orders contain the types of foundational *grundnorms* one associates with legitimate constitutional orders.[34]

Importantly, this is precisely where philosophers working in the orthodox mode argue that their services are necessary for achieving the goal of a normatively coherent system of international human rights law. If the legitimacy of international legal institutions is itself contested even within the practice (as it surely is in theory), then it seems patently self-defeating to appeal to the procedures of those institutions as the source of their moral authority. Instead, they argue, this situation points precisely and powerfully to the need for philosophically foundational work that can provide an account of normative legitimacy for international legal institutions, and arguments for the moral accuracy of the human rights norms they contain. As James Griffin puts it, in defense of orthodox theorizing: "No matter who we are, we cannot establish the existence of a human right just by declaring it to be one. We can get it wrong, and we owe attention, therefore, to what are the criteria for right and wrong here."[35] John Tasioulas makes a similar point in responding to Richard Rorty regarding real-world resistance to the demands of human rights law:

> He simply forecloses on the possibility that the human rights culture might achieve enhanced "efficacy"—higher levels of acceptance and compliance throughout the globe—precisely through being furnished with a rational justification that addresses these questions and is thereby able to win over individuals, states and cultures currently resistant to the idea of human rights or beset by confusion and perplexity about it.[36]

My response is that the methodology of looking to how international courts actually function is a step forward in taking these concerns seriously, not only at an abstract theoretical level, but concretely, regarding actual processes and outcomes of international law. A theory of institutional legitimacy or of human rights morality that engages with the concrete realities of these institutions is more likely to be effective both at alleviating real-world perplexity as well as overcoming real-world resistance. Without engaging with the actual processes of international law, for example, it is very easy to describe them in rough sketches or generalities that may or may not be accurate. For example, Alter's description of international courts as "enforcing higher order international laws against strongly legitimated domestic actors" is itself revealed by the case study to be only partly accurate, insofar as it shows that international venues may create new opportunities for certain domestic actors' voices to be heard, provide fertile ground for grasping the human rights significance of what they're saying, and create actionable remedies for existing human rights violations that may not be possible to achieve at the national level. This methodology can both put some concerns about legitimacy to rest, while vitiating others, as well as pointing the way toward the legitimate development of greater capacity for international law to articulate and advance human rights for women and other social groups in the future.

In this regard, it is helpful to remember the point that the institutions of international law, and human rights practice more broadly, continue to evolve. Darryl Robinson and Gillian MacNeil offer a practice-based framework that suggests a trajectory for the evolution of greater normative legitimacy for international criminal law over time. They argue that the development of international criminal law can be understood as consisting of three phases, each of which is more legitimate than the last. The first, consisting of the international courts established by the victorious allies after World War II, they label "victor's justice." These tribunals "entailed, inter alia, retroactive laws tailored to the crimes of one's vanquished foes."[37] The second phase, consisting of the ad hoc international tribunals, they refer to as Security Council Justice, which marked "a significant improvement over victor's justice" insofar as it was more impartial (not implemented by one side to the conflict). However, they note that the tribunals "tended to adopt sweeping principles and fairly open-ended definitions of crimes," a tendency that they see as following from the fact that these rules were designed by actors representing the international community "primarily to be applied to 'others' (the parties involved in the conflict)."[38] Finally, they characterize the ICC's Rome Conference as exemplifying "community justice," in which "all states are invited to shape rules that will apply prospectively."[39] They argue that the model of community justice, while it may still be aspirational, is more legitimate, as it involves more input from more states, and more consistent with the rule of law, insofar as rules are adopted prospectively.

On this view, the tribunals occupy a kind of transitional status in the development of normatively legitimate international criminal law. On one hand, this suggests that they are lacking full normative legitimacy. As my framework has emphasized, however, it is important not to lose sight of the fact that such institutions have resources for improving their own legitimacy over time. The institutionalized reforms recommended by the ICTY regarding the prosecution of sexual violence is (as I argued in the previous chapter) one example of this phenomenon. But Robinson and MacNeil's thesis suggests that this institutional bootstrapping may be a feature of international legal institutions in a broader sense. Again, the point is that attention to practice-based standards for the moral assessment of international legal institutions helps to ensure both the relevance and normativity of the assessment.

THEORY VS. APPLICATION

I have argued that philosophical theories of human rights morality should be institutional in the sense of making room for institutional moral reasoning as a source of moral discovery. If this is correct, then philosophers should regard the practice not solely as a consumer of moral principles, but also a potential producer of authoritative moral principles. Moreover, as I sketched in the previous subsection, the processes by which legal institutions may reflect on their own contextual values and improve their own epistemic position accordingly, as in the ICTY's self-reflection, constitutes an important methodological model for philosophy. The institutional reasoning inherent in the international tribunals not only provided an avenue for women's voices to be raised and heard, but responded to those voices to critique and improve its own contextual values, and as a result to institutionalize epistemically and legally better (because less-biased) procedures and norms. In turn, these results created a standard within international law that takes seriously norms of accountability for the violation of women's rights to bodily security, thereby enabling further change to deeply entrenched ideologies conducive to women's subordination.

In addition to my characterization of the practice as a potential source of authoritative moral principles, I also argued that philosophers need to attend to our own contextual values in theorizing human rights, including what questions about human rights are properly matters of philosophical inquiry, and our conception of the appropriate level of abstraction for philosophical work that attempts to address human rights morality. The question of abstraction is important, and provides the basis for an objection to my view from the direction of orthodox theorizing. This objection maintains that *Akayesu* provides no moral instruction, but rather merely the (perhaps belated) instantiation in law of what the correct morality of human rights, developed using traditional philosophical methods, would entail. While the philosophy of human rights should properly be worked out at an abstract conceptual level, how those human rights are to be instantiated requires further work within the practice and by those academics with more concrete expertise regarding how to institutionalize or "give effect to" the moral norms that philosophers articulate in their theories. This argument can concede that the contentious politics of women's activism to bring charges of sexual violence into the indictment in *Akayesu* provided a way for international human rights law to evolve, which in turn may have served to enlighten people with benighted beliefs about women's human rights. However (the objection goes), this is a different issue altogether than the question of morally reliable knowledge production, which is after all a matter of rational argument, not a matter of which views happen to win in international legal tribunals or the court of public opinion. Thus, according to this objection, my argument runs together popular moral education with our understanding of morality itself: of course contentious politics and other forms of institutional moral reasoning can advance the first, but rational argument and moral philosophy are the authoritative sources for the second.

Indeed, Pablo Gilabert argues that a distinction between "abstract" and "specific" rights is essential for synthesizing the insights of the orthodox approach (which he calls the "humanist" approach) with political, or institutional, perspectives. In Gilabert's view:

> The political perspective captures the point that human rights should (at least in some social contexts) have some institutional embodiment. The humanist perspective captures a characteristic feature of human rights as human entitlements, and concentrates on unearthing the general moral basis and content of them (their underlying human interests and values).[40]

Gilabert concedes that institutional moral reasoning is essential for devising morally acceptable and feasible ways of specifying the content of abstract moral human rights and ensuring that their institutionalization does not impose "unreasonable costs on those affected by it." However, his theory utilizes traditional philosophical methods to construct a theory of those moral human rights in the first place.[41]

John Tasioulas and Effy Vayena similarly argue that institutions are required for specifying the content of moral human rights. On their view:

> a fully adequate specification through pure moral reasoning is unavailable. Instead, a workable standard must, to a large extent, be the product of social decision-making, whether conventional or legal. This is especially so when addressing the difficult questions or priority-setting in the use of limited resources. Of course, any such specification through social fiat must operate within tolerably determinate parameters set by moral reasoning.[42]

Notice, however, that these arguments about the specification essentially reproduce and rely upon the same division of labor I criticized in Chapter 1. This is apparent not only in Tasioulas and Vayena's remark about how "moral reasoning" must set the guidelines for specifying human rights, but also in Gilabert's insistence on the priority of what he calls "humanist" reasoning about morality over institutional reasoning about specifying human rights. As he argues, "[t]o avoid circularity (or conventionalism) we cannot take for granted the specific institutions we are trying to assess. A deeper and more general layer of moral reasoning must be uncovered."[43] In the absence of a deeper account of the kind of moral reasoning they have in mind, these arguments appear to presume that (a) the only way to provide normative guidance to the practice is via a theory of moral human rights and (b) the conviction that philosophical theory about moral human rights not only can but should be done in abstraction from the institutional contexts within which that theory is intended to be normatively authoritative. These gestures toward recognizing institutional moral reasoning as a means of specifying abstract moral human rights therefore only reproduce the problematic reliance within orthodox theorizing on a disciplinary division of labor that is itself based on the overly dichotomized fact/value distinction that I criticized in Chapter 1.

Importantly, these methodological questions cannot be fully answered on the basis of arguments that presume the reliability of the very methods that are at issue. In addition to more explicit and sustained attention to methodology, then, philosophers need to adopt a broader perspective on what counts as a virtue for a philosophical theory of human rights morality. Given that the philosophy of human rights presents itself as providing normative guidance for the practice, we should be exploring ways of assessing the aptness of philosophical theories to the practice, and its usefulness within it. This will necessarily involve greater understanding of and collaboration with perspectives outside of philosophy.

CRIMINAL LAW, FEMINISM, AND HUMAN RIGHTS

I argued briefly in Chapter 1 that human rights norms are operative in branches of international law other than IHRL. Moreover, my case study assumes that the sexual violence jurisprudence at the ad hoc tribunals was in fact an advance in institutional understanding and recognition of women's human rights. I make the argument for these claims more explicit in this section.

As I argued earlier, human rights activism and advocacy on behalf of particular groups or issues may influence the development of branches of international law beyond human rights law, including by agitating for the creation of new legal venues (like the ad hoc tribunals and the ICC). Understood broadly, then, human rights practice can be construed for certain purposes to include at least certain aspects of international criminal law and international humanitarian law. The point is that what David Luban calls "human rights thinking" has been influential in areas of international law beyond human rights law. For example, as Luban argues, the influence of "human rights thinking" can be seen in "not only the evolution of ever greater humanitarian protections in IHRL, but also a gradual move toward regarding those protections as rights of the protected individuals and not of their states or collectivities."[44]

The relevance for human rights morality of international criminal law begins with the historical development of international criminal law, grounded in the human rights concerns of activists, which were instrumental in developing international courts in the first place. More important at a theoretical level is the substantive result that the activists were aiming to achieve, namely, that accountability for human rights violations is an essential component of institutionalizing human rights morality. Kathryn Sikkink has argued that one important driver of developments in international criminal law after Nuremberg was the work of activists seeking accountability for crimes committed by former government officials within their countries. According to Sikkink, these developments did not necessarily work within existing legal categories; rather, as she characterizes them, the pursuit of legal accountability for human rights violations blurred the distinction between human rights law and criminal law, while the fact that activists were pursuing international accountability for human rights violations within their countries also blurred the boundaries between domestic and international law.[45] A developmental pathway that transcends existing legal categories makes sense when we see the actors as individual human beings organized at the grassroots level in pursuit of justice and the protection of human rights. As Sikkink emphasizes, in pursuit of this goal, activists seeking accountability at home organized to build connections with international communities of other individuals, activist groups, non-governmental organizations, and international or transnational organizations.[46] This method of institutional development therefore emphasizes both the dynamic nature of international institutions and the influence of real human beings constructing those institutions in pursuit of distinctively moral aims.

On this account, there is an important respect in which the development of international criminal law may in some respects at least serve to institutionalize or "give effect to" human rights morality. It therefore could be argued that it is somewhat arbitrary for philosophers to focus only on international human rights law as the institutional or political manifestation of human rights morality. It is possible that philosophers have tended to focus exclusively on international human rights law because they see it (but not international criminal law) as explicitly using philosophical terms and concepts (namely, the idea of human rights), which they then view as an invitation to deploy expert philosophical analysis to guide and clarify those terms and concepts in law. A deeper focus on the aims and histories of the different areas of law, however, reveals more overlap between them in terms of human rights morality than might at first glance be apparent. If this is correct, then philosophers of human rights morality would do well to attend more closely not only to what seems distinctive about international human rights law, but also how it connects to other branches of international law (and, as Sikkink and others would argue, to domestic law as well). This perspective highlights the complex set of normative considerations (including accountability for human rights violations) that are relevant to theorizing and institutionalizing a political conception of human rights morality (as opposed to developing, more narrowly, a theory of moral human rights).

Finally, as we saw in Chapter 5, some feminist scholars like Janet Halley and Karen Engle critique feminist celebrations of the sexual violence jurisprudence at the ad hoc tribunals as a naïve and uncritical endorsement of the morality and effectiveness of the criminal law to achieve gender justice. In response, it is important to note that, as I argued earlier this chapter, the same legal and institutional strategies may be assessed along different evaluative dimensions. While pointing out possible adverse consequences of a particular legal strategy is an important component of an overall normative assessment of that strategy, a complete assessment will pay attention also to the potential good to be achieved and whether it might outweigh the bad. Moreover, even beyond consequences, there may be significant symbolic and other intrinsic goods to be achieved. In addition to the moral complexity of a summary assessment of a particular institutional strategy, it is important also to note that it may very well be impossible to make a determinate and accurate moral assessment of an entire institution. Institutions like criminal legal systems can go wrong or do good in different respects at the same time. It is also possible and often more plausible to point toward directions for incremental reform and development of an institution, rather than to suggest on the basis of one or a few dimensions of criticism that all aspects of a particular institution are flawed. Moreover, the practical consequences even of a negative assessment of an entire institution may not be clear, for example, if all the alternatives are worse. Importantly, my argument (like the arguments of other feminist scholars who find moral progress in the sexual violence jurisprudence of the tribunals) does not uncritically endorse any and all pursuit of putatively feminist ends using criminal law. Nor does it assume in advance that the successful pursuit of feminist ends via criminal law necessarily outweighs all possible adverse consequences. Rather, the point is precisely to engage in careful normative assessment of different aspects of the same institution in order to clarify the good that those institutions may contribute while also identifying potential harms and reasons for concern. Neither feminists nor human rights advocates therefore need to prove that human rights practice or international legal institutions are flawless before investing in the avenues toward moral progress that they make available.

CONCLUSION

Ultimately, I hope that my arguments in this book contribute to expanding the range of approaches and the methodologies that philosophers consider relevant to theorizing human rights. My primary methodological point is that engaging more with the real world of human rights culture and practice—including law, activism, and politics—will point philosophers to a richer conception of what that culture and practice is, and may help us think more clearly about which of our philosophical tools and approaches are relevant to solving the moral and conceptual problems inherent within it. It may also help point us toward neglected tools in the philosophical toolbox, toward questions or perspectives to which philosophers have not paid enough attention, and toward identifying valid forms of pluralism where we might currently see simply a mistake (e.g., different senses of "human rights" where we might be tempted to impose univocality). We can bridge gaps between philosophy and political theory, activism, and law, and between philosophers and people around the world concerned with moral and legal human rights (including but not limited to other academics, lawyers, or judges), by taking upon ourselves some of the work of answering their questions, demonstrating the relevance of our disciplinary tools to their inquiries, and better appreciating the lessons we can draw from their perspectives and modes of analysis.

Moreover, I have tried to surface some of the more practical, less abstract questions emerging from human rights practice that, on my view, may be very productive points of engagement for philosophical discussion. These questions may seem less philosophically significant than developing a theory that tells us what human rights we have and why, especially when this contribution is seen as essential for illuminating the entire moral aim and purpose of human rights practice. But in addition to a greater relevance to the practice, I also hope to show that philosophical analysis of these questions (provisional and contingent as they may be) does not boil down to descriptive reports about how the system currently works, nor are they a matter of "applying" a fully worked-out philosophical theory of moral human rights to (various aspects of) the practice. Rather, as I hope to have demonstrated, there are substantive and important moral questions being raised and debated within human rights practice and the disciplines that study it. Philosophers can learn from and contribute productively to helping to articulate the best formulations of the issues, while contributing tools and resources to help study them.

Finally, I intend the philosophical methodology I'm describing to constitute a call for further collaboration in which scholars from multiple fields and participants in the practice recognize and appreciate the normative thinking that takes place at both the theoretical level and within diverse areas of international law. Not incidentally, this perspective also beckons philosophers to develop an interdisciplinary commitment to active engagement with fields of study that possess greater expertise regarding the politics and processes of international law, in recognition of the interdependence between philosophical theory and understanding of the practice. In this way, I hope that this book is seen as an invitation to greater collaboration among philosophers, international lawyers, political scientists, activists, and others who share an interest in theorizing human rights practice.

NOTES

1. David Luban, "Fairness to Rightness: Jurisdiction, Legality, and the Legitimacy of International Criminal Law," in *The Philosophy of International Law,* ed. Samantha Besson and John Tasioulas (Oxford: Oxford University Press, 2010), 575.

2. Michael J. Matheson and David Scheffer, "The Creation of the Tribunals," *American Journal of International Law* 110 (2016): 173. See also "Achievements—Establishing the Facts," ICTY, accessed August 5, 2019, http://www.icty.org/en/about/tribunal/achievements.

3. Judge Vagn Joensen, "Commemoration Event—20th Anniversary of the ICTR," United Nations—International Residual Mechanism for Criminal Tribunals, a Compendium on the Legacy of the ICTR and the Development of International Law, accessed August 5, 2019, http://unictr.irmct.org/sites/unictr.org/files/publications/compendium-documents/20th-anniversary-commemoration-speech-pdt-joensen.pdf.

4. ICTY, "Achievements." Cited in Marko Milanovic, "The Impact of the ICTY on the Former Yugoslavia: An Anticipatory Postmortem," *American Journal of International Law* 110 (2016).

5. Milanovic, "The Impact of the ICTY," 235.

6. Milanovic, "The Impact of the ICTY," 235.

7. Milanovic, "The Impact of the ICTY," 146.

8. Sara Kendall and Sarah M. H. Nouwen, "Speaking of Legacy: Toward an Ethos of Modesty at the International Criminal Tribunal for Rwanda," *American Journal of International Law* 110 (2016): 223.

9. Kendall and Nouwen, "Speaking of Legacy," 223.

10. Kirsten Campbell, "Gender Justice Beyond the Tribunals: From Criminal Accountability to Transformative Justice," *American Journal of International Law Unbound* 110 (2016): 229. Indeed, recent interviews have shown that the sexual violence victims who testified in Akayesu's trial have faced steep challenges moving forward with their lives after the verdict, including material and economic deprivation to long-term mental and physical health issues. See Jina Moore, "This Is the Story a UN Court Didn't Want Three Rape Survivors to Tell," *Buzzfeed News*, December 18, 2016.

11. Rosemary Grey and Indira Rosenthal, "Gender-based Crimes: A Monumental Day for the ICC," IntlawGrrls: Voices on International Law, Policy, Practice, July 8, 2019, https://ilg2.org/2019/07/08/gender-based-crimes-a-monumental-day-for-the-icc/.

12. Victoire Mukambanda, "Rwandan Rape Survivor in 'The Uncondemned' Speaks Out," *Women's eNews*, October 19, 2016, https://womensenews.org/2016/10/rwandan-rape-survivor-in-the-uncondemned-speaks-out/.

13. I thank Jon Mandle for helpful comments and discussion on this point.

14. Catharine MacKinnon, "Rape Redefined," *Harvard Law and Policy Review* 10 (2016): 477.

15. Kathryn Sikkink, *The Justice Cascade: How Human Rights Prosecutions Are Changing World Politics* (New York: W. W. Norton & Co., 2011), 75.

16. Sikkink, *Justice Cascade*, 75.

17. MacKinnon, "Rape Redefined," 477.

18. Louise Chappell, "Women, Gender, and International Institutions: Exploring New Opportunities at the International Criminal Court," *Policy and Society* 22, no. 1 (2003): 8.

19. Sikkink, *Justice Cascade*.

20. Sikkink, *Justice Cascade*, Ch. 4.

21. Sikkink, *Justice Cascade*, 98.

22. Sikkink, *Justice Cascade*, 83 (emphasis original).

23. Julie Mertus, "When Adding Women Matters: Women's Participation in the International Criminal Tribunal for the Former Yugoslavia," *Seton Hall Law Review* 38 (2008): 1300.

24. Grace Harbour, "International Concern Regarding Conflict-related Sexual Violence in the Lead-up to the ICTY's Establishment," in *Prosecuting Conflict-Related Sexual Violence at the ICTY*, ed. Serge Brammertz and Michelle Jarvis (Oxford: Oxford University Press, 2016), 19.

25. Harbour, "International Concern," 21, citing Mertus, "When Adding Women Matters," 1300.

26. Karen Alter, *The New Terrain of International Law* (Princeton, NJ: Princeton University Press, 2014), 322.

27. Alter, *New Terrain*, 26.

28. Alter, *New Terrain*, 26.

29. Alter, *New Terrain*, 27.

30. Darryl Robinson and Gillian MacNeil, "The Tribunals and the Renaissance of International Criminal Law: Three Themes," *American Journal of International Law* 110 (2016): 204–5.

31. Robinson and MacNeil, "Tribunals," 204–5.

32. Charles Beitz, *The Idea of Human Rights* (Oxford: Oxford University Press, 2009), 196.

33. Alter, *New Terrain,* Ch. 8.

34. Alter, *New Terrain,* 283.

35. James Griffin, *On Human Rights* (New York: Oxford University Press, 2008), 5.

36. John Tasioulas, "Human Rights, Universality and the Values of Personhood: Retracing Griffin's Steps," *European Journal of Philosophy* 10, no. 1 (2002): 82.

37. Robinson and MacNeil, "Tribunals," 210.

38. Robinson and MacNeil, "Tribunals," 210.

39. Robinson and MacNeil, "Tribunals," 210.

40. Pablo Gilabert, *Human Dignity and Human Rights* (Oxford: Oxford University Press, 2018), 57.

41. Gilabert, *Human Dignity,* 53.

42. John Tasioulas and Effy Vayena, "The Place of Human Rights and the Common Good in Global Health Policy," *Theoretical Medical Bioethics* 37 (2016): 374.

43. Gilabert, *Human Dignity,* 59.

44. David Luban, "Human Rights Pragmatism and Human Dignity," in *Philosophical Foundations of Human Rights*, ed. Rowan Cruft, Matthew Liao, and Massimo Renzo (Oxford: Oxford University Press, 2015), 271.

45. Sikkink, *Justice Cascade*, 16.

46. Sikkink, *Justice Cascade*, 16.

Bibliography

Ackerly, Brooke. *Just Responsibility: A Human Rights Theory of Global Justice*. Oxford: Oxford University Press, 2018.

Ad Hoc Tribunals Oral History Project. *Oral History Interview with Patricia Viseur Sellers*. Waltham, MA: International Center for Ethics, Justice and Public Life, Robert D. Farber University Archives & Special Collections Department, Brandeis University, 2017.

African Rights. *Rwanda: Death, Despair, and Defiance*. London: African Rights, 1995.

Ahmed, Aziza. "Women's Rights, Human Rights and the Criminal Law, or, Feminist Debates and Responses to [De]Criminalization and Sexual and Reproductive Health." *American Society of International Law Proceedings* (2018): 87–90. DOI:10.1017/amp.2019.40

Ahmed, Aziza. "Janet Halley in Conversation with Aziza Ahmed: Interview." In *Beyond Virtue and Vice: Rethinking Human Rights and Criminal Law*, edited by Alice Miller, and Mindy Roseman, 17–38. Philadelphia: University of Pennsylvania Press, 2019.

Alston, Philip. "The Populist Challenge to Human Rights." *Journal of Human Rights Practice* 9 (2017): 1–15.

Alter, Karen. *The New Terrain of International Law*. Princeton: Princeton University Press, 2014.

Anderson, Elizabeth. "Pragmatism, Science, and Moral Inquiry." In *In Face of the Facts: Moral Inquiry in American Scholarship*, edited by Richard Wightman Fox and Robert Westbrook, 10–39. Cambridge: Cambridge University Press, 1998.

Anderson, Elizabeth. "Uses of Value Judgments in Science: A General Argument with Lessons From a Case Study of Feminist Research on Divorce." *Hypatia* 19, no. 1 (2004): 1–24.

Antony, Louise, and Charlotte Witt, eds. *A Mind of One's Own: Feminist Essays on Reason and Objectivity*, 2nd ed. Boulder, CO: Westview Press, 2002.

Applebaum, Paul S. "Saving the UN Convention on the Rights of Persons with Disabilities—From Itself." *World Psychiatry: Official Journal of the World Psychiatric Association* 18, no. 1 (February 2019): 1–2.

Askin, Kelly. "Women's Issues in International Criminal Law: Recent Developments and the Potential Contribution of the ICC." In *International Crimes, Peace, and*

Human Rights: The Role of the International Criminal Court, edited by Dinah Shelton, 47–63. New York: Transnational Publishers, Inc., 2000.

Bass, Gary. *Stay the Hand of Vengeance*. Princeton: Princeton University Press, 2000.

Beitz, Charles. *The Idea of Human Rights*. New York: Oxford University Press, 2009.

Beitz, Charles. "The Practice and Its Authority: An Elaboration." *Critical Review of International Social and Political Philosophy* (2020). DOI: 10.1080/13698230.2020.1859220

Berkeley, Bill. "Judgment Day," *The Washington Post*, October 11, 1998. https://www.washingtonpost.com/archive/lifestyle/magazine/1998/10/11/judgement-day/3ae2490b-c3c7-4c17-b43c-e96bbfc064e5/.

Brammertz, Serge, and Michelle Jarvis, eds. *Prosecuting Conflict-Related Sexual Violence at the ICTY*. Oxford: Oxford University Press, 2016.

Brownmiller, Susan. *Against Our Will: Men, Women, and Rape*. New York: Fawcett Columbine, 1975.

Buchanan, Allen. *Justice, Legitimacy, and Self-Determination*. Oxford: Oxford University Press, 2003.

Buchanan, Allen. "Taking the Human Out of Human Rights." In *Rawls's Law of Peoples: A Realistic Utopia?*, edited by Rex Martin and David Reidy, 150–68. Malden, MA: Blackwell Publishing, 2006.

Buchanan, Allen. "The Egalitarianism of Human Rights." *Ethics* 120 (2010): 679–710.

Buchanan, Allen. *The Heart of Human Rights*. Oxford: Oxford University Press, 2013.

Buchanan, Allen. "Why International Legal Human Rights?," in *Philosophical Foundations of Human Rights*, edited by Rowan Cruft, S. Matthew Liao, and Massimo Renzo, 244–62. Oxford: Oxford University Press, 2015.

Buchanan, Allen. "Reply to Talbott, Ackerly, Kelly, and Risse." *Law and Philosophy* 36 (2017): 191–213.

Buchanan, Allen, and Gopal Sreenivasan. "Taking International Legality Seriously: A Methodology for Human Rights." In *Human Rights: Moral or Political?*, edited by Adam Etinson, 211–29. New York: Oxford University Press, 2018.

Bureau of Justice Statistics. "Women Victims of Sexual Violence, 1994–2010." Last modified February 13, 2013. https://www.bjs.gov/content/pub/press/fvsv9410pr.cfm.

Burgess-Jackson, Keith. "A History of Rape Law." In *A Most Detestable Crime: New Philosophical Essays on Rape*, edited by Keith Burgess-Jackson, 167–95. New York: Oxford University Press, 1999.

Campbell, Kirsten. "Gender Justice Beyond the Tribunals: From Criminal Accountability to Transformative Justice." *American Journal of International Law Unbound* 110 (2016): 227–33.

Campbell, Tom, and Kylie Bourne, eds. *Political and Legal Approaches to Human Rights*. New York: Routledge, 2017.

Chappell, Louise. "Women, Gender and International Institutions: Exploring New Opportunities at the International Criminal Court." *Policy and Society* 22 (2003): 3–25.

Charlesworth, Hilary, Christine Chinkin, and Shelley Wright. "Feminist Approaches to International Law." *American Journal of International Law* 85 (1991): 613–45.

Chenault, Suzanne. "And since *Akayesu*? The Development of ICTR Jurisprudence on Gender Crimes: A Comparison of *Akaysu* and *Muhimana*." *New England Journal of International and Comparative Law* 14, no. 2 (2008): 221–37.

Clapham, Andrew. "Human Rights and International Criminal Law." In *The Cambridge Companion to International Criminal Law*, edited by William Schabas, 11–33. Cambridge: Cambridge University Press, 2016.

Convention on the Elimination of all Forms of Discrimination Against Women, December 18, 1979, 1249 United Nations Treaty Series 13; 19 I.L.M. 33 (1980).

Convention on the Rights of Persons with Disabilities, May 3, 2008, A/RES/61/106, Annex I.

Cranston, Maurice. "Are There Any Human Rights?" *Daedalus* 112, no. 4 (Fall 1983): 1–17.

Cruft, Rowan, S. Matthew Liao, and Massimo Renzo, eds. *Philosophical Foundations of Human Rights*. Oxford: Oxford University Press, 2015.

Cruvellier, Thierry. *Court of Remorse: Inside the International Criminal Tribunal for Rwanda*. Translated by Chari Voss. Madison: University of Wisconsin Press, 2010.

Darlington, Shasta. "Domestic Abuse, Shown Blow by Blow, Shocks Brazil." *New York Times*, August 7, 2018. https://www.nytimes.com/2018/08/07/world/americas/domestic-abuse-shown-blow-by-blow-shocks-brazil.html?module=inline.

Degener, Theresia. "A Human Rights Model of Disability." In *Routledge Handbook of Disability Law and Human Rights,* edited by Peter Blanck and Eilionóir Flynn (New York: Routledge, 2016): 31–49.

Des Forges, Alison. *Leave None to Tell the Story: Genocide in Rwanda*. New York: Human Rights Watch and Fédération Internationale des Ligues des Droits de l'Homme, 1999.

Doherty, Teresa. "Sexual Violence and the Role of International Courts." *New Zealand Journal of Public and International Law* 11 (2013): 693–705.

Elshtain, Jean Bethke. "Political Children: Reflections on Hannah Arendt's Distinction between Public and Private Life." In *Reconstructing Political Theory: Feminist Perspectives*, edited by Mary Lyndon Shanley and Uma Narayan, 109–27. University Park: Pennsylvania State University Press, 1997.

Engle, Karen. "'Calling in the Troops': The Uneasy Relationship Among Women's Rights, Human Rights, and Humanitarian Intervention." *Harvard Human Rights Journal* 20 (2007): 189–62.

Engle, Karen. "Feminism and Its (Dis)Contents: Criminalizing Wartime Rape in Bosnia and Herzegovina." *American Journal of International Law* 99 (2005): 778–816.

Engle, Karen. "Anti-Impunity and the Turn to Criminal Law in Human Rights." *Cornell Law Review* 200, no. 5 (2015): 1069–127.

Engle, Karen. "Feminist Legacies." *American Journal of International Law Unbound* 110 (2016): 220–26.

Etinson, Adam, ed. *Human Rights: Moral or Political?* New York: Oxford University Press, 2018.

Ferguson, Lucy. "Gender, Work, and the Sexual Division of Labor." In *The Oxford Handbook of Gender and Politics*, edited by Georgina Waylen, Karen Celis, Johanna Kantola, and S. Laurel Weldon, 337–61. Oxford: Oxford University Press, 2013.

Fleischman, Janet, and Binaifer Nowrojee. "In Rwanda, Too, Rape Was a War Crime and Must Be Punished." *New York Times,* July 25, 1996. https://www.nytimes.com/1996/07/25/opinion/IHT-in-rwanda-too-rape-was-a-war-crime-and-must-be-punished.html?searchResultPosition=1.

Fricker, Miranda. *Epistemic Injustice: Power and the Ethics of Knowing*. Oxford: Oxford University Press, 2007.

Gilabert, Pablo. *Human Dignity and Human Rights*. Oxford: Oxford University Press, 2018.

Grey, Rosemary, and Indira Rosenthal. "Gender-based Crimes: A Monumental Day for the ICC." IntlawGrrls: Voices on International Law, Policy, Practice (July 8, 2019). https://ilg2.org/2019/07/08/gender-based-crimes-a-monumental-day-for-the-icc/.

Griffin, James. "Discrepancies Between the Best Philosophical Account of Human Rights and the International Law of Human Rights." *Proceedings of the Aristotelian Society* 101 (2001): 1–28.

Griffin, James. *On Human Rights*. New York: Oxford University Press, 2008.

Griffin, James. "Human Rights and the Autonomy of International Law." In *The Philosophy of International Law,* edited by Samantha Besson and John Tasioulas, 339–55. Oxford: Oxford University Press, 2010.

Gourevitch, Philip. "After the Genocide." *New Yorker*, December 10, 1995.

Grossman, Nienke. "Sex on the Bench: Do Women Judges Matter to the Legitimacy of International Courts?" *Chicago Journal of International Law* 12 (Winter 2012): 647–85.

Gurbai, Sándor. "Beyond the Pragmatic Definition? The Right to Non-discrimination of Persons with Disabilities in the Context of Coercive Interventions." *Health and Human Rights Journal* 22, no. 1 (May 13 2020): 279–92.

Hagerty, Barbara Bradley. "An Epidemic of Disbelief." *The Atlantic* (August 2019).

Halley, Janet, Prabha Kotiswaran, Hila Shamir, and Chantal Thomas. "From the International to the Local in Feminist Legal Responses to Rape, Prostitution/Sex Work, and Sex Trafficking: Four Studies in Contemporary Governance Feminism." *Harvard Journal of Law and Gender* 29 (2006): 335–423.

Hampton, Jean. "The Case for Feminism." In *The Liberation Debate*, edited by Michael Leahy and Dan Cohn-Sherbock, 3–44. New York: Routledge, 1996.

Harbour, Grace. "International Concern Regarding Conflict-related Sexual Violence in the Lead-up to the ICTY's Establishment." In *Prosecuting Conflict-Related Sexual Violence at the ICTY*, edited by Serge Brammertz and Michelle Jarvis, 19–32. Oxford: Oxford University Press, 2016.

Hayes, Niamh. "The Impact of Prosecutorial Strategy on the Investigation and Prosecution of Sexual Violence at International Criminal Tribunals." In *Thematic Prosecution of Sex Crimes*, edited by Morten Bergsmo, 409–39. Beijing: Torkel Opsahl Academic EPublisher, 2012.

Hessler, Kristen. "Hard Cases: Public Health and Women's Human Rights." *Journal of Value Inquiry* 47, no. 4 (2013): 375–90.

Hessler, Kristen. "Women Judges or Feminist Judges?: Gender Representation and Feminist Values in International Courts." *Journal of Social Philosophy* 52, no. 4 (2021): 459–72.

Hurwitz, Deena, and Margaret Satterthwaite, eds. *Human Rights Advocacy Stories.* New York: Thomson Reuters/Foundation Press, 2009.

Hutchings, Kimberly. "Global Justice." In *New Directions in Political Science: Responding to the Challenges of an Interdependent World*, edited by Colin Hay, 231–49. Hampshire, UK: Palgrave Macmillan, 2010.

ICTY. "Achievements—Establishing the Facts." Accessed August 5, 2019. https://www.icty.org/en/about/tribunal/achievements.

Jarvis, Michelle. "Overview: The Challenge of Accountability for Conflict-related Sexual Violence Crimes." In *Prosecuting Conflict-Related Sexual Violence at the ICTY*, edited by Serge Brammertz and Michelle Jarvis, 1–18. Oxford: Oxford University Press, 2016.

Jarvis, Michelle, and Kate Vigneswaran. "Challenges to Successful Outcomes in Sexual Violence Cases." In *Prosecuting Conflict-Related Sexual Violence at the ICTY*, edited by Serge Brammertz and Michelle Jarvis, 33–72. Oxford: Oxford University Press, 2016.

Joensen, Vagn. "Commemoration Event—20th Anniversary of the ICTR." United Nations—International Residual Mechanism for Criminal Tribunals, A Compendium on the Legacy of the ICTR and the Development of International Law. Accessed August 5, 2019. http://unictr.irmct.org/sites/unictr.org/files/publications/compendium-documents/20th-anniversary-commemoration-speech-pdt-joensen.pdf.

Kendall, Sara, and Sarah M. H. Nouwen. "Speaking of Legacy: Toward an Ethos of Modesty at the International Criminal Tribunal for Rwanda." *American Journal of International Law* 110 (2016): 212–32.

Kendi, Ibram X. "Racial Progress Is Real. But So Is Racist Progress." *New York Times*. January 21 2017. https://www.nytimes.com/2017/01/21/opinion/sunday/racial-progress-is-real-but-so-is-racist-progress.html.

LaFont, Cristina. *Global Governance and Human Rights*. Assen, Netherlands: Koninklijke Van Gorcum, 2012.

Lang, Raymond, Maria Kett, Nora Groce, and Jean-Francois Trani. "Implementing the United Nations Convention on the Rights of Persons with Disabilities: Principles, Implications, Practice and Limitations." *Alter* 5, no. 3 (2011): 206–20.

Longino, Helen. "Can There Be a Feminist Science?" *Hypatia* 2, no. 3 (1987): 51–64.

Luban, David. "Fairness to Rightness: Jurisdiction, Legality, and the Legitimacy of International Criminal Law." In *The Philosophy of International Law,* edited by Samantha Besson and John Tasioulas, 569–88. Oxford: Oxford University Press, 2010.

Luban, David. "Human Rights Pragmatism and Human Dignity." In *Philosophical Foundations of Human Rights*, edited by Rowan Cruft, Matthew Liao, and Massimo Renzo, 263–78. Oxford: Oxford University Press, 2015.

Luping, Dianne. "Investigation and Prosecution of Sexual and Gender-Based Crimes Before the International Criminal Court." *American University Journal of Gender, Social Policy, and the Law* 17 (2009): 431–96.

MacKinnon, Catharine. "Crimes of War, Crimes of Peace." In *On Human Rights: The Oxford Amnesty Lectures 1993*, edited by Stephen Shute and Susan Hurley, 83–109. New York: Basic Books, 1993.

MacKinnon, Catharine. "Defining Rape Internationally: A Comment on Akayesu." *Columbia Journal of Transnational Law* 44 (2006): 940–58.

MacKinnon, Catharine. "The ICTR's Legacy on Sexual Violence." *New England Journal of International and Comparative Law* 14 (2008): 211.

MacKinnon, Catharine. "Rape Redefined." *Harvard Law and Policy Review* 10 (2016): 431–77.

Manne, Kate. *Down Girl: The Logic of Misogyny.* Oxford: Oxford University Press, 2018.

Matheson, Michael J., and David Scheffer. "The Creation of the Tribunals." *American Journal of International Law* 110 (2016): 173–90.

Matloff, Judith. "The War Crime No One Wants to Talk About." *New York Times,* September 22, 2020. https://www.nytimes.com/2020/09/22/books/review/our-bodies-their-battlefields-christina-lamb.html.

Mertus, Julie. "When Adding Women Matters: Women's Participation in the International Criminal Tribunal for the Former Yugoslavia." *Seton Hall Law Review* 38 (2008): 1297–326.

Milanovic, Marko. "The Impact of the ICTY on the Former Yugoslavia: An Anticipatory Postmortem." *American Journal of International Law* 110 (2016): 233–59.

Mitchell, Michele, and Nick Louvel, dirs. *The Uncondemned*. New York: Film at Eleven Media, 2015.

Mohamed, Hawa Aden. "When Laws Against Rape Aren't Enough." *New York Times,* January 30, 2018.

Moore, Jina. "This Is the Story a UN Court Didn't Want Three Rape Survivors to Tell." *Buzzfeed News*, December 18, 2016. https://www.buzzfeednews.com/article/jinamoore/this-is-the-story-a-un-court-didnt-want-three-rape-survivors.

Mukumbanda, Victoire. "Rwandan Rape Survivor in 'The Uncondemned' Speaks Out." *Women's eNews*, October 19, 2016. https://womensenews.org/2016/10/rwandan-rape-survivor-in-the-uncondemned-speaks-out/.

Nedelsky, Jennifer. "Receptivity and Judgment." *Ethics and Global Politics* 4, no. 4 (2011): 231–54. DOI: 10.3402/egp.v4i4.15116

Nowrojee, Binaifer. *Shattered Lives: Sexual Violence during the Rwandan Genocide and its Aftermath*. New York: Human Rights Watch, 1996.

Nussbaum, Martha. "Human Capabilities and Female Human Beings." In *Women, Culture, and Development: A Study of Human Capabilities*, edited by Martha Nussbaum and Jonathon Glover, 495–551. Oxford: Oxford University Press, 1995.

Obote-Odora, Alex. "Rape and Sexual Violence in International Law: ICTR Contribution." *New England Journal of International and Comparative Law* 12, no. 1 (2005): 135–59.

Okin, Susan. *Women in Western Political Thought*. Princeton: Princeton University Press, 1979.

Okin, Susan. *Justice, Gender, and the Family*. New York: Basic Books, 1989.

Oosterveld, Valerie. "Gender-Sensitive Justice and the International Criminal Tribunal for Rwanda: Lessons Learned for the International Criminal Court." *New England Journal of International and Comparative Law* 12, no. 1 (2005): 121.

Pogge, Thomas. *World Poverty and Human Rights*. 2nd edition. Cambridge: Polity Press, 2008.

Posner, Eric A. *The Twilight of Human Rights Law.* Oxford: Oxford University Press, 2014.

Power, Samantha. *A Problem from Hell: America and the Age of Genocide*. New York: HarperCollins, 2002.

Prosecutor v. Akayesu, Case No. ICTR 96–4-T, Judgment (September 2, 1998).

Pruitt, Lisa. "Taba Commune Sexual Assault Evidence Summary: An Analysis of Akayesu's and Kubwimana's Authority and Responsibility." October 25, 1996. Copy on file with the author.

Prunier, Gérard. *The Rwanda Crisis 1959–1994: History of a Genocide*. London: Hurst & Company, 1995.

Rawls, John. *The Law of Peoples*. Cambridge, MA: Harvard University Press, 1999.

Rawls, John. *A Theory of Justice*, rev. ed. Cambridge, MA: Harvard University Press, 1999.

Raz, Joseph. "Human Rights Without Foundations." In *The Philosophy of International Law*, edited by Samantha Besson and John Tasioulas, 321–37. New York: Oxford University Press, 2010.

Robinson, Darryl, and Gillian MacNeil. "The Tribunals and the Renaissance of International Criminal Law: Three Themes." *American Journal of International Law* 110 (2016): 191–211.

Russell, Camisha."The Race Idea in Reproductive Technologies: Beyond Epistemic Scientism and Technological Mastery." *Journal of Bioethical Inquiry* 12, no. 4 (2015): 601–12.

Sangiovanni, Andrea. "Human Rights Practices." *Critical Review of International Social and Political Philosophy* 25, no. 1 (2022): 50–65.

Schaffer, Johan Karlsson, and Reidar Maliks, eds. *Moral and Political Conceptions to Human Rights: Implications for Theory and Practice.* Cambridge: Cambridge University Press, 2017.

Sellers, Patricia Viseur. "Sexual Violence and Peremptory Norms: The Legal Value of Rape." *Case Western Reserve Journal of International Law* 34, no. 3 (2002): 287–303.

Sellers, Patricia. "Gender Strategy Is Not Luxury for International Courts Symposium: Prosecuting Sexual and Gender-Based Crimes Before International/ized Criminal Courts." *Journal of Gender, Social Policy & the Law* 17, no. 2 (2009): 327–35.

The Sentinel Project. "AIDS Intersects with Genocide." December 1, 2013. https://thesentinelproject.org/2013/12/01/aids-intersects-with-genocide/.

Sikkink, Kathryn. *The Justice Cascade: How Human Rights Prosecutions are Changing World Politics*. New York: W. W. Norton & Co., 2011.

Sreenivasan, Gopal. "A Human Right to Health? Some Inconclusive Skepticism." *Aristotelian Society Supplementary Volume* 86, no. 1 (2012): 239–65.

Stauffer, Dana J. "Aristotle's Account of the Subjection of Women." *Journal of Politics* 70, no. 4 (2008): 929–41.

Stein, Michael Ashley, and Janet E. Lord. "Monitoring the Convention on the Rights of Persons with Disabilities: Innovations, Lost Opportunities, and Future Potential." *Human Rights Quarterly* 32 (2010): 689–728.

Tasioulas, John. "Human Rights, Universality and the Values of Personhood: Retracing Griffin's Steps." *European Journal of Philosophy* 10, no. 1 (2002): 79–100.

Tasioulas, John. "The Moral Reality of Human Rights.' In *Freedom from Poverty as a Human Right*, edited by Thomas Pogge, 75–101. Oxford: Oxford University Press, 2007.

Tasioulas, John. "On the Nature of Human Rights." In *The Philosophy of Human Rights*, edited by Gerhard Ernst and Jan-Cristoph Heilinger, 17–59. Göttingen: De Gruyter, 2012.

Tasioulas, John. "Towards a Philosophy of Human Rights." *Current Legal Problems* 65, no. 1 (2012): 1–30.

Tasioulas, John. "Human Rights, Legitimacy, and International Law." *American Journal of Jurisprudence* 58, no. 1 (2013): 1–25.

Tasioulas, John. "On the Foundations of Human Rights." In *Philosophical Foundations of Human Rights*, edited by Rowan Cruft, S. Matthew Liao, and Massimo Renzo, 45–70. Oxford: Oxford University Press, 2015.

Tasioulas, John. "Exiting the Hall of Mirrors: Morality and Law in Human Rights." In *Political and Legal Approaches to Human Rights*, edited by Tom Campbell and Kylie Bourne, 73–89. New York: Routledge, 2017.

Tasioulas, John. "Philosophizing the Real World of Human Rights: A Reply to Samuel Moyn." In *Human Rights: Moral or Political?*, edited by Adam Etinson, 88–102. Oxford: Oxford University Press, 2018.

Tasioulas, John. "Saving Human Rights from Human Rights Law." *Vanderbilt Journal of Transnational Law* 52 (2019): 1167–207.

Tasioulas, John, and Effy Vayena. "The Place of Human Rights and the Common Good in Global Health Policy." *Theoretical Medical Bioethics* 37 (2016): 365–82.

UN Department of Economic and Social Affairs. *Handbook for Parliamentarians on the Convention on the Rights of Persons with Disabilities.* Geneva, 2007. https://www.un.org/development/desa/disabilities/resources/handbook-for-parliamentarians-on-the-convention-on-the-rights-of-persons-with-disabilities/chapter-one-overview.html

UN Department of Economic and Social Affairs: Disability. "Convention on the Rights of Persons with Disabilities (CRPD)." Accessed August 12, 2022. https://www.un.org/development/desa/disabilities/convention-on-the-rights-of-persons-with-disabilities.html.

UN Office on Drugs and Crime. Global Study on Homicide 2018. Vienna, 2018. https://www.unodc.org/documents/data-and-analysis/GSH2018/GSH18_Gender-related_killing_of_women_and_girls.pdf.

UN International Residual Mechanism for Criminal Tribunals. "Cases." Accessed August 12, 2022. https://www.irmct.org/en/cases.

Uvin, Peter. "Reading the Rwandan Genocide." *International Studies Review* 3, no. 3 (Autumn 2001).

Van Dam, Andrew. "Less than 1% of Rapes Lead to Felony Convictions. At Least 89% of Victims Face Emotional and Physical Consequences." *The Washington Post,* October 6, 2018. https://www.washingtonpost.com/business/2018/10/06/less-than-percent-rapes-lead-felony-convictions-least-percent-victims-face-emotional-physical-consequences/.

Van Schaack, Beth. "Engendering Genocide: The *Akayesu* Case Before the International Criminal Tribunal for Rwanda." In *Human Rights Advocacy Stories*, edited by Deena Hurwitz and Margaret Satterthwaite, 193–227. New York: Thomson Reuters/Foundation Press, 2009.

Wilson, Bertha. "Will Women Judges Really Make a Difference?" *Osgoode Hall Law Journal* (1990).

Young, Iris Marion. *Justice and the Politics of Difference.* Princeton: Princeton University Press, 1990.

Zraick, Karen. "Most Dangerous Place for Women Is the Home, U.N. Report Finds." *New York Times,* November 27, 2018. https://www.nytimes.com/2018/11/27/world/female-homicide-gender-violence.html?action=click&module=Latest&pgtype=Homepage.

Index

About the Author

Kristen Hessler received her PhD in philosophy from the University of Arizona. Her published work includes articles and chapters in political philosophy, feminist philosophy, global justice, environmental ethics, and the philosophy of public health. She was the world's first "extension ethicist," as a philosopher working for the cooperative extension service under the auspices of the Office of Biotechnology at Iowa State University, and she was recently a visiting researcher at the PluriCourts Institute at the University of Oslo, Norway. She currently teaches in the Philosophy Department at the University at Albany (SUNY).

Milton Keynes UK
Ingram Content Group UK Ltd.
UKHW011522080124
435668UK00005B/97

9 781498 592307